# Building
# Digital
# Libraries

# Building Digital Libraries

A How-To-Do-It Manual for Librarians®

**SECOND EDITION**

Kyle Banerjee and Terry Reese Jr.

ALA
Neal-Schuman

Chicago   2019

**KYLE BANERJEE** has twenty years of library experience and extensive systems knowledge. He has planned and written software to support library systems migration since 1996. He is the coauthor of *Building Digital Libraries* (2008) and *Digital Libraries: Content and Systems* (2006), and is the author of numerous other publications.

**TERRY REESE** is the head of digital initiatives at the Ohio State University Libraries. Over the past seventeen years, his research interests have centered on the changing nature of library metadata and the ways in which this data can be reused and transformed in different contexts. He is the author and creator of MarcEdit, a cross-platform library metadata editing tool that is designed to lower the technical barriers for users working with various forms of library metadata, and is the coauthor of *Building Digital Libraries* (2008), and is the author of numerous other publications.

ISBNs
978-0-8389-1635-3 (paper)
978-0-8389-1723-7 (PDF)
978-0-8389-1714-5 (ePub)
978-0-8389-1724-4 (Kindle)

**Library of Congress Cataloging-in-Publication Data**
Names: Banerjee, Kyle, author. | Reese, Terry, Jr., author.
Title: Building digital libraries : a how-to-do-it manual for librarians /Kyle Banerjee, Terry Reese.
Description: Second edition. | Chicago : ALA Neal-Schuman, an imprint of the American Library Association, 2019. | Series: How-to-do-it manuals for librarians? | Includes bibliographical references.
Identifiers: LCCN 2018001090 | ISBN 9780838916353 (print : alk. paper) | ISBN 9780838917145 (epub) | ISBN 9780838917237 (pdf) | ISBN 9780838917244 (kindle : alk. paper)
Subjects: LCSH: Digital libraries.
Classification: LCC ZA4080 .R44 2018 | DDC 027—dc23
LC record available at https://lccn.loc.gov/2018001090

Composition by Dianne M. Rooney in the Minion Pro and Interstate typefaces.

♾ This paper meets the requirements of ANSI/NISO Z39.48–1992 (Permanence of Paper).

Printed in the United States of America

23 22 21 20 19     5 4 3 2 1

# Contents

# Contents

# Acknowledgments

**When we created** the first edition of this book in 2006, cultural heritage organizations largely thought about institutional repositories in terms of publishing open-access content. These issues are still present, but the variety of needs that repositories must serve has expanded, as has the content they provide. Moreover, repositories have become a much more integral part of library operations—the long-term success of libraries and cultural heritage organizations partly depends on their ability to create and integrate digital library platforms into their identities.

As we considered writing this new edition, we wanted to address this shift in thinking and expand the book to explore the wider issues surrounding digital libraries and the infrastructure that makes them possible. We hope we've succeeded, and that this book will help practitioners and students understand how the landscape has changed for cultural heritage organizations. We further hope that this book will afford its readers a better understanding of how one can initiate and sustain digital endeavors in libraries.

As in other areas of life, many others have helped us throughout the writing of this book. Friends, colleagues, and family members endured our endless musings on technical and library topics and shared ideas that really changed how we look at things.

We are grateful to Rachel Chance and others working behind the scenes at ALA Neal-Schuman Publishing for their support. Our names might be on the cover, but our colleagues have put in an enormous amount of work to make this book much better than it otherwise would have been, while leaving us to work on the fun parts.

## Kyle's Notes

First and foremost, I want to dedicate my efforts to my dad. He always liked to say that people get so fixated on ants that they don't notice elephants walking by. The multitude of technologies, standards, methods, reports, and activities associated with digital libraries are as overwhelming as any swarm of ants, so I hope I can help you to discover the far more interesting and helpful elephants.

I feel lucky to have worked with Kate Thornhill and David Forero, who challenged me to think differently and who remind me why I joined this field in the first place. They looked over early drafts of my work and offered many insights.

I would also like to thank Terry, who has been a partner in crime both personally and professionally since we first met. His attitude and encouragement have helped me get excited about working every day, even after all these years.

Lastly, I'm grateful to Bonnie Parks, who has awakened things I didn't even know I had in me and has taken me in directions I never dreamed I would go.

## Terry's Notes

I would like to specifically thank my friends and colleagues at the Ohio State University Libraries, specifically Magda El-Sherbini, who has been a sounding board and trusted friend throughout my tenure there. I also would like to thank my coauthor, Kyle, who has pushed and prodded to make sure I'd make my deadlines, while still providing great suggestions and feedback throughout the process. More importantly, Kyle has been my friend and mentor since 2000, when we first met. I often wonder what I would have ended up doing had he not encouraged me to pursue my degree in library science, though I'm happy that he did.

Finally, I'd be remiss if I didn't mention my family. To my two boys, Kenny and Nathan, I really appreciate your interest in the process of writing this book. You may not have realized it, but the questions you guys have been asking over the past six months really helped me work on making my writing more accessible and filled with less techno-speak. And to my wife and partner, Alyce, I'm grateful for all her suggestions and patience throughout the writing process. If I accomplish anything in this world, it is due to the support and faith that she has always shown in me.

# Introduction

**Digital collections take** many forms and serve many objectives. This book aims to help you understand the broad issues surrounding institutional repositories (IRs), digital asset management systems (DAMs), online educational resources (OERs), and digital libraries. For the purposes of this book, the differences between these different types of collections are unimportant, and the terms "repository" or "digital repository" will be used to refer to any system that is used to organize, store, retrieve, and disseminate digital resources.

Understanding digital libraries is as much a matter of recognizing what you don't need to know as it is about learning what you do need to know. There are too many types of repositories to discuss them individually, so we focus on concepts that can help you understand any system. Commercial and open source systems designed to fulfill very divergent needs depend on a countless array of standards and technologies, so this book introduces you only to those that will likely be significant for your own project, with the expectation that you will consult specialized references for greater detail on specific tools, methods, standards, and technologies.

The first chapter of this book discusses creating a digital repository, including how to determine whether your library should create one at all, since building a repository requires a permanent commitment of resources that would otherwise be used to support other services. This chapter also discusses determining the scope or extent of your project, securing support for initial and ongoing expenses, and tools you can use to help get started.

Chapter 2 guides you through the questions that need to be answered to select a repository architecture. Every repository project is ultimately motivated by a vision of how a set of needs can be met. The architecture determines what can be added to the repository, how materials can be processed and enhanced to meet needs, how resources are navigated, and how they can be used. The architecture defines what user and staff workflows are possible, as well as the potential capabilities of the repository. This chapter concludes with suggestions on how to build a requirements list that allows a meaningful comparison of platforms.

Chapter 3 tackles the question of how to identify materials for your repository and develop workflows to incorporate those materials into collections. Once it is stored, the value of a resource is defined by the metadata that makes it findable and the structures and mechanisms that allow it to be used. This chapter helps you navigate the process of creating efficient workflows to structure, organize, and protect resources so they will be useful for many years to come.

Repositories exist to make resources available for future users—a challenging task given how formats are largely a reflection of the capabilities and understandings of the times when they were created. Chapter 4 discusses how to preserve materials so they can still be used as technology progresses.

Anyone building or maintaining a repository faces an alphabet soup of technical acronyms. Chapter 5 introduces you to standards and technologies for storing, organizing, sharing, and searching repositories. Chapter 6 elaborates on these themes, with special attention paid to metadata formats associated with general-purpose repositories, specific domains, and managing resources.

The value of a repository is measured by its use. Chapter 7 describes how information in repositories can be shared across different environments created for different purposes. This chapter discusses linked data, protocols for sharing and harvesting information, technologies for indexing and searching resources, and general-purpose technologies for manipulating information in a shared environment.

Authentication and authorization appear straightforward from a technical perspective. However, working with a variety of privacy and security needs, intellectual property requirements, data sources, user types, and mechanisms that cross organizational boundaries makes it challenging to set up access control. Chapter 8 discusses the deceptively simple task of authenticating staff and users, as well as managing mechanisms that provide them with convenient and appropriate access while honoring the needs of different rights holders.

Of course, a repository would be of little use if users cannot find and access content—the findability or discovery of content, both within an existing system, but within the larger information landscape. Chapter 9 looks at the current research and techniques for exposing content both within one's repository and to the broader research community.

This book's concluding chapter examines the future of repositories as library services continue their trend of consolidation, and the vast majority of resources that users need are owned and maintained outside the library. Special attention is given to operating in shared environments, and the chapter offers some thoughts for what might be in store as demand for maintaining a huge number of resources with a small number of staff using federated vocabularies continues to build.

# Getting Started

**The ultimate success** or failure of a digital repository is often determined in the planning stages. A repository must serve a real need. It must support user workflows and be structured and organized so that users can interact with resources as needed. It must be easy to maintain and capable of accommodating needs and resources that may not exist at the time the repository is designed.

On a basic level, a digital repository is a collection of digital resources. These materials may have been converted from an analog format such as paper, or they may have been born digital. They may consist of singular objects that are used individually such as documents, images, and video files, but they might also be complex objects consisting of related files as might be found in exhibitions, photos associated with releases, and learning objects. Some types of resources such as datasets, output from specialized devices, music associated with scores, and anything with a geospatial component may require specialized software or platforms to be useful.

Regardless of the type of resources they contain, the purpose of digital repositories is to allow information to be accessed and used. To accomplish this objective, a repository must preserve both objects and sufficient metadata to provide a context that can make those objects usable. The repository must also support a reasonable mechanism for ingesting, searching, using, and managing materials.

## Should You Build a Repository?

People charged with implementing digital repositories often focus immediately on the technical aspects of the endeavor. They read about standards and best practices, they write requirements, evaluate software, and explore hardware and services they might need to make their repository a success. While important, these steps represent only a tiny part of the planning process.

Before starting to build a repository, you need to say why it should even exist. From a user perspective, a repository is just another website. Countless websites already exist, so why is this one needed? What compelling service does it offer? Even presuming that the service is valuable and desired by users, why is this one so important that it should receive permanently dedicated staff and funding lines that represent a significant portion of the total budget—particularly given that most libraries have seen both their budgets and staff sizes shrink in recent years?

Just as any library would plan carefully before agreeing to take on the responsibility of absorbing and nurturing a new physical collection indefinitely, it must also do the same for electronic collections. Although there is a widespread tendency to think that digital materials take few resources to work with or maintain, implementing a digital repository is a major commitment that requires significant staff and funding resources.

When digital resources are involved, it is natural for people to want to build all the good features they have seen in other systems into their own. While it is perfectly reasonable to want the greatest level of functionality possible, it is important to be aware that every feature complicates configuration and increases long-term maintenance commitments.

Launching a repository is an exciting process, but long-term success depends on a viable long-term plan. Such a plan requires a realistic view of how much time and money are required. The library must have access to adequate technological resources, as well as sufficient expertise to set up, configure, and maintain systems properly. The library also needs adequate staff to perform acquisitions and processing tasks. If the resources are not sufficient to implement the plan, it may be necessary to adjust the goals downward to achievable levels. A high-quality repository with a modest scope is more valuable as a resource than an overly ambitious project for the simple reason that with the former, people can reasonably know what they can expect to find.

Acquiring and processing new electronic resources take time and significant staff resources. An acquisitions model which presumes that authors and others will consistently identify valuable materials and submit them using an online submission form is not realistic—relatively few people are motivated by library interests in archiving or in open access. Depending on nonexperts to create helpful metadata is equally unrealistic. History has yet to provide an example of a good library with a collection development policy based primarily on letting authors and users determine all acquisitions. Nor has any library succeeded in organizing a major collection by having ordinary information providers and patrons catalog and shelve materials in the way they believe will be most useful.

Repositories are dependent on technology, and it is easy to underestimate the costs of long-term system support. When a repository is new, people remember the planning process, they are familiar with the components used to build the repository, and it is easy to find people with detailed knowledge of how things work. As a result, most things function as designed, and while the repository is still new, problems are solved rapidly.

After some years have passed, however, supporting and improving the system become more difficult. The software for any digital repository will have many dependencies, and it may turn out years later that individual components are dependent on specific versions of software that are no longer maintained. This problem can occur with proprietary as well as open source software. Key players may no longer be available, and critical details will have been forgotten. Consequently, maintenance and troubleshooting that were previously simple can become very difficult, and complex operations such as systems migrations can become overwhelming. Once a system reaches the point where it cannot be supported properly, all of the resources in the repository are at risk of being lost.

Maintaining a digital repository in the long term is more complicated than maintaining an integrated library system (ILS). Over the past few decades, the ILS market has become relatively mature. Bibliographic, patron, and vendor data have become more standardized. Future migrations may be costly and complicated, but they are certainly feasible.

By contrast, digital repositories use divergent and incompatible methods to store complex information. It is still unclear which architectures will survive in the long term. It is important to design the repository so that it is easy to maintain using resources that will be available after some time has passed. In many cases, this means setting relatively modest goals. Sophistication and complexity can lead to difficulties, while simple, elegant designs tend to be more robust.

Before embarking on a repository project, you should ask yourself the following questions:

### Why is the repository needed?

When designing a repository, the most important questions to answer are why people would use it, who would use it, and what the impact of that use would be. The repository must identify the specific needs of specific user groups—all-encompassing mandates such as storing the output of an institution for anyone who might need it is not a viable purpose. Is the purpose to provide access to archival exhibitions, dissertations or articles, institutionally acquired images for use in marketing and presentations, datasets with complex structures, or specialized resources to support specific courses such as allowing students to interact with scores while they listen to music?

User needs drive the design process. The almost limitless possibilities must be reduced to a discrete set of capabilities that will be provided. When determining the purpose, it's important not to get bogged down in discussions about what could be done. Rather, attention must be focused on what will be done. Search boxes do not appear until code specifies their size, location, and appearance. Search results do not display until resources are acquired, encoded, structured, and made searchable. Patrons cannot even use text, images, or audio unless they have software that interprets the files presented by the repository.

Different purposes require different designs and technical infrastructure. Dissertations and articles may require embargo support, as well as the ability to provide access to supplementary data which require anonymization or access controls. Images for use in marketing and presentations may require the ability to manage large sequences contracted from individual photo shoots, access controls, and release forms that limit how and when they can be used. Datasets often require specialized metadata and ways for users to interact with resources. Music may require rights management as well as specialized data storage, display, and user controls. Each type of repository needs to interact with totally different workflows for acquisition and use.

### Is the library the appropriate entity to meet this need?

It's essential to articulate how the repository fits within the library's mission, priorities, and capabilities. Libraries have expertise in organizing and preserving certain types of information, but they lack the professional and technical resources to manage a wide variety of materials. Just as the post office isn't the best entity to provide e-mail service just because they have extensive experience delivering mail, the library isn't the best entity to manage and provide access to electronic resources simply because it has long been trusted to preserve and provide access to diverse physical resources.

Librarians are technically sophisticated and have strong organizational skills. However, their expertise, tools, and methods are largely oriented around needs surrounding bibliographic materials, and they are not usually equipped to provide services that require specialized technical knowledge, major computing facilities, or sophisticated access management. Many communities already have repositories designed around the needs of specific types of resources such as genomic or proteomic datasets. Researchers who need to provide supporting data for articles may be required to deposit their materials in specific repositories. Even cloud services designed for individual use are appropriate in many cases.

Even when libraries have the expertise and technical capability to provide a service, they should still examine whether it is appropriate to do so. Managing scientific datasets, extensive high-resolution video, e-mail, resources containing sensitive health or personal data, or information that is intricately connected to specialized platforms optimized for tasks such as mapping, bioimaging, and certain types of social media require the library to permanently commit support for specialized platforms and skill sets. Permanently dedicating limited resources for such services—especially when they duplicate services available elsewhere—delivers questionable benefits to library users.

The library does not become the appropriate entity to archive and manage a resource simply because no one else is doing so and the resource is deemed to be valuable. Just as many types of resources in the physical world are not preserved, the same is true of digital materials. It simply isn't viable to do everything people want, and so a serious examination is needed of how a project fits within the library's mission before permanently committing money and staff to maintain a custom application that awkwardly harvests and stores a specific resource, thus making money and staff unavailable for other priorities.

### How will resources be acquired, managed, and accessed?

The value that libraries contribute is in the selection, organization, and presentation of materials. They select materials that have value, they organize these materials in meaningful contexts, and they present them in ways that help the user. Just as a major difference between a museum and a landfill is that the former selects relevant items which are organized and presented in meaningful contexts, while the latter accepts whatever people bring, a repository must decide what it will contain and how to make those resources meaningful to users.

Digital materials present many of the same challenges as physical resources. Just as successful libraries have robust collection development policies and dedicate significant resources to catalog and organize physical resources, these things are also needed for digital materials—a successful outcome is unlikely if the collection development policy is to expect users to donate materials that they organize themselves. Regardless of format, the library plays a critical role in identifying materials that are organized into useful contexts and managed so that they are relevant for users. Nothing lasts forever, so an important component of a plan is to describe what happens when the library needs to get rid of objects or collections via deaccessioning or transferring the assets to another institution.

Some types of resources present special acquisition and processing challenges. Large files of any sort are difficult to transmit over network connections. Complex objects and those consisting of many items present ingestion, metadata, organization, and display issues. Many types of resources are produced by specific systems that the repository needs to interact with. The appropriate mechanism depends on many factors, but the library should not assume that a web form that allows users or staff to upload files one at a time or even in bulk will suffice.

Libraries have limited resources that only allow them to acquire and protect a small percentage of the world of information. It is therefore very important that library-managed repositories are supported by well-scoped collection development policies that ensure users will be able to interact with target collections as intended.

Discussions with stakeholders will help you understand which workflows the repository must interact with, as well as how resources might be added, modified, and used. Be aware that stakeholders often have unreasonable service expectations. For example, if departments submit photo collections or datasets consisting of thousands of files, these collections need good metadata to be useful. But content providers don't have the time or experience to create well-structured metadata, and library staff lack the domain expertise and time to create it for them. Regardless of a system's full capabilities, a major limiting factor is the completeness and consistency of the metadata, and the repository plan has to be built around what people will actually work with and do rather than what one might imagine they could work with and do.

## Selling the Project

A digital repository needs support from all areas in an organization. While projects to create digital repositories often generate considerable enthusiasm, they will have a significant impact on the services an organization provides, as well as the staff responsible for maintaining those services. For this reason, buy-in from an organization's stakeholders, staff, and users is critical to success. One of the first jobs of those planning a digital repository is to garner this support.

*How will you get support for the repository project?*

Many repository projects consist of a small number of individuals who advocate for a project and effectively get people to let them do it. However, a successful proposal needs support throughout the organization—from users and staff to the administration, which in turn requires each of these groups to have some ownership of the project.

The key to a successful repository project is to engage the people who will ultimately use it early in the process so you can understand how resources need to be acquired, managed, and used. Doing this requires identifying people in all areas who will ultimately be involved. These people will help you answer questions such as:

- Why will people use the repository?
- Who is going to use it?
- How are they going to use it?
- What type of resources will it contain?
- How big is it expected to grow?
- How can resources be maintained?
- How will access and intellectual property rights be managed?
- What systems does it need to interact with for ingesting, discovering, and using materials?
- Who is responsible for what parts of its operations?
- What workflows does it need to support?
- What special capabilities does it need?
- How are objects and collections that are no longer needed identified, and what happens to them?

Key stakeholders must agree on the worth of the repository and the viability of the plan because their buy-in is critical to securing funding. Answering these questions allows planners to refine the repository proposal, generate enthusiasm for the project, and engage those individuals who are necessary for a successful outcome.

### How will staffing needs be met?

You will also need to establish how to fulfill the different staff roles needed to run the repository services. A wide range of skills is needed:

- Help users become aware of and take advantage of services
- Provide overall administration
- Manage objects
- Metadata and vocabulary support
- Technical support

One person can fill multiple roles, but it is unrealistic to expect one person to fill all of the roles. Working with users is time-consuming but essential. Most users don't realize how repository services can help them, let alone that the library will be hosting the services. Working directly with users is also critical for understanding how their needs are or are not being met.

Objects are useful only when they are findable within a useful context. The context of an object within a repository is provided through navigation, structure, and metadata, so even highly engaged users need help creating and managing metadata, working with vocabularies, and establishing relationships between objects.

Even if the repository is hosted by a vendor, significant resources are needed for technical support. All systems require those who manage them to implement regular improvements, and users and staff need to load, modify, and change things in bulk as well as individually.

### How will start-up funding needs be met?

Repositories require start-up expenses for which one-time capital requests or grants can be pursued. In either of these cases, the library needs to demonstrate that the repository meets compelling needs, and it needs to provide a sustainable funding model, as described later in this chapter. This is where early work with stakeholders to learn what they actually need proves essential. A much more compelling case can be made when key users themselves appeal directly to funders via letters of support and other means, and they articulate how the repository meets their own critical needs.

For example, a repository could publish the scholarly output of an institution, data to meet funder requirements, or help a marketing or communications department easily find and manage videos or photos they've contracted for (which saves valuable time and avoids the need to pay to re-create material they can't find). Storing documents, images, recordings, and other resources can help those engaged in development work tell the story of the institution in much more compelling ways in order to help potential donors understand what they can be a part of. If your institution has paid infringement claims because departments used copyrighted images on web pages, it would save money to have a collection of approved images that departments could use. Researchers who need a place to mount data to comply with funder requirements or simply prevent repeating expensive processes to re-create datasets could potentially save money. New legal or institutional mandates are relevant, but these do not guarantee any financial or staff support.

It's a good idea to bring in stakeholders even if the purpose of the repository is to perform a function that libraries have historically performed well, such as providing access to theses and dissertations. To achieve broad support and enthusiasm for the project, it's critical to engage the user community. Don't just ask what they want—have them be active participants in the process. Reach out and spend time learning what they do, what they want, and what they need. Invite them to help select the system, and listen to what they say. It's very possible that the system they want you to build is very different than the one you would normally want to build.

What you learn from users affects your plan as well as initial and ongoing expenses. Except where relatively simple materials are concerned, it's not realistic to expect even the most sophisticated hardware and software to be able to organize all of the data the way people need them. Providing even basic access to simple images and text files requires the time-consuming creation and maintenance of metadata. The addition of these access points becomes much more difficult and time-consuming with video and more complex objects such as datasets, and to be useful, these resources often require extensive specialized metadata.

Certain design and functionality choices imply a long-term commitment to specific technologies that may or may not meet future needs and which may not themselves be viable in the long term. Repository designers should focus their activities on materials that can reasonably be expected to be maintained through future technology cycles. For each type of resource, planners need to know how they will obtain, process, and provide long-term protection for that type of resource using available methods and tools. As of this writing, there are no reliable methods for archiving certain types of materials, such as interactive resources, because these are often dependent on specific software products. Chapter 3 discusses approaches that can be used when there is a need to archive materials that are especially problematic, as well as how to identify appropriate technologies for a digital repository project.

### How will ongoing operations be funded?

The funding model plays an important role in securing support and is closely tied to the purpose of the repository. People accustomed to free Internet services funded by advertising and personal information often believe that repository services are cheap and easy to provide. The reality is that repositories are expensive. Maintaining growing and increasingly complex collections takes significant time and money, as does incorporating new materials. To be sustainable, funding for a repository must grow as its collections and scope do. If the library simply adds high-resolution video without considering what this means for long-term storage and delivery costs, it may well find the resources allocated to the repository overwhelmed after a short time.

Building and maintaining a repository require the library to permanently commit significant staff and financial resources—it's not reasonable to expect ongoing technology, service, and staffing costs to be absorbed by existing operations. This means that the library must secure a source of recurring funding, redirect staff and money from existing library services, operate on a cost recovery basis, or employ a combination of these approaches.

For most libraries, the only way to secure a new permanent budget line is to convince funders to redirect monies from another budget line. This is difficult because repositories are expensive propositions from the perspectives of common metrics such as cost per item or cost per use. Under normal circumstances, the library must demonstrate that the repository is worth cutting some other program to fund it, either because the value proposition is so compelling or because doing so saves money overall—and the work done to enlist the support of users for start-up funding will prove helpful here as well. In addition, a request for permanent funding needs to include a plan for accommodating growth so that the resources provided will continue to meet needs over time.

A credible growth and cost model is essential for securing support. It may be possible to support limited repositories such as those that provide access to small collections of images, documents, and sound files with a regularly budgeted amount that is slowly adjusted for inflation. If your repository will store large high-resolution video or image collections, scientific datasets, or other system-intensive resources, regularly budgeted recurring funds will most likely prove inadequate to meet ongoing needs unless retention schedules are implemented to manage growth or fees are implemented to help others prioritize what is kept. Growth can be limited via retention schedules or other mechanisms and the cost can be shared by users or depositors. Funders will not allocate money unless they are convinced that the amounts budgeted will cover the intended costs. Users will only support projects when the short- and long-term costs are acceptable.

## Getting Your Repository off the Ground

Building a repository is a complex process involving many people, so you will need to define the repository's purpose, scope, and requirements, as well as create policies and track progress. As you would expect, a number of tools are available to assist you with these tasks. Regardless of any tool or process, you must choose one of relatively few options for a given repository project. You will have the same technical and staffing constraints regardless of any plan adorned with matrices, checklists, and diagrams.

As you explore repository platforms, you'll encounter an overwhelming variety of standards and models, a few of the better-known ones of which are discussed in this book. Standards and models can be fully "supported" in noncompliant ways, so it's important to make sure your needs are being supported. The tools introduced in this chapter are essentially documents spanning hundreds of pages and saying that you need to be able to get resources and descriptive, structural, and administrative metadata into and out of the system reliably. If you can do those things, your repository can survive inevitable technology cycles whether or not your repository supports any particular model or standard.

Be aware that the tools presented here are predicated on assumptions geared towards the library's interests in preserving information and metadata. This must be a component of any sustainable repository, but it's important for this need to not overshadow the reason why the repository is being created in the first place. Use gives repositories their value, so user needs must take priority over the library's operational concerns.

It is virtually impossible to be involved in digital archives and not come in contact with the Open Archival Information System (OAIS) reference model, which has become ISO Standard 14721:2012. OAIS is relevant because it is general enough to encompass almost any kind of archiving, and it provides the conceptual framework for a growing number of digital preservation efforts. As a conceptual model, OAIS does not address implementation details. OAIS is concerned primarily with preservation and does not address the use cases that repositories are designed to address. Not all systems can be made OAIS-compliant, and the importance of compliance depends entirely on the purpose of the repository.

The Trusted Digital Repository (TDR) checklist, which is ISO Standard 16363, is used to audit and certify digital repositories. TDR is based on OAIS and contains specific criteria that can be documented. Like OAIS, TDR concerns itself with preservation and is not designed to accommodate use cases surrounding specific types of materials. TDR is useful for documenting the preservation capabilities of a repository or what those should be, but it offers no guidance for selecting platforms for specific purposes.

The Metadata Encoding and Transmission Standard (METS) uses the eXtensible Markup Language (XML) to contain the structure of digital objects and associated metadata. PREMIS is a dictionary to support the long-term preservation of digital objects. PREMIS allows you to describe who owns an object, whether the digital object is authentic, what has been done to preserve it, what you need to use it, and rights management information. The idea is that PREMIS metadata along with descriptive metadata in a schema such as Dublin Core or VRA Core can be put in a METS wrapper within an OAIS-compliant repository that can be audited with TDR, DRAMBORA (Digital Repository Audit Method Based on Risk Assessment), or some other auditing tool, as figure 1.1 illustrates.

The preceding three paragraphs may look like alphabet soup, but the tools and standards themselves are filled with much less accessible jargon and acronyms that make reliably managing data and objects appear more complex than it is. It

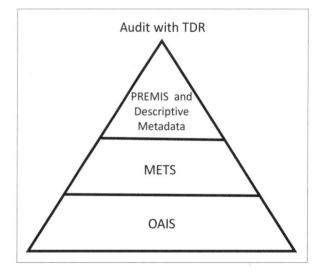

**FIGURE 1.1**

Preservation Standards Work Together

is important to be aware of the problems the standards are designed to help you address, but don't let them derail your repository project. None of these standards addresses critical issues such as:

- How to ingest resources
- How to assign consistent and complete descriptive, structural, technical, and administrative metadata
- System behavior for objects or metadata

In other words, those standards do not address the most important aspect of your repository—namely, the user needs it is designed to address. These standards only help with preservation, and even then only in an abstract way.

As of this writing, most open source and commercially available platforms are not OAIS-compliant. This does not mean that libraries should avoid these platforms. Rather, it means that your repository plan should be built around actual needs, and you shouldn't let your process get bogged down in a set of requirements defined for another purpose. Your repository will be successful if the users can interact with resources the way they need to, and you have the capability to migrate the objects and metadata necessary to use those resources to another platform.

## Resources

OAIS: https://public.ccsds.org/pubs/650x0m2.pdf

PREMIS: www.loc.gov/standards/premis/index.html

DRAMBORA: www.repositoryaudit.eu/participate/

TDR: https://www.crl.edu/archiving-preservation/digital-archives/metrics-assessing-and-certifying/is016363

# Choosing a Repository Architecture

2

**Some design choices** preclude others. Power and flexibility come at the expense of simplicity, speed, and ease of maintenance. The ability to handle a wide variety of resource types may preclude support for the functionality and workflows associated with specialized resources.

The best architecture for a repository depends on the purpose of the repository and its anticipated use. Because the platform determines how information is added, processed, stored, searched, and used, it has an enormous impact on the user experience as well as on all staff functions relating to the repository. For this reason, understanding the opportunities and challenges conceptually and the technically divergent approaches that exist is essential to making a good choice.

## Questions to Ask before Choosing an Architecture

Planners must have a solid understanding of what fundamental needs the repository serves and who will interact with it before identifying a repository platform. Virtually all repositories support a certain set of basic functions, such as adding, processing, managing, storing, and disseminating resources. Because the way in which these functions are implemented determines what can be done and how, it is critical to translate how people expect to interact with the repository into a set of platform requirements.

For example, if materials need to be protected, access controls are essential. If your library lacks the expertise or technical resources to install the repository, you'll need a system that can be hosted or maintained by a vendor. If data that requires protection for privacy, intellectual property, or other reasons will be stored, data controls are required. If users need to be able to manipulate large numbers of objects in the system, it must support bulk operations in a workflow they would find acceptable. If support for provenance or genealogy is required, appropriate metadata and navigation support are necessary.

To choose an architecture, the planning group must create a list of requirements. A list of requirements must be exactly that—a list that describes what you minimally need for the system to be usable. The list should be as short as possible, with highly desired functionality stored elsewhere. The most effective way to create this list is to directly involve staff and users in defining requirements, identifying questions to ask vendors, and system selection. The key to improving outcomes is to ensure that key stakeholders take ownership of the project.

## Who Are the Users and What Do They Need?

The users and their needs define the scope of your project and what you need in terms of financial, staff, and technical resources. For this reason, the most important question to answer before choosing an architecture is what need the repository serves.

The answer to this question defines requirements such as:

- Who are the users?
- What is in the repository?
- How will users interact with the repository?
- How will objects be added, retrieved, and maintained?
- Metadata and vocabulary support?
- What access and rights management are needed?
- Will integration with other systems be required?
- What is the system's capacity?
- Will preservation capabilities be needed?
- How are objects removed?
- What happens to the repository and its contents when it is no longer needed or supported?
- How will funding for the repository be maintained?

Best practices and standards such as OAIS inform the requirements-building process, but these things are tools that have the ultimate purpose of supporting user needs. For this reason, it's essential to work closely with users to understand their objectives, the materials they need, and their workflows.

For example, if the current workflow for image-processing staff is to use specific software for processing, adding metadata to, and managing images, the best repository workflow may be for them to continue to add metadata as they have been doing. These staff may be unwilling to change how they accomplish this specific task, since their existing workflow may be more efficient or integrate more seamlessly with other processes.

More broadly, fundamentally different needs require fundamentally different solutions. Communities that need to publish data and research require a very different system and must support different workflows than faculty requiring support for online educational resources, or staff needing to centrally manage an image archive or a peer-reviewed journal. As a practical matter, most libraries can only support a few systems. However, adapting systems that were designed for intrinsically different use cases is difficult, expensive, and often leads to unsatisfactory solutions that are difficult to migrate from later.

## What Types of Collections Will It Contain?

Part of understanding who your users are and what they need is identifying what types of collections your repository will contain. Is access needed for individual documents, images, and videos, objects consisting of multiple files, or something else? What are the relative size and quantity of these resources, what formats are they in, and what metadata are needed to manage and describe them? What formats will they need to be in for reuse by the users of the system? Do they contain sensitive information that must be tightly controlled?

The answers to these questions impact the underlying architecture as well as software options. If the repository will contain huge video or data files, neither hosted services requiring files to be uploaded over the Internet nor locally hosted services requiring uploads using web browser-based forms will be practical, because the uploads would take much longer than most users are willing to wait. Such files will likely mean users need to be able to stream, manipulate, or otherwise interact with objects without downloading them. Proprietary formats as well as large files in universally supported formats will require viewers, derivative copies, or other arrangements to be usable. Materials associated with any kind of specialized workflow may impact both repository software and architecture choices. Sensitive materials may require sophisticated access controls and audit logs of when items are accessed or modified.

## How Are Assets Acquired?

All repositories were initially designed to meet the needs associated with specific resource types, which are in turn associated with specific methods for ingesting materials and metadata. For example, some common platforms were initially designed to support needs such as sharing research, serving as a journal publication platform, disseminating images, supporting music education, or performing a number of other tasks. The repository project will be much more successful if the process needed for ingesting objects and metadata is compatible with what the system is designed to do.

- Are objects added one at a time or in batches?
- Is there technical, descriptive, or administrative metadata that must be added, or is this metadata already provided upon ingestion?

- Is metadata extracted from the objects themselves, uploaded in a separate process, or is it keyed in?
- What requirements are there for the metadata in terms of structure, format, and content?
- What operations such as normalization into standard formats or generation of derivatives are necessary for new resources?
- What opportunities for automation are available?
- Who will be managing which parts of the metadata?

Of the questions in the list above, the most important regard the addition of metadata and batch support. Metadata provides the context for resources which makes them useful, so special attention needs to be devoted to the addition of metadata, since the success of the repository ultimately hinges on the ability to efficiently provide the metadata needed to use and manage resources. Are the needed data fields supported, and can the required fields be completely and efficiently populated?

If support for batch operations is required, are the batch operations provided sufficient, and can they be made compatible with existing workflows or ones that could be realistically implemented? Even if an application programming interface (API) is provided that allows the library to design a custom interface, all tools must ultimately interface with humans and the way they actually work.

### What Rights Management and Access Controls Do You Need?

All systems require access controls, if only to define who can assign rights as well as upload and modify data and objects. Support for access controls varies widely across systems and includes the ability to restrict the ability to create, view, modify, download, and perform operations on collections, objects, or metadata based on factors such as:

- user
- group
- role (e.g., administrator, staff, collection manager, student worker, authenticated user, general public, etc.)
- network location
- object or metadata properties such as being protected by embargo, the Health Insurance Portability and Accountability Act, or the Family Educational Rights and Privacy Act
- other factors

Rights management potentially involves identity management systems, authentication protocols, and the storage of staff and user data. Legal and institutional requirements that dictate where and how data and user information can be stored can have an enormous impact on what systems can be used and where they can be hosted. To go live, the repository architecture that is selected must support required access controls and rights management, so it is important to consider these factors early in the decision-making process.

### How Does the Repository Handle Preservation?

A viable preservation strategy is necessary to provide long-term access to resources. Files and metadata must be protected against corruption or modification, and measures must be taken to ensure that resources are still usable through technology transitions. The OAIS model and the TDR checklists discussed in chapter 1 can be helpful, though possibly overwhelming for smaller libraries. Chapter 4 discusses preservation in detail.

Table 2.1 depicts a grid developed by the National Digital Stewardship Alliance that serves as a concise preservation guide and which is useful when considering repository systems. All things being equal, greater levels of preservation are better. However, in practical environments, it's important to be mindful of the following:

- The purpose of the repository is to make resources usable. Preservation is a tool that promotes use, but it is important to keep focused on the primary purpose of the repository—namely, use.

- The repository is the sum total of the people, procedures, and infrastructure that support it. Needs may be best satisfied by a combination of systems, so it is unnecessary to find a single system that does everything.

- Some resources, especially more complex ones, are difficult to separate from the platform they are in. It's desirable to maintain as few systems as possible, but some resources may be safer in special-purpose platforms rather than transferred to a system that may require both objects and metadata to be restructured or reformatted.

- Preserving resources requires much more than copying files to tape or online storage. Preserving resources means you know backups are not corrupted, and you can fully recover them years later if all hardware and software are lost.

- Even when files can be preserved perfectly, storing resources in their native format is likely to cause serious problems in the future unless they are in a widely supported archival format. Converting files to an archival format inevitably results in a loss of use or information, and leaving them in any other format requires emulation or specialized software for them to be usable. Legal and technical barriers

**TABLE 2.1**

NSDA Levels of Preservation

| | **LEVEL 1**<br>Protect your data | **LEVEL 2**<br>Know your data | **LEVEL 3**<br>Monitor your data | **LEVEL 4**<br>Repair your data |
|---|---|---|---|---|
| *Storage and Geographic Location* | Two complete copies that are not collocated. For data on heterogeneous media (optical discs, hard drives, etc.), get the content off the medium and into your storage system. | At least three complete copies. At least one copy in a different geographic location.<br><br>Document your storage system(s) and storage media and what you need to use them. | At least one copy in a geographic location with a different disaster threat.<br><br>Obsolescence monitoring process for your storage system(s) and media. | At least three copies in geographic locations with different disaster threats.<br><br>Have a comprehensive plan in place that will keep files and metadata on currently accessible media or systems. |
| *File Fixity and Data Integrity* | Check file fixity on ingest if it has been provided with the content.<br><br>Create fixity info if it wasn't provided with the content. | Check fixity on all ingests.<br><br>Use write-blockers when working with original media. Virus-check high-risk content. | Check fixity of content at fixed intervals.<br><br>Maintain logs of fixity info; supply audit on demand.<br><br>Ability to detect corrupt data. Virus-check all content. | Check fixity of all content in response to specific events or activities.<br><br>Ability to replace/repair corrupted data.<br><br>Ensure no one person has write access to all copies. |
| *Information Security* | Identify who has read, write, move, and delete authorization to individual files. Restrict who has those authorizations to individual files. | Document access restrictions for content. | Maintain logs of who performed what actions on files, including deletions and preservation actions. | Perform audit of logs. |
| *Metadata* | Inventory of content and its storage location. Ensure backup and non-collocation of inventory. | Store administrative metadata.<br><br>Store transformative metadata and log events. | Store standard technical and descriptive metadata. | Store standard preservation metadata. |
| *File Formats* | When you can give input into the creation of digital files encourage use of a limited set of known open formats and codecs. | Inventory of file formats in use. | Monitor file format obsolescence issues. | Perform format migrations, emulation, and similar activities as needed. |

SOURCE: www.digitalpreservation.gov:8081/ndsa/activities/levels.html

(e.g., when the resource and the platform are difficult to separate) may prevent either of these solutions from being viable in the long term unless policies and procedures are regularly assessed to ensure that resources are in usable formats.

- Some levels depicted in the table are intrinsic to certain platforms. For example, many repositories can interact with cloud-based storage solutions with robust archival support. If files are cryptographically transferred to a write-protected area that is designed to detect and repair corruption, they are safe.

- Metadata is essential to long-term success because it provides the context necessary to find and use resources. It also helps you recover from errors and understand the history of the object. However, it is expensive and difficult to generate.

- A repository can support only a limited number of formats, and emulating environments is sometimes not technically or legally feasible. In the physical world, libraries collect, maintain, and preserve resources only when they have the capacity to do so. This principle is still important with digital resources.

### How Will the Repository Be Managed?

People are a critical component of every repository—however capable the platform, individuals make the decisions and do the work that determine what can be added to the repository, how it is managed, and how it can be used. For any repository, the following questions must be answered:

- Who provides oversight for the repository as a whole?
- Who decides what content will be added?
- Who oversees the incorporation of resources into the repository?
- Who creates content?
- Who is responsible for individual resources and collections?
- Who supplies technical expertise to maintain the repository and advise on the management of specific resource types?
- Who addresses curatorial issues that emerge over time?
- Who manages compliance to ensure that access and retention are handled properly?

### Other High-Level Platform Decisions

A number of other high-level decisions need to be made before choosing a repository architecture. High-level architecture decisions as to whether the repository should be optimized for specific types of resources, based on open source or proprietary software, hosted locally or remotely, and based on virtual or real machines, must be based on users' and institutional needs rather than on broad generalizations.

#### Special-Purpose or General Platform?

Different products are optimized for different purposes for the simple reason that they were initially created to attain different goals. For example, consider the three early platforms adopted by libraries: DSpace, CONTENTdm, and Bepress. All three theoretically provide access to all types of resources, but each is much better suited for some purposes than others because they were designed to perform different tasks and are based on fundamentally different assumptions.

DSpace was initially conceived as a way to disseminate research throughout user communities, and it is still best suited to that task. According to this community-based model, it is assumed that resources can be understood, described, and organized best by experts who are not necessarily part of the library. In contrast, CONTENTdm is based on a highly centralized model for managing images, with tools to support the workflows that are often found in libraries. Rather than relying on authors to choose and organize what belongs in the collection, library staff fulfill these functions. Bepress was specifically designed to disseminate scholarly information primarily in textual format, so the system presumes a publishing workflow, has built-in support for features required in publishing such as embargo support, and emphasizes search engine optimization.

The functionality offered by each platform is very different, as is the staff and user experience, because each platform is based on a different assumption of who is responsible for doing what and how tasks are performed. Platforms have been created for publishing journals, creating exhibitions, storing and manipulating specialized data types, managing licensed or sensitive images, storing music to support educational programs, and many other diverse purposes. The platform, resources, and metadata are closely related, and optimizing them for certain purposes makes them unsuited to other purposes. However, not optimizing them for any purpose can lead to situations where they don't align with user needs, are difficult to use, or require extensive modification or are difficult to maintain.

## Open Source or Proprietary?

Open source software (OSS) is software created under a license that allows the user to modify and distribute the code. Open source software may be maintained by a group of companies or individuals, but it might also be maintained by a single company or individual. In contrast, proprietary software is owned by one or more individuals or companies and has restrictions on its use. Under normal circumstances, the code is not provided, nor are modifications permitted.

Even if your library lacks the ability to support open source software, support can often be contracted—often from those who produced the software. If you need the ability to modify functionality, many companies allow you to contract custom development, while others allow you to modify the application yourself. It is important to be aware that future migrations become more challenging as the level of customization increases.

It is usually unnecessary to decide whether the repository should be open source or proprietary before selecting a platform. The practical differences between OSS and proprietary software depend on the specifics of an individual situation. Either open source or proprietary software may:

- have better functionality
- be easier to customize for your needs
- have better vendor support
- have better user community support
- be more secure

- integrate better with other systems
- be fixed quickly when bugs are discovered

However, there are inherent differences between open source and proprietary software. For example:

- Procurement is completely different. Many institutions require a request for proposal (RFP), contracts that must be vetted by a legal office and signed only by certain individuals, and other requirements for proprietary products or services exceeding a certain dollar amount, but they require no particular process for OSS.

- Unless you contract a third party to maintain OSS, no outside party can be held responsible for performance, data breaches, or certifications required by your institution.

- Unless you contract with a third party, your library must have the skills needed to install, maintain, and update your software, as well as migrate all materials out.

- OSS provides access to the code, so extracting resources and data will be possible if your institution has the technical expertise. If a proprietary product does not offer export capabilities or an API with the requisite functionality as part of the product, future migrations may require the assistance of the vendor.

- If your library has the expertise, it may modify OSS tools for the specific workflows and features needed by the organization.

## Cloud-Based or Locally Hosted?

The term "cloud computing" has no formal technical meaning but is commonly used to describe services provided somewhere else, maintained by someone else, and delivered over a network. The term often implies redundancies to prevent failures, but lacking any specific meaning, the onus is on the consumer to determine what is meant when the term is used. A cloud service may or may not be:

- hosted in a secure data center
- more reliable than a locally hosted service
- better maintained than a locally hosted service
- more secure than a locally hosted service

Cloud services vary dramatically, and being "cloud-based" offers no inherent advantages over locally hosted options—in fact, many institutions maintain local clouds. A "local cloud" is typically a cluster of computers managed by your organization and configured to provide resiliencies to failures by the use of redundancies over a network. However, vendor-maintained cloud services on encrypted systems in secure data centers may be easier to use, more reliable, and more secure than any locally provided option.

When deciding whether cloud-based services are appropriate for your application, consider:

which institutional resources need to connect to the service and which policies apply. Many institutions do not allow internal systems to connect to outside services. This could affect authentication and directory services, billing, file transfer, and integration with other locally provided services.

data regulations at your institution. Even if data is encrypted and the vendor has no access to it, you may be prohibited from transporting certain types of data or at least required to go through an exception process.

size of files. It is not practical to transfer large datasets, high-definition video, and other large resources over a network connection outside of your institution—especially if staff or users need to be able to manipulate these objects.

Because the term "cloud" doesn't carry any specific meaning aside from service being delivered over a network, it is important to base decisions on how the service meets your needs rather than on whether or not a service is described as being a "cloud" service.

## Real or Virtual Hardware?

Recovering files is easy, but recovering systems is difficult. Unless you need specific real hardware connected to your service, virtual hardware is usually a better choice. Virtual environments offer the following advantages over real hardware:

Avoid the procurement and de-accessioning processes that are associated with physical hardware. Bids, purchase orders, shipping, inventory, installation, and surplusing at end of life are not necessary.

Greatly simplified disaster recovery. Identical hardware is not necessary to recover from hardware failures, and entire pre-configured systems can be launched within minutes. Testing disaster recovery is also simplified—it is only necessary to verify that images launch properly. Backups can be made with services running.

Easily relocate services to other environments. Services can be moved across departments as well as into or out of the institution.

Improve uptime.

Simpler upgrades. Successful experiments can be incorporated into the production image, while unsuccessful ones are quickly rolled back. Multiple different images can be kept.

Lower cost. Rather than buying hardware to accommodate the maximum anticipated use, you can provision only what is necessary and provision more or less as needs dictate.

Avoid vendor hardware lock-in.

On the same hardware, virtual machines are inherently slower because the emulation layer consumes resources. In addition, services hosted by virtual machines in shared environments may affect each others' performance. However, most repositories will perform well in a properly managed virtual environment.

## What Data Model Does Your Repository Need?

A data model is an abstraction that organizes elements and standardizes how they are related to each other. For purposes of creating, maintaining, and migrating repositories, it is important to be aware of the following:

Data models are only relevant to the extent that you can organize resources and their associated metadata into a form that supports the functionality you need, and you can export this same data in a manner that can be made understandable to future systems.

Data models do not define the contents of elements, how systems interact with elements, or any other aspect of system behavior. As a result, the underlying data model is only one factor of many that determine whether a system meets a need.

Most systems have their own data models, and as of this writing, no widely supported data model yet exists. Even when different systems have the same data model, there is no guarantee that they can share information.

Data and resources can usually be migrated from one data model to another, particularly when the migration is across systems that are designed to perform similar tasks.

A system may be fully compliant with a data model even if it doesn't claim to be so.

A system may meet both user and library needs even if it does not support the desired data model.

For the purpose of understanding data models, consider the Portland Common Data Model (PCDM). The PCDM is a simple but flexible model specifically created for repositories in that it is designed to express structural relationships between objects, as well as provide access control. A few things are particularly interesting about PCDM:

- It formalizes structures that can be found in systems that have been around for many years—including paper-based ones that predate computerization.

- It is designed for general use and was created with library use cases in mind. It may or may not be appropriate for specialized repositories.
- It is extensible, meaning that it provides an architecture for incorporating new functionality.

The PCDM is a minimalist data model by design. It defines only three types of things:

1. Collections
2. Objects
3. Files

and four types of relationships:

1. Has Member
2. Has File
3. Aggregates
4. Has Related File

Details about how PCDM allows these things and relationships to be used are available at https://github.com/duraspace/pcdm/wiki.

To understand how a repository that does not support a desired data model may be a good choice while a repository that does support that data model is a poor choice, consider a case where a library needs to control access to individual files or groups of related files based on network ID, group membership, and network location. Let's also suppose that file owners need to be able to grant permissions to groups and users.

For such a need, PCDM seems ideal because it allows access metadata to be attached to Collections, Objects, and Files. However, PCDM does not specify what access metadata is attached to records or how it is implemented. If a PCDM-compliant system lacks a concept of file ownership, the library cannot use the system. Likewise, if the system does support the concept of user ownership but is unable to communicate with organizational identity management systems, support the creation of necessary groups, or allow access based on network location, the library cannot implement the system.

Let's suppose another system that is not PCDM-compliant supports the desired authentication functionality, but permissions can only be allocated at the individual file level. If automation can be used with existing metadata fields in a reasonable workflow for users and staff to achieve the desired effect, the system might be an excellent choice, and future migrations to systems that support the desired data model would still be possible.

Small differences in system behavior can make a big difference in how people use a system, as well as their willingness to interact with it at all. For this reason, addressing crucial implementation details effectively is much more important than conforming to models and standards successfully used in environments where needs may be different than in your own library. So long as resources and metadata can be transformed to a usable form and converted to a desired form in the future, your library can implement a system and expect to be able to migrate in the future.

# Building the Requirements List

The answers to the questions above will enable you to build a preliminary requirements list. Requirements are ultimately driven by user and staff workflow. For a repository to be successful, users must be able to discover and use resources the way they need, and staff must be able to maintain the system and the resources it contains. A useful requirements list must reflect how technical, staffing, financial, and user realities can address the needs the repository exists to meet. The processes for ingesting, describing, establishing linkages between, using, and maintaining resources must be realistic as well as feasible.

A requirements list should reflect what is minimally needed, with desired functionality listed separately. The list below outlines a few features that are relevant for most repositories.

## *General*

- Accepts content in formats required by the user community
- Performs acceptably under anticipated growth and usage for life of product
- Maintains appropriate security for resources and metadata
- Ensures appropriate privacy
- Monitors system and resource health
- Accessible to staff and patrons with disabilities
- Interface offers user experience appropriate to materials

## *Metadata*

- Support for descriptive, technical, structural, and administrative data necessary to discover, identify, use, relate, and manage resources. Support for necessary vocabularies is highly desirable.
- Customize metadata to meet local needs
- Allows for systematic use of metadata

### Automation

- Supports bulk ingest, export, and maintenance of resources and metadata for use, analysis, or migration purposes
- Leverages embedded metadata and standards appropriate to materials
- Machine interface to interact with outside systems
- Supports protocols to interact with required outside systems
- Programmable and/or language-based method to manipulate data

### Access Control

- Authenticates using required authentication systems
- Supports appropriate controls for staff, user, and automated functions
- Supports required rights, privacy, and life-cycle controls
- Reports access settings of objects in the repository

### Resource and Data Management

- Maintains version control if appropriate
- Converts to appropriate formats
- Conforms with legal and institutional storage requirements
- Ensures integrity of resources and metadata

The most important aspect of choosing a repository architecture is to ensure that it is designed to meet the needs at hand. A repository's platform, policies, procedures, resources, and metadata are closely related. For this reason, platform choice must be driven by the needs identified as the reason for creating the repository, while taking into account the ability of the library to support it in terms of expertise, time, money, and institutional support. Asking the right questions early in the process will maximize your chances of success.

# Acquiring, Processing, Classifying, and Describing Digital Content

3

**The value of a repository** is determined by how it selects, organizes, and presents information. While libraries have successfully used a number of powerful tools such as approval plans, OCLC cataloging, the MARC format, electronic resource management systems, and knowledge bases for traditional library resources, the analogous standard procedures for identifying, processing, and organizing other types of digital materials are less developed.

## Planning Workflow

Libraries depend on a variety of procedures to incorporate books, journals, database packages, and other resources into their collections. A collection development process determines which materials will be added to or removed from the collection based on what users need and what the library has. An ordering and acquisitions process determines how libraries locate and obtain desired items wherever they may be. Other processes make these items findable and usable, whether they are physically managed by the library or made temporarily available with records, metadata, knowledge bases, and other tools.

Workflows define the physical and conceptual processes that occur when libraries acquire new materials, organize or manage the collection, and provide access. They determine who does what: what level of staff is needed, what specific skills these staff need, and what actual tasks they perform. Managing a library collection is a complex operation. Most people have difficulty finding things that they recently bought for themselves, even though they decide where those things are kept. However, these same people expect to easily find library resources regardless of when they were acquired, their format, or given the fact that their accessibility might depend entirely on decisions made by one of hundreds of staff members working at the library over the years. Reliable workflows and procedures make finding library resources possible.

The conceptual challenges of incorporating digital collections are similar to those for incorporating traditional resources. A mechanism to systematically identify materials to add to the collection must exist. These materials must be maintained and delivered in a manner that will be accessible to users over time and through technology changes. The items must also be described using metadata or a catalog record. As with physical resources, some digital resources must be handled individually, while others may be processed in batches.

Libraries develop a variety of workflows that are optimized to address the practical challenges presented by different types of resources. Digital repositories vary significantly in terms of purpose, what they contain, and the technical and personnel resources available to support them. For this reason, the processes for selecting, acquiring, processing, and organizing digital materials vary with the type of resource, as well as with how they will most likely be used. Although there are many ways to develop workflows, the most effective approach is often to identify what major tasks need to be accomplished and then to determine how those tasks can be broken down into discrete procedures. Once the tasks have been identified, the library can decide who will do them and how.

Repository design must reflect how people need to use the repository—that is, user workflow. When designing a repository, it's tempting to construct a data model that supports desired workflows and then add a user interface to that. However, the front and back ends of systems are intimately related, so using this process can lead to a system that's optimized for library rather than user purposes—and this is problematic when specialized resources are involved.

Instead, the process should begin with an understanding of what the ideal user experience is, and then a practical plan needs to be devised to create the data and technical infrastructure necessary to support that use. Every user experience depends on proper metadata and linkages between objects, and the success of the repository depends on this process being realistic and sustainable.

The degree to which automation can simplify workflow depends on the specific resources and tools available, as well as the technical capabilities of those using the repository. Even with a very high level of automation, human intervention will still be necessary to establish certain linkages between items, whether that involves a controlled vocabulary to identify related photos, or structural metadata that allows users to traverse a dataset.

The metadata that relate items to each other and which determine how they can be found and used are what give objects their value—otherwise no one will be able to use them or know they exist. But creating metadata requires both time and expertise. It is not realistic to expect content providers who are not metadata experts to provide this information, nor is it realistic to expect library staff without domain knowledge to create this information. Rather, the strategy needs to be to have library staff leverage the metadata provided by domain experts as well as the metadata extracted via automation. Workflows for ingesting and processing materials need to be based on realistic scenarios if the repository is to succeed.

## Collection Development

Once a rough framework has been established for how materials will be incorporated into the repository, repository planners must establish how content will be selected and acquired. The selection process is critical, but it is frequently neglected because many planners fail to appreciate how different the process for selecting digital content can be from the familiar process for selecting physical content.

For paper resources, selection and acquisitions are heavily influenced by a publishing model that has been slowly evolving for over 500 years. Publishing and distributing paper resources is a complex and expensive process. Because publishers and distributors lose money if no one is interested in a book or journal, mechanisms are built into the publication process to ensure that an item in question is of value to enough customers to be marketable. By its nature, the publication process imposes a minimal level of quality and directly contributes to the traditional association of good libraries with large collections. It also has led to a variety of mechanisms such as catalogs, approval plans, and other ways to help librarians learn about and obtain materials that might be of interest to users.

The Internet and rapidly advancing technology lowered the barriers to distributing works to the point that anyone can completely bypass the publication process and distribute virtually anything to a worldwide audience at negligible cost. Aside from dramatically increasing the number of authors, materials need not be edited, marketed, or be of any interest to any particular audience. Distribution is so decentralized that it is not reasonable to believe that librarians can rely heavily upon marketing literature, catalogs, approval plans, or other mechanisms used with print resources for purposes of identifying materials for inclusion in the collection. Consequently, they must find other means of learning about and acquiring resources that should be added to the collection.

Adding materials to the collection simply because they are available, requiring content providers to submit resources, or expecting librarians to discover resources through serendipity are three common methods that usually prove unsatisfactory unless used in combination with other techniques. Acquiring resources because they are available electronically makes no more sense than acquiring resources simply because they are available in paper form. Content providers cannot be expected to consistently provide resources because many of them will either not be aware of the library's need to archive materials or they simply don't care. It is unrealistic to depend primarily on individuals encountering useful resources primarily by means of serendipity. For these reasons, the workflow itself needs to include a reliable means for systematically identifying high-value resources that users expect, while avoiding low-value materials that clutter up search results.

Just as it is common in physical libraries to use different selection methods for different types of resources, it is appropriate to use a combination of methods to identify materials for inclusion in a digital collection. Selection is a time-consuming process that requires an understanding of what resources are available and what practical challenges they present, given the goals of the repository and the technology it is based on.

For a selection process to be successful, the following questions must be addressed:

### What resources are desired and where are they?

The success of a repository depends on the effective identification of materials that are relevant to the purpose of the repository. For this reason, the single most critical aspect of the selection process is to define as clearly as possible what should be included and where it can be found. The selection process must address a number of questions: How will selectors identify desirable resources? Who is the target audience? Are the resources in a physical collection waiting to be digitized? Are they oriented towards a particular topic or purpose? Are they in a CMS (content management system) or database? Who currently creates and maintains the resources? Are they part of a collection now, and if not, are they scattered across multiple websites? If they are stored in multiple systems, how do selectors know where to find them? What formats are they in? Who is going to use the collection and for what purpose?

The answers to these questions vary greatly from one digital repository to the next, so there is no "best" way to identify resources. If the purpose of the repository is to provide specialized information on a given topic, the first task is to identify where the desired information is and who maintains it. If it turns out that the resources in question are created and/or maintained by a small number of content providers, it may prove feasible to ask content providers to manually or automatically help identify useful resources. On the other hand, if the resources are created and/or maintained by a large number of individuals with diverse interests, it is unrealistic to expect consistent assistance in identifying relevant items, so alternative methods need to be explored.

### How will different versions of documents be handled?

Depending on what type of resources a repository includes, version control can be a serious issue. Although many resources are not changed after they are created, digital resources are inherently different from their physical counterparts because they can be easily modified. If the collection development policy includes resources that might be changed, which version(s) will be kept? The decision to retain or not retain different versions of resources has enormous implications for workflow, staffing, systems resources, and access.

If every version of a resource is retained, procedures need to be developed so that the repository staff know when a new version is available. Time will need to be spent processing the document, and systems resources will need to be allocated accordingly. Even if changed resources can be easily identified, and staff and systems resources are plentiful, how will users search for and use these materials—if seven versions of a resource are available, how do users and staff choose which one they interact with?

Retaining only a single version of a resource has its own problems. If only the most recent version is retained, a means to replace previous versions and to make appropriate changes to metadata is necessary. Similarly, a mechanism for informing the staff of updates must exist. Although confusion with duplication in the repository is reduced when only one version is kept, problems could emerge when a version that a user cited as an authoritative source is replaced. A similar problem will occur when the library only retains the first version that it encounters, but a user cites a later version.

### Who should participate in the selection process?

Will specialists locate and identify works to include in the repository, and if so, how will they accomplish this? Will an automated or semiautomated process identify resources of interest? Will content providers be expected to submit resources via a web page? The process of determining which resources are desired, where they are, and what tools exist to detect them should help identify who should be involved in the selection process.

Just as it is extremely useful in the physical world to have people with subject expertise help select materials in those topics, it is also very useful to have people who can be considered experts help select digital resources. We tend to focus on the technical aspects of digital collections, which often means that a web developer, programmer, or systems administrator is put in the role of curator. This is akin to having a printer or bookbinder select the books in a collection. In other words, make sure the staff involved are playing to their strengths.

### What tools exist to help automatically detect resources?

Can systematic ingestion tools (e.g., web spiders, data extractions from a CMS or other system, scripts, or other tools) be used to identify desirable materials? Identifying digital resources is often a difficult task, so multiple methods should be employed simultaneously. Automated tools can be very useful for identifying desirable resources, but in most cases, the identification process will still involve a significant amount of manual labor. For example, if systematic ingestion is used, how will the desired resources be separated out from the vast bulk of undesirable resources?

## Acquiring Content

Once a method for selecting content is determined, a mechanism using one or more of the following three methods for acquiring that content must be established:

- Content providers submit materials
- Staff collect materials
- Automated processes ingest materials individually or using batch processes

Ingesting discrete items such as articles, documents, images, video, and sound files is generally easy. However, acquiring digital resources is often a complex task that requires substantial compromises for the following reasons:

- Resources frequently consist of many components with complex relationships
- A resource may lack obvious boundaries
- The components of a resource may be distributed across systems
- A resource may be closely integrated with a specific platform or it may dynamically change when it is used

There are many potential methods for addressing the challenges presented by complex resources, but most fall into one of four general approaches:

1. *Object requirements:* Adopt a collection development policy that excludes troublesome resources
2. *Transform:* Reformat and restructure materials so that they are easier to process and preserve
3. *Kick the can down the road:* Presume that future technological advances will solve the problem
4. *Outsource:* Contract responsibility for preserving the resource to an outside party

## *Object Requirements*

All of these approaches have substantial advantages and disadvantages. Limiting the types of resources that can be added to the repository greatly simplifies workflow, storage, access, and long-term preservation. However, limiting the types of resources to be acquired has the effect of excluding items on the basis of administrative convenience for the library, rather than on the basis of the value of the resource. On the other hand, libraries have always required that certain physical prerequisites be met as a condition of materials being added to the collection. Most libraries don't accept materials that are falling apart or have some other problem which means they can only be preserved at a very high cost (if at all). Few libraries accept unreadable and obsolete tape, cylinder, punch card, or disk media. It is common for libraries to accept only materials that can be made available over the long term, and there is no compelling reason to abandon this long-standing practice simply because a resource is accessed by computer.

## *Transform*

As a strategy, reformatting materials limits the types of resources that can be added to a repository and offers most of the same advantages that simply accepting only certain formats does. It is important to remember that digital objects are inherently abstractions. When collecting, preserving, and disseminating these objects, it is literally impossible to share the original object as stored as bits on the original media. Instead, we make copies of those bits at some level of abstraction. In some cases, this is simple. For example, usually when word-processed files are involved, the textual content—hopefully with layout and formatting—must be kept but the bitstream itself is irrelevant. This agreement is important because word-processing technology constantly changes. Word processors only read a limited number of versions, and software to interpret formats that were once dominant such as WordStar and WordPerfect can be difficult to obtain. Fortunately, most libraries concerned with archiving documents save them in a much more stable format such as Unicode, Portable Document Format (PDF), or one of the other common file types used by the National Archives and Record Administration and described at https://www.archives.gov/preservation/products/definitions/filetypes.html.

Transforming inevitably results in a loss of information and functionality, and converting some resources is difficult. Simple objects consisting of individual images, audio, and video files are often straightforward from an ingestion and processing point of view. However, even textual documents can contain embedded images, spreadsheets that contain formulas which reference other documents, and other objects that are difficult to store and preserve. Other types of objects—especially those associated with specific platforms—often present complex challenges.

Nonetheless, as chapter 4 explains, migrating resources to an archival format as they are incorporated into the collection is usually the most practical approach. By supporting only a small number of formats chosen for their archival qualities, libraries can significantly reduce the likelihood of information loss while dramatically simplifying future migrations. Any digital object that is kept long enough will require either a transformation or the development of an emulation environment which only moves these same problems to the emulator.

This process sounds straightforward, but it's sometimes difficult to implement. Consider a simple example in which a main document is a table of contents with links to component subdivisions. These subdivisions also contain dependencies (images, stylesheets, etc.) as well as links to supporting documents that may or may not be in HTML. If, for instance, the document is within a page containing global navigation links, then instructing the software to make copies of everything down to a depth of three links could result in the retrieval of many hundreds of files. Some of these may be in proprietary formats that will be unreadable in a few years. Other pages may "talk" to live services that cannot be archived or even intentionally designed, so they cannot be copied easily. Likewise, if the original site encapsulated the entire resource or it uses Adobe Flash or other proprietary technologies to create navigational elements or other critical aspects, some features in the stored version of the resource may not work as desired.

## Kick the Can down the Road

Ignoring the problem by assuming that technological advances will later resolve problems is the riskiest strategy of all. Historically, libraries do not have a good record of fixing issues that were unresolved during technology transitions. For example, when libraries converted from card to online catalogs, many cards at large libraries were not converted for a variety of reasons, so these resources were not findable in the online catalog. Not surprisingly, the labor that couldn't be found to transfer them to the online environment during the initial conversion also couldn't be found years later when other priorities had emerged. Additionally, the important contextual knowledge needed to successfully transition may be lost over time. Most librarians have not used a card catalog since the 1990s, and it's safe to say that only a minuscule percentage of the cards that remain unconverted ever will be.

Likewise, few computer, audio, or video materials ever get converted, so they become unusable as the hardware and software necessary to use them becomes unavailable. It is unlikely that libraries will suddenly acquire the considerable additional staff and money needed to identify all materials in problematic formats and take the action that is necessary to make them usable—especially since many libraries already struggle to meet current demands. For this reason, hoping that some unspecified future development will solve problems is not a realistic preservation and access strategy. To prevent the loss of resources, it is highly recommended that repository planners address access, processing, or preservation issues as early as possible. Emulation can mitigate the effects of technology cycles, but this method also suffers from shortcomings, such as possibly requiring users to be familiar with obsolete technologies, not being viable for objects depending on proprietary hardware or software, and bringing into question how the emulators themselves will survive technology transitions.

## Outsourcing

The option of contracting responsibility for preserving some resources to outside parties may seem counterintuitive. However, just as the principle of access has been displacing that of ownership for purposes of evaluating library collections, there is nothing inherently wrong with digital repositories relying on third parties to provide access to certain resources. Conceptually, this method is similar to purchasing database access in that it effectively outsources a portion of the collection to an entity that is better equipped to manage it. Moreover, it is now common for libraries to outsource operations that were once considered core library operations, and libraries now frequently turn to vendors to host systems for virtually all aspects of library operations, including repositories.

Contracting responsibility for providing perpetual access to materials is appropriate in certain cases, particularly for interactive resources that are data- or software-driven. As chapter 4 describes, two basic strategies can be used to ensure that resources will be available when technology changes: emulation and migration. For a variety of reasons, it is not feasible to emulate complex software environments:

- Even in a perfect world where emulators are free and work perfectly, they may require users to master completely unfamiliar technology for which no documentation is available.

- Creating emulators is very expensive. Just as formats become obsolete, emulators also become obsolete, since the environments they run on change, requiring yet more emulators for them to run in.

- Software environments often contain proprietary technology that cannot be replicated or licensed in perpetuity.

- Software environments may be designed to interact with specific hardware that no longer exists and cannot be synthesized.

- Knowledge and access to the source code needed to make modifications may no longer be available.

When emulation cannot be used to archive interactive resources based on databases or services distributed across multiple machines, these resources simply cannot be migrated.

Relying on third parties does not necessarily require the library to even pay to have access to important resources maintained. In its simplest form, the library need only create a formal agreement with the entity that maintains the data, and this agreement establishes that the data are important and must be maintained indefinitely. In certain cases, relying on organizations with an inherent interest in the resource to be responsible for preserving that access is appropriate as well as cost-effective. Just as it is perfectly reasonable to trust the Patent Office to provide perpetual access to patents and that the appropriate departments will maintain court proceedings, entities vested in the ongoing provision of an information service, such as specialized scientific communities, are often in a better position than the library to provide access to that service. Having said this, other organizations have different priorities than libraries, and providing access to such materials from other access mechanisms can be difficult unless their systems are designed to be used in this way.

## Organizing Content and Assigning Metadata

An object's value is ultimately defined by use, and people must find objects before they can use them. For this reason, metadata must be assigned to or extracted from acquired objects so they may be searched and relationships between them understood. The first step in developing a workflow for adding or extracting appropriate access points is to consider what types of materials will be added, who will use them and how, how they will be searched, and what the expected size of the repository will be. If the repository consists of Portable Document Format (PDF) documents or simple image files that are uploaded to a server, the processing required will be substantially different from processing web pages or an eclectic collection of multimedia resources. Likewise, completeness and consistency of metadata are far more important for repositories that contain millions of items than for collections containing only a few thousand items.

A repository's usefulness depends heavily on how well it associates similar items and allows users to find what they need. There are many ways to organize electronic resources, but one of the time-tested ways to provide access is to create or extract metadata that is embedded in the resource or stored in a separate record. All repository software relies on metadata to help users find things—in fact, the traditional library catalog card is metadata printed on paper.

The quality and completeness of metadata are critical to its usefulness. Although it's administratively convenient to store information in its original form and rely on automated means to identify access points, this approach rarely leads to adequate long-term access. Resources—especially nontextual ones such as those consisting of images, video, or sound—lend themselves poorly to keyword searching. File formats become obsolete or require users to install software which may be expensive or difficult to find, if it is available at all. Even if resources already contain metadata, one cannot assume that it is useful.

Even when only textual resources are concerned, searching representations of objects satisfies a different need than searching objects themselves via full-text search—imagine trying to find a book, article, or other resource if the title, author, or subjects you wanted to use to find it weren't separately recorded and you could only use keywords against a search interface to find what you needed.

User- or author-provided metadata is often not helpful and sometimes does more harm than good. To be useful, metadata must be consistent and provide access points within the context of the collection. Authors and patrons are usually unaware of how their work fits in with other resources or how it will be used. Consequently, they typically supply terms that reflect their own interests and views rather than those of the broader user community that the repository exists to serve. Metadata must be consistent to be useful, so if similar resources aren't described with a similar level of accuracy, specificity, and completeness, it won't be possible to predict which search strategy will be most successful. Web search-engine companies such as Google have known this for a long time and ignore user-supplied metadata for that reason.

Providing full cataloging of electronic resources is often impractical, but it is important to develop procedures that produce metadata which is consistent enough in terms of quality and completeness to reliably identify resources. The methods used by major search engines often prove ineffective for digital repositories because the algorithms these search engines depend on only work effectively with very large numbers of resources. Search engines base their results on factors such as the number of linked resources, click-through activity, formatting, and a number of statistical criteria. These methods are highly effective when used on huge numbers of heavily used documents. However, these same methods provide much less satisfactory results when used on small collections containing predominantly low-use resources.

## Structuring Content

Metadata can be used to organize works into virtual subcollections, but it's sometimes desirable to impose a structure on a resource that was not present in the original source materials. For example, many organizations issue newsletters, bulletins, regular reports, and other materials in a pattern that follows a serial publication pattern. The organizations' websites frequently include a link to the current issue, and links to older issues may or may not be provided. If these issues are simply treated as electronic documents, the effect would be similar to creating a new record in a traditional catalog for every issue. Aside from filling the catalog with enormous amounts of duplicate data, navigating and locating specific issues become awkward, since a frequently produced publication could easily be represented by hundreds of entries in the repository. An obvious solution is to create a record or index page listing the issues in reverse chronological order even if the original publisher provides no similar navigational tool.

Although electronic serials can be made navigable with the appropriate metadata, such a solution requires the system to properly interpret and sort a wide variety of enumeration schemes. These various enumeration patterns would invariably need to be entered as plain text because there are too many different patterns for a system to list them all. Also, the serial title would need to be entered exactly the same way in each record. Otherwise, even minor discrepancies would cause different issues to appear under different titles—which would make it effectively impossible to browse issues.

Likewise, digital resources are even more likely than physical resources to consist of many individual components. With paper materials, the indexes, appendixes, and other supplementary materials are usually bound with the main work. However, digital resources might store different sections of text and supplementary material in separate files, particularly when the supplementary material is in a different format from that of the main document. It's possible to express the relationships between the various components with metadata, but it's very difficult to do this in a way that will allow the work to be used as an integrated whole. As is the case with serials, the slightest typographical error can separate the components from each other. Again, to make the resource usable, a separate record aggregating the resources or even an index page listing the components in an appropriate order might be far more helpful than complex metadata.

Despite the challenges it presents, good-quality metadata is usually the core of any good organizational scheme. Metadata can store information about the format, purpose, associated people and organizations, time, place, relationships with other resources or collections, and any other appropriate information. It is important to be aware that the system has to be able to interpret the metadata for it to be useful—there is little if any value in storing information that systems do not use. With few exceptions, storing metadata that current systems cannot use is unproductive.

For example, over the years, catalogers have spent enormous amounts of time meticulously encoding cryptic fixed fields that store information about various types of illustrations and tape formats, as well as whether the item contains conference proceedings, is a Festschrift, or contains bibliographical references. No major integrated library system (ILS) uses any of these fields or a number of others that are equally obscure. Most of these fields are ignored outright, and there is no patron demand to see or search them. Consequently, it is unlikely that this information will ever be usable. It is not difficult to imagine scenarios in which some obscure bit of information would be useful. However, the fact that someone might conceivably find a use for the information does not justify storing it. Storing information "just in case" someone may need it at a later date takes resources that would probably be better spent providing information and services that people already need.

As metadata becomes more detailed and complete, the possibilities for searching and organizing a collection increase. However, creating elaborate metadata is expensive and time-consuming, and it is also prone to errors and omissions. Metadata must be applied consistently to be useful, or systems will either ignore it or normalize it to a simpler form. For example, in addition to the cryptic fixed-length fields described above, the MARC standard for bibliographic records defines literally dozens of variable-length note fields. Despite the fact that notes in the catalog record are stored as free text, different MARC fields are used for notes depending on whether they concern bibliographical resources, summaries, translations, reproductions, access restrictions, file types, dissertations, or a number of other things notes may be written about. Each MARC field is associated with a separate numeric tag and may contain a myriad of subfields. Guidelines for inputting notes exist, but the notes themselves vary considerably in terms of structure and completeness. This should not be surprising, given that cataloging rules change over time, practices vary from one library to the next, and notes consist of free text. To compensate for the variability of how notes are input, the vast majority of systems treat almost all note fields identically. In other words, catalogers at many institutions spend countless hours encoding information that will never be used. The notes may be useful, but the specific fields, indicators, and tags are not. The lesson to be learned is that repositories should only require metadata that can be entered consistently.

Consistent metadata structures are essential, but it is also important to ensure that the contents of various metadata fields are normalized as much as possible. This means that when subjects, names, organizations, places, or other entities are associated with a resource, those who assign metadata should select from an authorized list of preferred terms rather than type in free-text entries. A way to add or suggest new preferred terms should be available, and new terms should be curated before being added to the authorized list.

To help users, metadata must categorize resources, and categorizing requires entering these resources consistently. If the documents created by an author named James Smith appear in the repository under "Jim Smith;" "Smith, James;" "J. T. Smith;" "Smith, James T.;" "Smith, J."; and a number of other variations, finding documents that he authored and distinguishing him from other authors with similar names will be difficult. Likewise, if subjects are not entered consistently, documents about the same topic will be assigned different subject headings—this makes it significantly harder to find materials about a resource or topic. Authority control can seem slow and expensive, but it is worth the trouble. Without it, a database will fill up with inconsistent and unreliable entries.

When determining how to use metadata to organize resources, repository planners should take reasonable steps to ensure that the metadata is compatible with that used in other collections that users will likely want to search. There are so many sources of information that it is unreasonable to expect people to search each one individually; the repository should be designed so that it can be included in federated searches.

The best way to give users the capability of searching the repository and other collections simultaneously is to employ a robust metadata scheme that is applicable to as many different types of resources as possible. Simple but versatile metadata schemes, such as Dublin Core, are most likely to prove robust enough to meet the evolving needs of many repositories. Alternatively, the repository should use metadata that can accurately be translated into Dublin Core or other widely used formats. Be aware that all metadata schemes, including Dublin Core, have disadvantages. For example, the simplicity that makes Dublin Core easy to use also means that it cannot express many concepts and relationships, making it unable to meet many needs. It does not define how data are entered, so the data can be inconsistent even if the fields themselves aren't. (Key metadata schemes are covered in detail in chapter 5.) Particularly complex and nonstandard metadata should be avoided because generating them is expensive, and they can create compatibility problems when used with other systems or when the time comes to migrate to another platform.

## Crowd-Sourcing

Many users have a knowledge of specific resources that library staff lack. They may know when and where a photo was taken or be able to identify the people in it. They may have expertise on documents that allows them to assign topics more effectively. They may know how to describe data in a way that makes it more useful for those who need it. Even when they don't bring specific expertise, they can provide labor to help with time-intensive tasks.

In addition to these benefits, allowing users to contribute metadata and descriptive information provides a mechanism for volunteers and others to engage with collections more directly. However, it's important to consider a number of issues before allowing users to contribute metadata:

- *How do you convince people to contribute?* People already have many demands on their time, so they need an incentive to participate. Strengthening the collection and improving access are rewarding, but libraries pay staff for a reason. The process for contribution needs to be rewarding enough that people will want to do it. Breaking down tasks into discrete projects and small, fun steps using games or other mechanisms may be part of the solution.
- *How do you ensure the quality and consistency of contributions?* How do you ensure that the information provided is correct, in a standard format, and at the right level of analysis?

    To be useful, metadata must be consistent within the context of the collection. For example, if three people add metadata to a collection, and one person provides broad headings, one provides very specific headings, and the third applies every heading she can think of, search results will be very inconsistent. If the people assigning headings refer to people, organizational units, geographical entities, and concepts in different ways, the results will be inconsistent. Different users have different levels of knowledge and are willing to invest different amounts of effort, and some may apply metadata designed to further personal or political objectives rather than to help the library.

To mitigate these issues, the library needs to train contributors, edit their contributions, identify contributions, and provide version control. Except for the fact that users do not need to physically access materials to contribute metadata and provide descriptions, the challenges of having users contribute metadata for digital collections are identical to those for having them contribute metadata for physical collections.

## Resource Identification

Part of the ingestion process needs to involve creating identifiers so the resources can be retrieved later. Identifiers are a little less straightforward than may appear on the surface. All repository systems automatically create identifiers, and most provide "permanent" Uniform Resource Locators (URLs), but these often become problematic in future systems after the resources are migrated. Moreover, the question of what identifiers to create and what metadata to associate them with arises when an object consists of many components.

Understanding identifiers requires familiarity with some jargon—you will hear about URLs, Uniform Resource Names (URNs), and Uniform Resource Identifiers (URIs). People are most familiar with URLs because they use them every time they access a resource on the Web.

Here are the important things to know:

- URIs are text identifiers that identify a resource. A URI may or may not include a network location.

- All URLs are also URIs. A URL must include a network location.

- All URNs are also URIs. URNs unambiguously identify resources but do not include a network location.

- When sharing information about how to access resources, you should use URIs that will be the same after you migrate rather than URLs that are different for each repository platform.

Figure 3.1 demonstrates the difference:

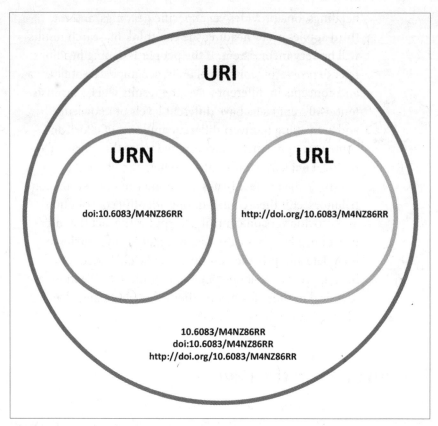

**FIGURE 3.1**

Differences between URI, URL, and URN

URNs and URIs do not need to look like computer addresses—they only need to be unique strings. For example, ISBNs and ISSNs are URNs and therefore are also URIs by definition. In figure 3.1, all the forms of the identifier are URIs. The string 10.6083/M4NZ86RR is a URI, but it is not a URN because it is not explicitly identified as a DOI—that same string could be used to identify resources that is not a DOI (Digital Object Identifier). The string doi:10.6083/M4NZ86RR is a URN because it unambiguously identifies the resource as a DOI and can be resolved using a mechanism of choice. The string http://doi.org/10.6083/M4NZ86RR is a URL because that takes someone directly to the resource on a network. Notice that while a URL uniquely identifies a resource on the network, these are subject to change because the object may be moved.

Handles, DOIs, and PURLs (Persistent Uniform Resource Locators) are all URIs that use an unchanging identifier to direct users to a resource. Identifying an object and directing a user to that object are separate functions, but it is desirable to use the identifier to do both. A PURL is just an address on the Web that redirects the browser to another address. PURLs look like regular URLs. Consider the following entry for

http://purl.oclc.org/digitallibraries/book

The http://purl.oclc.org is the PURL resolver, and the /digitallibraries/book is an arbitrary string that points to a record for this book. If it is desirable to have the PURL point only to the latest edition, the address that the PURL points to can be changed without affecting the original URL. The advantage of using a PURL over a regular URL is that a PURL resolution service is likely to be more stable. If a resource is migrated, the access URL will most likely be different even if the same domain name is used, but the structure of the PURL will remain the same.

Like PURLs, the Handle System provides a level of indirection to resources. It is different than PURLs in that rather than consisting of arbitrary strings which are managed on a central service, handles consist of a naming authority and a name managed on a distributed service. Consider the following URI:

10.6083/M4NZ86RR

The 10.6083 is the naming authority, and the name of the object is M4NZ86RR. To access it, the value needs to be routed through a proxy handle server, for example:

http://hdl.handle.net/10.6083/M4NZ86RR

which points to exactly the same place as the PURL above.

A Digital Object Identifier is a specific implementation of the Handle System—by definition, all DOIs are also handles. In fact, the handle above resolves as a DOI because it was originally created as one:

http://doi.org/10.6083/M4NZ86RR

http://hdl.handle.net/10.6083/M4NZ86RR

resolve to the same Internet address. Notice that the two different URLs are both URIs that point to an object with the same DOI—10.6083/M4NZ86RR (which is also a URI). The DOI never changes, but the URL can even if the doi.org and hdl.handle.net domains are very stable. For this reason, it is best to store URIs that are resolved to URLs on demand rather than URLs that may someday be inaccurate.

DOIs are different from handles in that they have metadata assigned to them, can express relationships, and are specifically designed to identify objects such as articles, reports, datasets, and other resources. The DOI technology platform is designed to be easy to use for large numbers of resources.

PURLs, handles, and DOIs are different from identifiers such as International Standard Book Numbers (ISBNs) and International Standard Serial Numbers (ISSNs) in that they are actionable and are designed to take users directly to a resource rather than merely identify them. However, be aware that redirected links receive lower rankings in search engines—and moreover, semantic information in the URL cannot help the resource be found.

If a library simply assigns unique identifiers on its own without using the PURLs, handles, or DOIs, the objects will still be findable, presuming those identifiers are indexed, since these identifiers will behave like ISBNs or ISSNs. However, such an approach presumes a separate search for each item rather than providing a single address that works anytime and anyplace.

## Setting Up Workflow

Acquiring, processing, and managing documents requires considerable human judgment and manual labor, so time, money, and staff effectiveness can be maximized if tools are optimized to accommodate workflows. Simply limiting the need for clicks and keystrokes by displaying information that staff and users interact with in the most prominent positions and by programming intelligent default system behavior and default values can significantly simplify and improve processing.

The workflow for acquiring and processing digital resources is often complicated and labor-intensive. The production and distribution of electronic resources may be decentralized, so knowing what to acquire can be problematic. Once materials are identified, they may consist of multiple interdependent files that require reformatting. Moreover, navigating a digital resource is inherently more difficult than browsing a physical volume that has an obvious structure and extent.

Identifying, obtaining, reformatting, cataloging (i.e., creating metadata), and properly protecting digital resources can be very time-consuming. However, the value of a repository lies more in how it organizes, presents, and preserves resources than in how many resources it contains. Therefore, to reach its full potential, a repository must have both well-conceived workflows that support its goals and tools optimized to facilitate those workflows.

## Batch Processes

Automating processes can save considerable staff resources and improve the consistency of the information. However, automation works best for repetitive tasks. Nevertheless, a number of tasks can benefit from at least partial automation. Automation can easily be used for a variety of tasks such as:

- Identifying materials to include in the repository
- Extracting embedded metadata
- Reformatting or renaming files
- Structuring resources and metadata
- Normalizing dates and other content
- Using application programming interfaces (APIs) to perform content analysis on materials
- Creating derivative and archival copies

Some reformatting processes are inherently problematic and inevitably result in a loss of functionality or usability. For example, if a spreadsheet references cells in other documents or contains formulas, these need to be converted to static values unless users will be expected to view the information using particular versions of the spreadsheet software. If the data are converted to static values, staff must ensure that the document can still fulfill its original purpose.

# Rights Management

Rights management must be built directly into the standard workflow unless the same provisions apply for all resources. Even if all materials in the repository may be freely used, this needs to be clearly communicated to users and staff. Depending on what is needed, rights management can be as simple as statements in the repository or within the metadata for the objects themselves. However, special workflows or functionality might also be needed to support rights management, requiring:

- Limiting access to authorized users
- Embargoing or expiring content
- Managing documents, releases, and other materials associated with rights
- Allowing the use of digitally rights managed (DRM) protected content
- Providing differential access

Users, content creators, and repository administrators benefit when rights are standardized. The easiest solution is to follow your institution's existing policy. If that does not exist or cannot be applied to your project, you'll need to work with users and content creators to see what rights management is needed. If possible, use standard and widely used licenses such as one of the Creative Commons licenses from https://creativecommons .org/. Be prepared to address practical needs. For example, a communications unit funded on a cost recovery basis cannot be expected to donate high-resolution materials for the library to give away for free. However, they might be willing to provide lower-resolution or watermarked images that may be useful for limited purposes if a mechanism that allows them to continue to finance their operations through the sale of full-resolution images is provided.

After identifying what rights management is needed, a collection policy needs to define what types of rights it supports, make these statements clear and obvious to users, and then the system can be adjusted to provide whatever support is needed. It is not recommended to allow content providers to define rights themselves. The inevitable result will render some items useless (a surprisingly common request by donors is to suppress items forever) or simply confuse people with too many different statements—which prevents the rights from functioning as needed.

Rights and access management is a complex topic discussed in chapter 8.

## Protecting the Integrity of Resources

Ensuring the integrity of resources is an essential part of acquiring and processing items. This issue is related to but separate from preservation, which is discussed in chapter 4. The idea of preserving integrity is simple—namely, ensuring that the resources and the content they contain are still usable after being added.

Operationalizing integrity is less straightforward because the goal of integrity is to replicate an experience with a resource rather than preserve a digital artifact as one would preserve a physical resource. Digital items differ from physical items in that the former don't exist in the normal sense of the word. A file typically takes the form of magnetic or electrical charges and often doesn't even occupy a contiguous area on a disk or in memory. There is no such thing as moving a file—it can only be copied from one place to another. Each time this happens, the bitstream is broken apart and modified as it is encrypted, mixed with transport protocol information, and recombined when rendered through software. By definition, any software used to view a document formats the information it is given.

To function, all repositories require that individuals have appropriate permissions to add and modify objects at certain points in the process. The ingestion process needs to allow legitimate reformatting and modification of resources while preventing illegitimate modification.

Many repositories employ checksums to help ensure the integrity of resources. However, the following should be kept in mind about checksums:

- Checksums only help identify modified files. They cannot help repair modified files except for purposes of identifying other copies that have not been modified.
- If checksums are kept with the objects, they only help identify inadvertent modification, since those who intentionally modify files can simply provide new checksums.
- Any legitimate modification of a file, such as creating a preservation copy or modifying the internal metadata, requires generating a new checksum.
- Checksums provide no additional value if files are transferred to an area where they are protected from modification, and deletion and transfers are validated with digital signatures.
- Regularly comparing checksums incurs significant disk activity that impairs performance.

- Modern file systems provide highly effective error correction and extremely reliable storage solutions that do not require external programs to be used.

- Higher safety can be achieved by using storage designed to preserve integrity that depend on cryptographic signatures to transfer and maintain files more conveniently, efficiently, and reliably than locally developed scripts. Numerous commercial solutions such as Amazon Glacier are available at low cost.

While libraries frequently modify files containing predominantly textual content so they will be much easier to manage, this practice is much less common for other types of files such as images, audio, and video—even when the file modified is a derivative copy. Many file formats, including all widely used image, audio, and video formats used in library repository systems, support internal metadata. Internal metadata affects the findability, usability, and migratability of resources, yet the dominant thinking as of this writing is still that such modification somehow alters the object in undesirable ways. Modifying the metadata does not modify the rest of the file at all, and retaining inaccurate and incomplete metadata within objects is of questionable value.

Having said this, there are workflow and administrative benefits to retaining files in a specific state, and the benefits of updated internal metadata can be achieved through mechanisms such as retaining multiple versions or outputting the latest and most complete internal metadata when the object is rendered or migrated.

# Preservation Planning

**Preservation is often** the last thing considered as part of a digital library platform. It is the part of the project that is hidden from users and organizations, and it is something that people don't think about until content needs to be migrated, or serious issues occur requiring systems or content to be restored. It is in these moments that the failure to plan for preservation can have long-term costs and ramifications for an organization and personal individual careers.

Why does preservation often get ignored? There are many reasons, but these are the most common ones:

1. A fundamental misunderstanding within organizations and their information infrastructure staff of what preservation entails.

2. Organizational paralysis, given the broad scope and fuzzy workflows related to preservation work.

3. Preservation is viewed as a software and systems problem, when in reality, it's very much a people problem.

We'll take a closer look at why these three themes often push organizations to ignore preservation planning, essentially placing the digital library platform's long-term fate on hope and luck. This is a recipe for disaster, but one that far too many organizations currently employ. The focus on the access of content, the ability to build new collections, and serve new users tends to override the long-term planning needed to preserve that access for future generations. And to be clear, preservation is all about access—without access, it's hard to argue that successful preservation of content is occurring. So while the two concepts of preservation and access are often viewed separately, they should go hand in hand, as the success of one directly affects the other.

For digital preservation planning to be successful and sustainable, it cannot be the job of just one person or one system. It must represent a cultural value that permeates every aspect of an organization's digital strategy. And to be clear, this is hard. Digital preservation is difficult. It's more than difficult—in many ways, it's impossible when viewed in the same light as preservation within an analog space. It requires a significant shift for cultural organizations that have traditionally focused on the preservation of a physical object to move to a digital space where preservation is focused on the long-term curation of an object's digital content and digital representation.

## What Is Digital Preservation?

Let's start with what preservation is not—backing up data is not a preservation plan. This is often a point that needs to be clarified for many in the information technology space, since data backups are the way in which IT staff protect data on a network. Data backups are an integral part of a digital preservation plan, but they cannot be the preservation plan. The difference isn't simply one of semantics, but one of goals. When organizations perform data backups, these backups are designed to restore production data quickly so that access to a specific program or dataset can be resumed. For example, if the server that stores your e-mail account is corrupted, the organization managing the system needs data backups to restore your information efficiently. In a sense, data backups are a passive action—they are a function of the system that works with them.

Digital preservation is an active process. Preservation is concerned not just with making copies of the content, but with the ability to provide long-term access as well. Preservation data must be actively curated, selected, handled, and even repaired (migrated) in order to preserve long-term access. While preservation does involve many of the same processes that are found in doing data backups, the need to provide long-term access complicates the process, and injects a human, curatorial element into the preservation process.

And when considering preservation, it is this active process of curation that is important to remember. A successful preservation repository cannot be a digital attic, a place in which to just toss digital objects. Preservation requires the curation and maintenance of the context of objects, which means the development of an active collection development strategy. Strategies built around the hoarding of digital content will be apt to fail, since this approach creates a disincentive to actively curate content. For digital repository managers, this is particularly important, since organizations have historically been so starved for active community participation in their repository platforms that they accept nearly any content and effectively create a digital dumping ground. This simply places unrealistic expectations on the organization's ability to provide long-term access, and dilutes the repository's overall impact. It also places the repository owners in a difficult position, since they are ultimately responsible to develop a cohesive preservation plan around an organizationally dysfunctional collection development plan.

So, what exactly makes up a good digital preservation plan or strategy? It should follow some basic guidelines:

1. For preservation to occur, long-term access must be guaranteed. Materials that cannot be accessed have not been preserved.

2. Preservation requires the maintenance of useful context, because context provides objects with meaning. This context may involve Dublin Core metadata, Archival Information Packages (AIPs), file structures, and/or otherwise structured and formatted data so people can use it in their own contexts.

3. Preservation does not end when a digital object has been saved—this is when it begins. Digital preservation requires the constant curation of content, evaluating not only the validity of the data through fixity checks, but also the continual evaluation of how the content fits into the collection development strategy, accessibility options, and long-term risk identification (i.e., file formats).

4. Digital preservation is messy, and that's okay. The process is always an imperfect one. Organizations should strive to do the best they can, while making the best use of their resources to ensure the long-term access and security of content.

5. Preservation is much more about people than systems, even if preservation activities are often tied to specific software or services. These certainly are helpful, and they are tools that enable organizations to do large-scale preservation activities at scale. But ultimately, successful digital preservation programs hinge on people and their ability to make the best decisions they can and then carry them out. Too often organizations become paralyzed by the perfect, and in this space, there is no one perfect solution. There are certainly best practices, but even these practices need to recognize that the boundaries around digital content are never fixed—they are mutable. This mutability requires not only flexible systems, but individuals who are able to work and thrive in a space that will likely be constantly changing.

One of the common misconceptions around digital preservation planning is that it is largely a systems issue that can be fixed with storage and resources. This goes back to the basic mindset that preservation is generally equivalent to data backups, and that we can assume that our digital objects are safe as long as data backups are being completed. As the above illustrates, this just simply isn't true. Unless access and active evaluation are parts of a preservation plan and process, an organization isn't really doing long-term preservation planning, but rather, just backing up bits.

## Preserving the Content and Context, Not the Medium

Preserving digital objects is significantly different from doing so in the analog world. One major difference between digital and analog preservation is that digital preservation should not be tied to a digital object's physical medium or carrier. Some cultural heritage organizations spend significant resources attempting to preserve the physical media that digital objects are stored on—tape drives, floppy disks, CDs, DVDs, flash drives, memory cards, and other media. But this process is a fool's errand because these media eventually become obsolete and fail. These physical media may have value as historical artifacts, but they have little preservation value. Digital data begins to degrade from the moment it is written onto a physical medium, and it continues to degrade with each subsequent reading. Physical media will become less relevant as a growing number of resources are transmitted over networks, though they will continue to play a role for the foreseeable future. This means that organizations must be clear about what they are trying to preserve and begin to plan on how that preservation will take place.

Digital preservation focuses primarily on digital content and the digital representation of that content. For example, let's say that you create a doodle in GIMP[1] and save the content as a PNG (Portable Network Graphics) format and store this item in a digital preservation system. What are you trying to preserve? Do you want to preserve the content, forever, as a PNG and preserve just the raw bits for some later user to attempt to decode? Do you want to retain the original compatibility with GIMP? Should you be concerned with the representation of the data, that is, preserve the visual display of the doodle so that it renders the same in fifty years as it does today? These are all questions that archivists and digital library designers are asking themselves every day, and this is why so much work is being done in the areas of software emulation and migration.

### Software Emulation

Software emulation approaches digital preservation as a bit-level problem. Organizations seek to preserve the original, true format of a digital object. In the above example, there is the PNG-formatted file of my doodle. The system would then seek to preserve the PNG format in perpetuity. The challenge with this approach is that file formats change, they become deprecated, or unsupported, and they disappear. And this happens all the time. Consider Microsoft's popular MS Word Document format. This format is nearly ubiquitous in the document-editing space, but Microsoft continually removes support for older versions of the software. Currently, any files created prior to 1997 would be unable to be opened in a current version of MS Office. And files created in their older MS Works format require significant conversion and would likely no longer render properly in the current software. Before Microsoft Word was dominant, Corel's Wordperfect format was used everywhere and before that, everyone used MicroPro's WordStar. Nowadays, most people who didn't use computers in the 1980s and 1990s haven't even heard of these programs.

All disciplines contend with file obsolescence, and unreadable files have no use. In libraries and other cultural heritage organizations, PDF files have been favored for storing or creating document-based content. PDF is another format that is notorious for making significant changes between file versions, and PDF viewers continually drop support for reading older PDF documents. Even the so-called archival PDFs—documents stored in PDF/A—have been shown to be much less durable than originally conceived, since the PDF/A document format has multiple versions which impact the ability of a PDF reader to properly represent content stored in the container.

This approach assumes that so long as data is preserved at a bit level, access to both the original content and experience can be re-created through software emulation. And this is an approach being used today. At the iPres conference in 2016, Espenschied, Stobbe, Liebetraut, and Rechert[2] presented a paper on exhibiting historical digital artwork through emulation. The paper detailed the researchers' attempt to restore the original digital experience of Olia Lialina's net art piece, *My Boyfriend Came Back from the War.* The presentation and paper document the technical design and challenges related to using emulation to achieve the result.

Copyright law and software licensing models limit the use of emulation as a preservation strategy at the operating system, application, and file levels. However, projects like the Software Conservatory and large emulation and archiving projects like those found with the Internet Archive[3] or the Web Archiving Project[4] demonstrate that emulation likely will play a role in the long-term preservation of content, but likely will not be the primary mechanism for providing long-term access to cultural heritage information. These solutions tend to be software- or project-based, meaning that organizations counting on emulation as a long-term solution will likely find that content will remain inaccessible to users for the foreseeable future.

As useful as it is, emulation is not a silver bullet. Aside from requiring people to know how to use the emulated environment, emulation presumes that the resources are self-contained. The growing number of dynamic, distributed, and cloud-based resources present challenges that cannot be readily met simply by emulating servers and software.

### Format Migration

Format migration requires preservation to be an action verb, not a passive operation. Within archives and museums, this ties closely to the idea of curation. Just as physical artifacts require long-term curation, repair, and so on, digital assets need to be regularly treated to ensure that materials remain available and accessible. Considering the doodle example above, format migration would take a very different approach to emulation. Rather than attempting to emulate the environments used to create the original doodle, format migration converts the digital content away from the deprecated digital container format to a supported one. And like the Microsoft Word example, this happens all the time. When a user opens a file in the older MS Word binary document format, the software often will prompt users with newer software to upgrade to the newer file format. By following the file format upgrade path, content can generally be placed into a new file format that preserves the original format and user experience.

This approach comes at the cost of compatibility, since files migrated to new formats may not be accessible by users with older software or older systems. This is often the case in the Microsoft MS Word document example. In fact, in 2013, when Microsoft first introduced its "open" document format, all software older than 2013 was unable to view or edit the new file format. This created significant incompatibilities between document formats, and caused several problems within the MS Office ecosystem due to the large number of users working with older versions of the Office Software Suite. These issues required Microsoft to go back and upgrade all versions of MS Office back to 2010 in order to enable support for the new MS Office document formats. But this kind of document conversion underlines the real concerns for organizations related to file migration. Organizations must weigh not only the technical merits of a file format or container, but also the availability of software and systems that can utilize a format. Again, if preservation is tied to access (and we believe that it is), then migrating content to the very best preservation format doesn't necessarily promote long-term preservation, if that format isn't accessible save for a very niche set of hardware or software.

As you can see, emulation and format migration are complicated issues for preserving simple individual files consisting of documents and static images. The process becomes exponentially more difficult as the metadata, structure, and linkages within the objects become complex, or the objects are integrally tied to particular platforms.

Whether one chooses to primarily rely on software emulation, file migration, or a combination of the two really depends on the digital object itself. Should the digital object and the preservation of the original format be part of the preservation process, or is digital preservation primarily the preservation of the digital content and experience? And can an organization universally agree on one approach, or will the organization use a multiplicity of approaches based primarily on the preferences of the curator?

At the Ohio State University Libraries (OSUL), curator preference plays a large role in determining if the original digital object should be preserved, or if file migration can be used as a primary strategy around digital preservation. Within the OSUL environment, preservation and access are closely tied together, so while byte-level preservation occurs for all master files, the master files themselves may have been migrated from other content types. But this doesn't always occur. Within the Ohio Congressional Archive, a

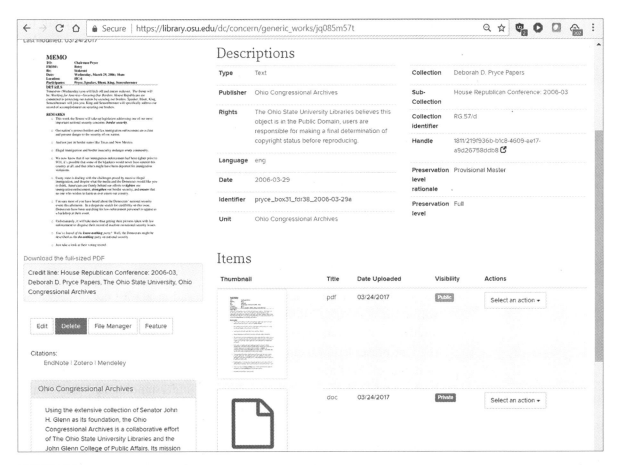

**FIGURE 4.1**

The Ohio Congressional Archive: Multiple Preservation Masters case has been made that the original digital object, regardless of format, has significant historical value. (See figure 4.1.)

Generally, these documents are MS Word files, meaning that in a number of years, it is very likely that these "master" preservation files will be inaccessible using current software. In those cases, OSUL will have to rely on software emulation to provide access to the original source, or "master" content, should a user request it. At the same time, the organization has adopted a policy that in these cases a more modern master file has been developed. In this case, the format selected has been a PDF/A. This file is used to generate an accessible copy of the content, but it also functions as the de facto preservation copy, since this file will be actively curated and migrated should the need arise.

If this example at OSUL sounds messy, it is . . . and it's pretty common within cultural heritage organizations. It also underlines an important fact around digital preservation: there is no one correct way to set up one's preservation system; nor is there any one organization that is doing it right. Preservation is a messy, moving target . . . and it is this messiness, the fuzziness of the workflows and the process, that cause many organizations to throw up their hands and decide that this will be an issue for some future administrator or future curator to solve. But this will never be a perfect or straightforward process. Has anything related to preservation, even in the analog era or since, ever been a perfect or straightforward process? No. We have an idea of what the best practices might be, some guidelines that we use to keep content safe, and then we move forward and do the best we can.

## Why Preservation Doesn't Happen

There are many reasons why preservation or the development of a preservation plan doesn't happen within an organization. Above, we identified three general reasons why this might be case.

### Language Difference between IT and Cultural Heritage Staff

As noted earlier, data backups are not preservation, at least not preservation within the context of cultural heritage organizations. When librarians and archivists talk about preserving content, there is an implicit understanding that preservation includes the long-term access to content. The commingling of preservation and access is a fundamental pillar of the cultural heritage profession. However, this implicit understanding isn't universally shared, and this leads to many misunderstandings between information technology and cultural heritage staff related to preservation planning. At the Ohio State University Libraries, this difference in cultures was one of the early challenges when crafting a digital preservation strategy. In order to move forward, the organization's systems staff and archival staff needed to come together to develop a shared set of language around preservation tasks and goals. This process forced the library/archival staff to identify those implicit assumptions that were being made around preservation, while at the same time, the process allowed library/archival staff to gain a better understanding of how the institution's system staff discussed the preservation of content in their space. By coming together and developing a shared language, the organization was able to start moving together, rather than often being at odds within itself.

## Getting Comfortable with Good Enough

One thing that becomes painfully obvious when starting a digital repository or library program is that someone is almost always doing it better than you are. If you are at a small organization, you are likely looking at a larger organization and wishing you could work on a bigger scale or have more resources. If you are at a larger organization, there will be peers with better websites, better tools, or novel workflows. The fact is that everyone is learning in this space. This means that changes can happen swiftly, and that guidelines or best practices can shift as new formats or research is done. The guidelines that we use for preserving digital video today may not be the same guidelines that we use in 3–5 years (in fact, they likely won't be). This often can leave organizations wanting to wait to see how things shake out. But this isn't a good preservation strategy, and likely will put an organization's collections at long-term risk. So, what can an organization do? The answer is—something, and now. Preservation will always be a moving target, filled with data and system migrations. For organizations developing a digital library, it is imperative that they pick a path, and then move forward consistently, understanding that things will and should change in the future.

## People, Not Software, Enable Preservation

Cultural heritage institutions have seen preservation as a curator- or archivist-centric process—at least in the analog world. Physical materials must be handled, described, repaired, and regularly evaluated. However, in the digital world, the opposite appears to be true, since most often, preservation activities are cached as functions of systems. Can Fedora identify at-risk content? Does Rosetta provide automated data migration? How does the system ensure long-term access? People are part of the equation, but in the digital preservation context, they are often described as tools of the system that has been put in place. This is a paradigm that needs to change. Just like in the analog world, digital preservation is a very people-centric process. Yes, digital preservation practice will be very reliant on the tools and services that the digital library platform provides, but these systems are just tools to be leveraged; they should not drive or determine the extent of the digital preservation plan.

| |
|---|
| Level 6. Information Preservation |

| |
|---|
| Level 5. Information Processes |

| |
|---|
| Level 4. Information Organization |

| |
|---|
| Level 3. Storage Validation |

| |
|---|
| Level 2. Storage Management |

| |
|---|
| Level 1. Safe Storage |

**FIGURE 4.2**

Digital Preservation Maturity Model

# The Maturity Model

The development of a digital preservation plan and system requires an organization to identify the level and preservation activities that it will be able to support. For most organizations, different material types will likely have different preservation activities associated with them. For example, an organization's plan to support high-resolution digital video would likely differ greatly from how it would handle digital texts or photography. Likewise, for institutions hosting repositories or storing digital data, the level and preservation activities that an organization could apply to a preservation TIF file would likely be very different from those for a GIS data file.

To help cultural heritage organizations better understand and define the level of preservation activities that can be supported, the Digital Preservation Maturity Model[5] was developed. The model breaks down preservation activities into six different activities. (See figure 4.2.)

The Maturity Model defines a basic set of services that allows organizations to communicate to stakeholders what they can expect for materials managed within the organization's repository or digital library. These levels define the following activities.

### Level 1. Safe Storage

The organization will provide bit-level storage with an agreed-upon level of reassurance that the bits are protected against simple storage failure.

### Level 2. Storage Management

The organization will optimize the storage management to ensure that the bits are moved to the most appropriate location. Decisions related to bit location are done based on issues such as storage durability, cost reduction, cloud versus local storage, or performance.

### Level 3. Storage Validation

The organization provides support for multiple object storage, plus fixity checking to validate storage security. Object fixity is checked on storage, at access, and at regular intervals to confirm that objects have not been changed due to bit rot or tampering. If a failure is identified, the corrupted file is replaced by an alternate good copy.

### Level 4. Information Organization

The organization incorporates information hierarchy organization, descriptive data management, and simple processes for the uploading, locating, and downloading of information.

### Level 5. Information Processes

The organization will provide efficient and flexible business processes to automate the activities associated with information management. These include flexible workflows and the availability of application programming interfaces (APIs) to enable integration with external tools and identify management systems.

### Level 6. Information Preservation

The organization ensures that the repository system provides functionality to ensure that information stored remains usable and accessible to anyone who requests it. This includes providing strategies to ensure that content is readable for as long as it is managed by the system.

By utilizing this model, which combines the principles of the Trusted Digital Repository (TDR) checklist and the Open Archival Information System (OAIS) reference model introduced in chapter 1, digital library managers can evaluate their own systems and begin to determine the current capacities and the level of both minimal and optimal digital preservation activities within the system. Once these have been determined, library managers can begin to establish baselines for stakeholder versus internal content, as well as outline supported preservation material types and their level of preservation versus ad hoc formats accepted into the repository infrastructure for long-term bit-level management.

## Preservation File Formats

It is important to note that file formats and the development of new file formats is a dynamic and changing area of study. While formats handling the preservation of digital imagery have changed very little over the past decade, content types related to high-resolution audio and video are constantly shifting as new container formats and new and better algorithms are made available or placed into the public domain. As one considers the Maturity Model, one important part of a digital preservation plan will be the definition of digital formats that the system supports as "master" preservation content. These "master" files represent the materials that an organization will perform the highest level of digital preservation activities upon, including, and up to, the migration to new encoding formats or the emulation of rendering software, for a particular material type. For digital repositories, this service level will define how the organization will actively curate the content going into the future. And like anything related to digital preservation, the evaluation of file format support should happen regularly as new and better digital containers are developed to support the long-term preservation and access mission of the organization and cultural heritage community.[6]

| MATERIAL TYPE | PREFERRED FORMATS | DESCRIPTION |
|---|---|---|
| **Electronic Text**<br><br>*Electronic text includes all text-based digital content, including traditional monographic content, serial content, musical scores, theses and dissertations, etc.* | 1. XML-based markup with included DTD/Schema files like TEI or EPUB<br>2. PDF/UA<br>3. PDF/A<br>4. Plain-Text | XML-based markup would be the best format for storing text-based content for long-term preservation. However, these formats are also the most difficult to provide support for in many of the current-generation digital library systems. Most digital library systems currently don't provide good support for XML-marked-up content, outside of supporting markup for metadata creation and storage. This lack of support is generally related to the lack of good readers that can parse and render the marked-up content to the user.<br><br>In the absence of XML-based markup, the use of PDF/UA, PDF/A, or plain-text would be the most acceptable preservation formats. PDF/UA is preferred, since it requires all data to be UTF-8 encoded. |
| **Imagery**<br><br>*Digital imagery includes photography taken through digital capture or high-resolution scans of analog content* | 1. TIFF[7]<br>2. JPEG2000[8]<br>3. PNG[9]<br>4. BMP[10] | A wide range of digital image formats are potentially available, including many not in this list. Some of those include JPEG, GIF, PSD (Photoshop), and CRW (Camera Raw formats)—however, these are not included in the list of preferred formats due to questions related to open patents or the proprietary nature of a particular image format. While they cannot always be avoided, proprietary formats should generally be avoided when selecting supported master preservation formats due to the limited numbers of readers and likely limited format migration pathways. |
| **Audio Files**<br><br>*Audio files include audio captured through digital audio capture or the conversion of analog-based audio files.* | 1. WAV[11] (at highest level of capture)<br>2. MP3[12] | Like digital image formats, audio and video formats have a wide range of format types that could potentially be used for preservation purposes. For audio captured through a digital recorder, the software or capture device will likely make available a raw, uncompressed, digital format. This format may or may not be in a proprietary file format. For the purposes of digital preservation, the creation of an uncompressed, WAV file created at the highest native resolution may provide the best format for long-term support and access.[13] |
| **Video**<br><br>*Digital video, either captured natively or through the digitization of film-based media* | 1. DPX[14]<br>2. AVI[15] | For digitized video, AVI[16] is currently the most commonly used container format for providing the preservation of video content. This format is well supported, and supports the creation of uncompressed video media. It should be noted, however, that a wide range of formats like MFX[17] and the Matroska[18] are being paired with the AVI wrapper to provide a more robust format (better metadata embedding) for digital audio capture.<br><br>Recommendations for natively digitized content can be a bit murkier. Organizations like the National Archives and the Library of Congress both point to the use of DPX. |

Of course, digital library managers are likely to run across a wide range of data types that are not covered in the table above. These range from proprietary data found in CAD drawings, to datasets in JSON or delimited formats, to databases like MS Access or SQLite, or web pages in WARC[19] format. Digital library managers will need to determine what their organizational capacity will be with regard to the long-term preservation of various digital content, as well as determine if there are any limits to the type of content that an organization can accept. And while it is unlikely that an organization or library can provide the highest level of preservation curation for all content, digital library managers should strive to provide at least Level 4 preservation activities for all content managed within an organization's digital library.

## Cloud-Based Digital Preservation Services

A question that often gets asked when developing digital libraries is whether to use a cloud-based or a local infrastructure. While there are good reasons why an organization may choose one infrastructure over another, there are no inherent differences between them for the purposes of digital preservation issues. "Cloud-based" has no technical meaning and really only refers to services provided elsewhere and delivered over a network, and both local and cloud storage are just storage. There are cloud-based services that protect file integrity using cryptographic signatures, geographically distributed replication, and robust maintenance procedures. However, this is not inherent to a service being on the "cloud." Having said this, a growing number of aggregated cloud-based preservation cooperatives have developed within the cultural heritage landscape. As of this writing, several different services exist, including:

- DPN or the Digital Preservation Network (http://dpn.org/)
- MetaArchive Cooperative (https://educopia.org/community/metaarchive)
- HathiTrust (https://www.hathitrust.org/)
- AP or Academic Preservation Trust (http://aptrust.org/)

These aggregate services offer a different type of digital preservation opportunity by leveraging the scale of their networks. They also do different things. DPN, for example, is somewhat unique because this service is designed as a permanent preservation option. Organizations select content for deposit and fund preservation activities on that content for a twenty-year period. Following that period, the organization can either continue to fund preservation activities, or turn the content over to the DPN network. The trust then provides perpetual preservation activities for the content, ensuring that it is preserved for future scholarly researchers. This does not replace an institution's own local preservation systems or planning. Rather, the DPN functions as a long-term permanent preservation system that is designed, in theory, to outlast individual systems, technology, and potentially, organizations. Whether this type of aggregation is successful in the long term will be worth watching. While the sentiment behind the cooperative is definitely admirable, it is hard to imagine the cooperative outliving many of its founding members, whose history extends back for many decades.

Other aggregations like MetaArchive, the HathiTrust, or the AP Trust provide a more traditional membership-based aggregation to support disaster recovery. MetaArchive uses a private LOCKSS[20] network to enable member organizations to keep multiple copies of their digital assets across multiple institutions, geographically distributing their digital content and providing many of the Level 1–3 preservation functions within a larger aggregated system. Cooperatives like the HathiTrust provide this type of aggregated content management for specific digital content (digital text), but the HathiTrust also takes on the management of the preservation masters for its membership, distributing the cost of this management across all of its members.

Just like in the analog world, where large cultural heritage organizations have come together to create large print repositories or share in the long-term management and preservation of analog content, organizations are more and more looking to aggregations in the digital world to leverage the same kinds of economies of scale. It's hard to know which of these aggregated models will have the greatest longevity.

## Summary

Of course, this has been just a shallow overview of the large digital preservation landscape. While formats and models are important for developing the initial preservation plans, understanding why preservation is important, and understanding some of the inherent biases that have shaped many cultural heritage organizations' long-term preservation strategies should be your next step. Over the course of writing this chapter, Trevor Owens, the head of digital content management at the Library of Congress, posted a preprint of a forthcoming book entitled *The Theory and Craft of Digital Preservation*.[21] In reviewing the preprint, it covers many of the issues noted in this chapter in much greater depth, and provides a treatment of the history and craft of digital preservation that is nuanced and timely. If you find yourself building or managing a digital library or repository, or you need to learn more about digital preservation from a cultural heritage perspective and want to go beyond the topics discussed in this chapter, Owens's book is highly recommended.

## Notes

1. GIMP—GNU Image Manipulation Program, https://www.gimp.org/.
2. Dragon Espenschied et al., *Exhibiting Digital Art via Emulation* (Bern, Switz: ipres, 2016), www.ipres2016.ch/frontend/organizers/media/iPRES2016/_PDF/IPR16 .Proceedings_3_Web_Broschuere_Link.pdf.
3. Internet Archive Software Collection, https://archive.org/details/software.
4. Web Archiving Project, https://www.webarchive.org.uk/ukwa/.
5. Preservica, "Digital Preservation Maturity Model: White Paper," 2014, http:// preservica.com/uploads/resources/Preservica-White-Paper-Maturity-Model-2014 _NEW.pdf.
6. Library of Congress, "Recommended Formats Statement," www.loc.gov/preservation/ resources/rfs/.
7. Wikipedia, "TIFF Format," https://en.wikipedia.org/wiki/TIFF.
8. Wikipedia, "JPEG 2000," https://en.wikipedia.org/wiki/JPEG_2000.
9. Wikipedia, "PNG File Format," https://en.wikipedia.org/wiki/Portable_Network _Graphics.
10. Wikipedia, "BMP," https://en.wikipedia.org/wiki/BMP_file_format.
11. Wikipedia, "WAV File Format," https://en.wikipedia.org/wiki/WAV.
12. Wikipedia, "MP3 File Format," https://en.wikipedia.org/wiki/MP3.
13. National Archives, https://www.archives.gov/preservation/products/products/aud-p1 .html.

14. Wikipedia, "DPX File Format," https://en.wikipedia.org/wiki/Digital_Picture_Exchange.

15. Wikipedia, "AVI File Format," https://en.wikipedia.org/wiki/Audio_Video_Interleave.

16. National Archives, https://www.archives.gov/preservation/products/products/vid-p1.html.

17. Library of Congress, "MFX Container Format," https://www.loc.gov/preservation/digital/formats/fdd/fdd000013.shtml?loclr=blogsig.

18. Library of Congress, "Matroska Container Format," https://www.loc.gov/preservation/digital/formats/fdd/fdd000342.shtml?loclr=blogsig.

19. Library of Congress, "WARC File Format," https://.www.loc.gov/preservation/digital/formats/fdd/fdd000236.shtml.

20. LOCKSS Network, https://www.lockss.org/.

21. Trevor Owens, *The Theory and Craft of Digital Preservation* (forthcoming, Johns Hopkins University Press, 2018), www.trevorowens.org/2017/06/full-draft-of-theory-craft-of-digital-preservation/.

# General-Purpose Technologies Useful for Digital Repositories

5

**As noted in previous** chapters, planning for and implementing a successful digital library platform require buy-in and support throughout the organization. In part, this is because the digital library touches all aspects of the organization, but more importantly, digital technologies will continue to displace and replace many of the aspects of a traditional library. While libraries continue to play a key role as community connectors and shared spaces, the digital library platform is increasingly becoming the de facto method for cultural heritage organizations to disseminate information. While concepts such as workflow and acquisitions planning are easier to understand because they directly relate to tangible information objects, what is often overlooked or not fully considered is the role that metadata plays in creating a successful digital library. If the value of a digital library is measured by the content found within it, then the success of the digital library platform will be defined by its ability to surface information to the library's users. Digital content is of little value to a potential user if that information cannot be found. And for more and more users, this means finding information outside the library by utilizing familiar tools embedded in social media, search engines, and personal digital assistant services. The availability, flexibility, and quality of one's metadata will ultimately determine the relevancy of one's digital repository within this expanded information ecosystem. This chapter focuses on some of the technologies that make up today's digital library platforms. Some of these technologies are old, familiar technologies such as XML and XSLT, while others have become more ubiquitous as the library community has sought to move away from locally developed standards to native web standards in order to support the greater reuse of technologies created outside of the library community. This push has raised the profile of standards like JSON, and a reconsideration of OAI-PMH for more web-native standards like ResourceSync, or community efforts around rich semantic metadata using standards like Schema.org. These next few chapters will attempt to focus on the technology, specific metadata schemas, and the tools necessary to utilize those schemas both inside and outside the context of the digital library platform environment.

## The Changing Face of Metadata

The foundation of any digital library platform is the underlying metadata structures that provide meaning to the information objects which the platform stores. However, this isn't new for libraries. Libraries have traditionally treated the creation and maintenance of bibliographic metadata as one of the core values of the profession. We organize, categorize, and bring meaning to content. Likewise, libraries have consistently evolved to support innovative ways of promoting the findability of resources. As repositories of cultural heritage information, libraries have always needed to be able to create access points between an organization's indexing system and the physical location of the piece. How this metadata is created, captured, and stored has changed throughout the years as printed catalog cards gave way to the ILS (integrated library system) and the MARC (machine-readable catalog) metadata schemas. As library metadata moved from print catalogs to online catalogs, organizations like OCLC were formed to enable shared metadata creation and a common set of bibliographic descriptive standards. From within the library community, standards like AACR2 and RDA recognized the changing face of metadata and helped to create a homogeneous metadata ecosystem around the MARC schema, allowing metadata from one institution to be used by another. In these efforts, libraries and their partners have been so successful that many have difficulty seeing a need to move away from the status quo, and even more libraries struggle to embrace new metadata models as more and more information is born digital. At the same time, the role that libraries play in their communities continues to change. Libraries have long since surrendered their roles at the center of their users' information universe. While they still play important roles as content providers and preservers of the historical record, libraries are now only one of many trusted information organizations. This shift has required libraries to rethink how they provide access to materials, since their users have come to expect digital access to content. As organizations develop digital library platforms, this shift can be difficult, since organizations often must find ways to reconcile the metadata utilized within their digital platforms with their legacy systems and data capture procedures, while at the same time, they must work to enable greater data interoperability with the variety of non-library communities that now inhabit the information landscape.

Given the vital importance of library metadata and the continued need to produce and maintain rich bibliographic systems and environments, many cultural heritage organizations have struggled to keep up. Metadata is expensive and difficult to create . . . and is largely transparent to the user when done properly. This had led to a shift in many organizations, as many have moved to minimize the staff used to create metadata within the library. Unfortunately, this has left many organizations unequipped to evaluate the metadata requirements necessary to develop a digital library platform. Legacy bibliographic metadata has become so homogenous and print-centric that many organizations lack the metadata expertise in-house to evaluate new and emerging metadata frameworks, or they have no one on their staff with enough familiarity to use the new metadata schemas. Moreover, many organizations have difficulty integrating new metadata schemas and bibliographic descriptive guidelines into existing workflows that are designed primarily for the acquisition and processing of print materials. As noted in previous chapters, when building a successful digital platform, libraries need to create new workflows and new acquisition processes to accommodate the dynamic nature of the materials. So too must an organization look at the metadata requirements for a digital repository. Individuals like Roy Tennant, senior program officer at OCLC, have long argued that for libraries to truly integrate their digital content, their bibliographic infrastructure must change dramatically. This change must include both the metadata creation and delivery methods of bibliographic content. The days of a homogenous bibliographic standard for all content has ended; the present and the future will likely see more specialized descriptive formats created and utilized within cultural heritage organizations, and it will be up to new and emerging systems to find ways to support these changing requirements and descriptive needs. Like many systems outside of the library community, the future direction of digital library platform software will be defined less by the ability to support very specific metadata formats or descriptive standards, and more by the system's ability to be generally metadata-agnostic, and support a wide range of data models and descriptive rules. This is obviously much harder to do, and is achieved outside the library community through the use of semantic data principles and RDF data models. Whether this can be achieved within the library community remains to be seen. But at the very least, this means that organizations will need to look beyond MARC or any particular metadata format, and instead focus on the ways in which digital library platform software supports and relates together data created using different data models.

## XML in Libraries

Cultural heritage organizations have long been early implementers of XML-based descriptive schemas. Early on, these communities identified many of the potential benefits that XML-based metadata schemas could have for libraries. This led many libraries to be early adopters of efforts like TEI, EAD, MODS, FGDC, and so on. What's more, as the lines between the library and the publishing community have blurred, more libraries have found themselves producing digital publications or digitizing their existing analog collections. Issues relating to document delivery, indexing, and display have pushed the library community to consider XML-based markup languages as a method of preserving digital and bibliographical information. Today, XML-based schemas have become ubiquitous within the digital publication systems used by libraries, and the conversation has shifted away from a discussion of the benefits of such systems, and toward the need to develop systems that take greater advantage of the rich or semantic web. Before looking at how XML (eXtensible Markup Language), and to a lesser degree,

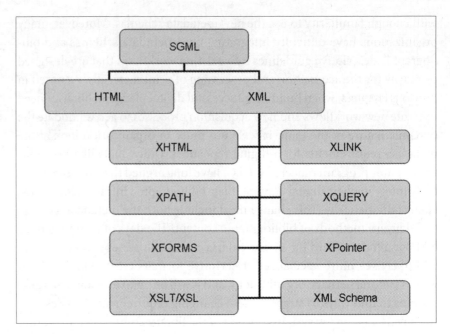

**FIGURE 5.1**

XML Family Tree

linked data, are being used in libraries today, we must first take a step back and look at XML in general. For many, the definition of what XML means has become understandably muddled. The definition of XML has been extended to include not only XML, but the many technologies that have come out of the XML specification. This is very much like the definition of MARC today. Like XML, the term "MARC" is often used to represent the bibliographic descriptive rules and interpretations used to create a MARC record. MARC21 users equate the MARC field 245 with a title—even though the MARC specification itself makes no such determination. In part, it's this fusion of rules and specification that often makes MARC difficult to work with outside of the library community. In reality, the MARC format is, at its most basic, just a container for the data. The Library of Congress developed MARC as a distribution format that could be used to capture information from a card catalog in digital form for transfer to other systems. In the same way, many tend to fold technologies like XSLT, XLink, or XQuery—all technologies that have been developed out of the XML schema—as part of the XML definition. While simplistic, figure 5.1 shows an abbreviated version of the XML family tree. From the tree, one can see the many different technologies that have been derived from the XML specification.

## XHTML

XHTML marks what many hope will be the next evolution of the HTML markup language. It was designed as an extension of the HTML4 document type which is XML-conforming, meaning that such documents can be viewed, edited, validated, and acted upon by XML tools, and it became a part of the HTML5 vocabulary with the revision in 2014.[1] The interest behind XHTML lies in its strict validation rules and the ability to process documents using XML parsing engines and XPath. What's more, due to its strict adherence to XML validation, browsers have an easier time processing XHTML documents. Since XHTML is XML-conforming, it must respect XML's strict set of document validation rules relating to tags and character data. This is very different from the implementation of HTML, which is in many respects a sloppy markup language that has been loosely interpreted by today's web-browsing technology. It's this promise of markup standardization and strict validation that continues to excite those developing for the Web. Additionally, the fact that XHTML documents can be validated and acted upon by XML tools and technologies like XPath and XQuery should not be underestimated. XHTML documents give web developers the ability to build documents for display, while still allowing the documents to be parseable and actionable by other groups and users. For institutions wanting to make their content available for users to build services or "mash-ups" on top of their collections, but which lack the expertise to provide a fully functional web-based API (application programming interface), offering content in XHTML can help to expose their collections or services. Within the library community, XHTML implementations are becoming easier to find. Many ILS systems offer an interface that renders against an XHTML schema, though the most public and widely used XHTML resource in the library community is OCLC's WorldCat.org service.[2] WorldCat.org provides a publicly searchable portal to the OCLC digital properties. However, what's more interesting is OCLC's decision to have WorldCat.org generate content in XHTML. By providing content in XHTML, OCLC has provided a minimal tool set necessary to parse, extract, or embed data from the WorldCat.org project into other services. For example, using an XPath statement (which will be defined and explained below), one can easily extract the holdings libraries from a document. So how do we identify XHTML records? We can identify XHTML records by the document type defined at the top of the source code. If we look at the source for the following record: www.worldcat.org/oclc/26557254&referer=brief_results, we will find the following statement at the top of the XHTML file:

```
<!DOCTYPE html PUBLIC "-//W3C//DTD XHTML 1.0 Transitional//EN"
"http://www.w3.org/TR/xhtml11/DTD/xhtml11-transitional
.dtd"><html xmlns="http://www.w3.org/1999/xhtml" xml:lang="en"
lang="en">
```

The source code identifies itself as XHTML to the web browser in the first line of the source, the DOCTYPE statement which defines the DTD (document type definition) that defines the parsing rules and elements that can legally be used within the document. As an XHTML document, each element or tag can be parsed using an XPath expression, in which the HTML tag is represented as the root tag in the XML tree.

## XPath

XPath is a methodology for addressing parts of an XML document. XPath is a technology designed to be utilized with XSLT and XPointer.[3] It defines a syntax by which XML data can be extracted and acted upon. In a conceptual sense, an XML document is really like a tree, with each element a different node on the tree. XPath defines a method for accessing the individual nodes on the tree. For example, consider the following XML snippet:

```xml
<?xml version="1.0" encoding="utf-8" ?>
<book>
        <item>
        <title>Pride and Prejudice</title>
        <author>Jane Austin</author>
        <publication_date>1813</publication_date>
        <language>eng</language>
        <format>text</format>
        </item>
        <item>
        <title>Pride and Prejudice</title>
        <author>Jane Austin</author>
        <author type="screenwriter">Deborah Moggach</author>
        <publication_date>2015</publication_date>
        <language>eng</language>
        <format>film</format>
        </item>
        <item>
        <title>Pride and Prejudice</title>
        <author>Jane Austin</author>
        <publication_date>2017</publication_date>
        <language>eng</language>
        <format>text</format>
        </item>
</book>
```

XPath statements furnish a process to access an individual node within an XML file by naming its location in relation to the root element. In this case, a process looking to extract the *publication_date* and *format* from the *second item* tag group would create an XPath statement that navigated the document nodes. In this example, however, the node *item* is not unique—but it appears multiple times at the same level within the XML document. XPath accommodates this by allowing access to the *item* group as elements of an array. XPath arrays, however, differ from traditional array structures in that XPath utilizes a state at 1, while an array in PERL, C, or C# would start at zero. Accessing the second node from our above example would use the following statement: */item[2]/publication_date,* which illustrates how the data in the second item node would be addressed. When coupled with XSLT, XPath gives an individual or a process the ability to loop or extract items from the XML document to retransform the data to something new. When dealing with XML-based metadata formats, XPath and XQuery represent the two primary methods for working with metadata. Currently, most metadata crosswalking is done utilizing XSLT stylesheets. These stylesheets make liberal use of XPath statements to process elements within the XML document in order to extract or transform the XML document into some other useful format. The Library of Congress, for example, is producing a number of XSLT stylesheets which make liberal use of XPath statements to provide crosswalking functionality between MARC21XML (and XML representations of MARC21) and other metadata formats like MODS and Dublin Core. These crosswalks can be found at the Library of Congress's MARC website at www.loc.gov/marc/.

## XForms

XForms was designed by the World Wide Web Consortium (W3C) as a technology to replace the current form methodology found in HTML 4.0. It was designed to work as a companion technology with XHTML.[4] Unfortunately, there are very few real-world implementations utilizing XForms, in part because many current-generation browsers only lightly support the protocols, and current development tools do not take advantage of the XForms syntax. With that said, XForms, like XHTML, represents the future of HTML and web development, so the technology should be monitored as it continues to mature and becomes more universally supported.

## XSLT

XSLT (eXtensible Stylesheet Language Transformations) represents one of the technologies that can be used to generate display elements from XML.[5] XSLT's primary function is to translate XML metadata to other document types—whether those are HTML or another XML format. Essentially, an XSLT document is made up of XPath statements, constructed in the form of "templates" that are used to process specific elements within an XML or XHTML document. In chapter 7, we will take a closer look at the mechanics of XSLT and how it can be used in the crosswalking of XML metadata.

## XLink

The XLink specification defines the methodology for the creation and description of links between XML documents.[6] In essence, the XLink syntax simply provides HTML linking between XML documents. However, unlike traditional HTML links, XLink treats links as objects that can have properties and actions associated with the link itself.

### XQuery

XQuery represents an attempt to build a general-purpose query language for XML documents. In some ways, it is analogous to SQL (Structured Query Language) when dealing with databases. XQuery is an attempt to create a query structure that is independent of the surface XML schema.[7] So how is it different from XPath? As noted above, XPath functions by treating an XML document as a tree, where each XML tag represents a branch on the tree. XPath statements navigate these trees by calling or processing specific branches, and the attributes that make up a specific tag. XQuery essentially works to solve the same problem (extracting and parsing XML data), but attempts to do so by using a structured query language rather than as part of an XML tree. As a result, XQuery has developed with its own set of functions and methods that can be used to act upon extracted XML data, providing a very SQL-like experience when processing XML documents. In many cases, the choice of XPath or XQuery comes down to a matter of personal taste, as well as support within the tools being used to process XML data. Some users will like the more structured processing language found in XQuery, while other users more familiar with the traditional HTML DOM (Document Object Model) element-processing approach will likely prefer using XPath processing. In either case, XPath and XQuery offer users the ability to process XML documents using the approach that best fits their learning style.

### XPointer

XPointer is a methodology for dealing with XML fragments.[8] XPointer is a technology that is utilized in conjunction with XPath within XSLT documents.

### XML Schema

XML Schemas represent an attempt to create a methodology for defining XML tag structures for automated processing.[9] The use of XML Schemas is currently part of an ongoing debate regarding how to best structure and define XML documents. XML documents currently can be defined using a number of methodologies, and at present, the W3C and the Dublin Core organization are taking a close look at XML Schema and how this technology can be used to generate application profiles to allow for the automated processing of XML documents. At this point in time, a truly automated solution for XML documents still remains an elusive goal.

At the top of the tree in figure 5.1, we find SGML (Standardized General Markup Language). SGML represents the genesis of current-day markup languages. Ironically, SGML was initially conceived by Ed Mosher, Ray Lorie, and Charles Goldfarb in 1969, the same year that the Library of Congress originally released the first MARC specification. Originally, Mosher, Lorie, and Goldfarb set out to develop a markup language that could be used for structuring legal documents to a standardized format. They were working for IBM at the time, and the goal of the project was to create a method of structuring documents so that those documents could be read and acted upon by a computer. At the time, this action was mainly limited to the formatting and reformatting of data for publication—but the underlying concept would allow the documents to become more useful because tools could be built to act upon the structured data. In 1970, IBM extended the project to encompass general text processing and SGML was born. In the early 1990s, a group from CERN developed HTML, a small subset of SGML for the publication of linked documents on the Web. This metadata schema provided a common tag set for created markup for online publication, and it quickly became the lingua franca for publishing on the World Wide Web (WWW). Finally, in 1996, a group known as the XML Working Group was formed out of the W3C with the goal of creating a subset of SGML that would enable generic SGML objects to be processed over the WWW in much the same way that HTML is now (W3C, www.w3.org/TR/REC-xml/).

In figure 5.1, we see a number of items located below XML. These represent a number of technologies or metadata schemas that have been developed out of the XML specification. What's important to note is that XML is, in large part, simply a markup language for data. In and of itself, XML has no inherent functionality, outside of the meaning and context that it brings to the data that it describes. Now, this in and of itself is a very powerful function. The ability to give elements within a document properties and attributes allows one to enhance the available metadata by creating context for the document elements. What's more, XML is not a "flat" metadata structure, but one that allows for the creation of hierarchical relationships between elements within a document. An XML document can literally become a digital object in and of itself. This is very different from a markup language like MARC, which functions solely as a container for data transfer. As a "flat" data structure, MARC lacks the ability to add context to the bibliographic data that it contains. Moreover, data stored in XML has the ability to exist separately from the object that it describes and still maintain meaning, given its contextual and hierarchical nature. However, as stated above, XML is in essence simply a fancy text file. What makes XML special and useful as a metadata schema is the ancillary technologies currently built around the XML specification that can be used to interpret meaning from the various properties and attributes of a given element. At the heart of these technologies is the XML parser. Currently, a number of different XML parsers exist, including Saxon, a Java XML/XSLT parser; libxml, the Gnome XML parsing library; and MSXML, the XML parser currently built into the Windows operating system. These XML parsers offer users two primary methods for interacting with an XML document: DOM (Document Object Model) and SAX (Simple API for XML).

1. *DOM*—The Document Object Model should be familiar to anyone who does web development using JavaScript. DOM is a platform-neutral interface with the content

and structure of a given XML document. Conceptually, DOM breaks down an XML document as nodes in a tree. Each tag represents a different "branch," and attributes its "leaves," if you will. Within the DOM model, the entire XML document is loaded into memory to construct the DOM tree. As a result, the Doocument Object Model represents a very inefficient method for accessing large XML documents. While it makes data access easier and more convenient through the DOM interface, it comes at a big cost. All XML processing done utilizing XPath, XQuery, or XSLT utilizes DOM processing, meaning that most XML transformations are done using the DOM architecture.

2. *SAX*—The Simple API for XML was initially developed as a Java-only processing method. Within the SAX model, the XML file is read sequentially, with events being fired as the parser enters and leaves elements within the document. Since the document is read sequentially, it is much less memory-intensive, since only small chunks of an XML document will be loaded at any one time. However, unlike DOM, the parser does not have access to any element within the XML tree, but only the specific data that is being read at that moment.

Because of DOM's flexibility and convenience, many XML processing technologies are built around the DOM application model, while coding libraries and tools that break XML down into programmable "objects" tend to use a more SAX-based model for reading and interacting with data. In chapter 7, we will take a closer look at XSLT and how it is used to perform metadata crosswalking between one metadata framework and another.

Early on, a number of libraries looked to the work being done by the W3C and the XML Working Group as a method for bridging the access gap between print and digital resources. Many of these projects continue to play a major role in how XML-based metadata schemas are utilized today.

- The Lane Medical Library at Stanford University initiated a project in 1998 with the purpose of exploring metadata schemas that could better represent digital objects. Through the Medlane project, the Stanford group developed one of the first MARC-to-XML crosswalks and developed XML-MARC, one of the first MARC-to-XML mapping software tools. Using this tool, the Medlane Library was able to test the feasibility of migrating large existing MARC databases into XML. In many respects, the work done at Stanford would be a precursor to the work that the Library of Congress would eventually undertake—creating an official MARCXML crosswalk as well as the eventual development of the MODS metadata framework.

- Prior to the work that the XML Working Group would eventually accomplish in 1996, the Online Archive of California (OAC) was already doing research on how SGML could be used to create archival finding aids. Between 1993 and 1995, a full one year before the XML Working Group would be established, the OAC published a prototype finding-aid syntax known then as the Berkeley Finding Aid Project. Using this prototype, the OAC developed one of the very first union databases composed primarily of encoded finding aids—showing early on some of the benefits that could be gained through the utilization of structured metadata. This prototype would eventually be developed into what we know today as EAD (Encoded Archival Description), which is the lingua franca of the library archival community.

- Developed in 1987 by the Association for Computers in the Humanities, TEI was initially developed to provide a standard-based format for moving formatted text into an XML markup language. Humanities scholars needed an agreed-upon markup language to enable the development and reusability of digitized text-based documents for long-term research purposes. In 1999, the University of Virginia and the University of Bern proposed the creation of a committee to oversee the continued development and expansion of the markup language. Libraries working with TEI realized that if expanded, the format could provide more than just a markup language; it could provide an essential component for the digital preservation of text-based content.

Today, libraries make use of XML nearly every day. Today, we can find XML in their ILS systems, in image management tools—in many facets of the library.

In figure 5.2 we see an example of how a current ILS vendor, in this case Innovative Interfaces, is utilizing XML to make bibliographic metadata available directly via the WWW. In this case, the process demonstrates the ILS vendor's localized XML format for the record. This information is available via a durable URL. The vendor also provides data in MARCXML for users working with the system's limited read-based programming interfaces. In figure 5.3, we see how the Ohio State University is utilizing the OAI (Open Archive Initiative) harvesting framework via its Samvera-based application to make a collection's metadata available for public data harvesting. And in figure 5.4, we see an example of an ILS vendor, in this case Ex Libris's Alma system, that has provided API integration to enable the ability to read and write data into their system utilizing MARCXML wrapped around a localized data format. In all of these examples, the availability of the XML interfaces offers digital library developers additional opportunities for integrating information from these disparate systems together. Moreover, technologies like OAI provide a way for other organizations to harvest and

```xml
<?xml version="1.0" encoding="UTF-8"?>
<!DOCTYPE IIIRECORD SYSTEM "http://library.ohio-state.edu:80/dtd/iiirecord.dtd">
<IIIRECORD>
  <RECORDINFO>
      <RECORDKEY>b7397200</RECORDKEY>
      <CREATEDATE>09-11-2013</CREATEDATE>
      <LASTUPDATEDATE>04-17-2014</LASTUPDATEDATE>
      <REVISIONS>8</REVISIONS>
      <PREVUPDATEDATE>03-13-2014</PREVUPDATEDATE>
  </RECORDINFO>
  <TYPEINFO>
    <BIBLIOGRAPHIC>
      <FIXFLD>
          <FIXLABEL>LANG</FIXLABEL>
          <FIXNUMBER>24</FIXNUMBER>
          <FIXVALUE>eng</FIXVALUE>
      </FIXFLD>
      <FIXFLD>
          <FIXLABEL>SKIP</FIXLABEL>
          <FIXNUMBER>25</FIXNUMBER>
          <FIXVALUE>0</FIXVALUE>
      </FIXFLD>
      <FIXFLD>
          <FIXLABEL>LOCATION</FIXLABEL>
          <FIXNUMBER>26</FIXNUMBER>
          <FIXVALUE>tho </FIXVALUE>
      </FIXFLD>
      <FIXFLD>
          <FIXLABEL>COPIES</FIXLABEL>
          <FIXNUMBER>27</FIXNUMBER>
          <FIXVALUE>0</FIXVALUE>
      </FIXFLD>
      <FIXFLD>
          <FIXLABEL>CAT DATE</FIXLABEL>
          <FIXNUMBER>28</FIXNUMBER>
          <FIXVALUE>12-31-2013</FIXVALUE>
      </FIXFLD>
      <FIXFLD>
          <FIXLABEL>BIB LVL</FIXLABEL>
          <FIXNUMBER>29</FIXNUMBER>
          <FIXVALUE>m</FIXVALUE>
      </FIXFLD>
      <FIXFLD>
          <FIXLABEL>MAT TYPE</FIXLABEL>
          <FIXNUMBER>30</FIXNUMBER>
          <FIXVALUE>a</FIXVALUE>
      </FIXFLD>
      <FIXFLD>
          <FIXLABEL>BCODE3</FIXLABEL>
          <FIXNUMBER>31</FIXNUMBER>
          <FIXVALUE>-</FIXVALUE>
      </FIXFLD>
      <FIXFLD>
```

**FIGURE 5.2**

XML Display from an ILS

index the bibliographic metadata from a digital repository into an outside local system. This opens up the possibilities for information from one's digital collections to be indexed by other systems. For example, as of this writing, the Digital Public Library of America (DPLA) utilizes OAI-PMH to enable cultural heritage institutions to share content with the project. Likewise, OCLC enables cultural heritage institutions to utilize OAI-PMH to ingest metadata from digital platforms directly into their WorldCat service. For cultural heritage organizations, the ability to share metadata through

```xml
<?xml version="1.0" encoding="UTF-8" ?>
<?xml-stylesheet type="text/xsl" href="/dc/assets/oai2-75ace0fb753c2bca031c7d863b5bc072c2248a1302eddf9101c97125a401bc10.xsl" ?>
<OAI-PMH xmlns="http://www.openarchives.org/OAI/2.0/" xmlns:xsi="http://www.w3.org/2001/XMLSchema-instance" xsi:schemaLocation="http://www.openarchives.org/OAI/2.0
  <responseDate>2017-07-30T15:40:15Z</responseDate>
  <request metadataPrefix="oai_dc" verb="ListRecords">https://library.osu.edu/dc/api/oai</request>
  <ListRecords>
    <record>
      <header>
        <identifier>oai:library.osu.edu:dc/g733fx36w</identifier>
        <datestamp>2016-10-05T11:13:21Z</datestamp>
        <setSpec>unit:ByrdPolarResearchCenterArchivalProgram</setSpec>
      </header>
      <metadata>
        <oai_dc:dc xmlns:oai_dc="http://www.openarchives.org/OAI/2.0/oai_dc/" xmlns:dc="http://purl.org/dc/elements/1.1/" xmlns:xsi="http://www.w3.org/2001/XMLSche
          <dc:creator>Mercer, J.</dc:creator>
          <dc:date>1965</dc:date>
          <dc:description>Erratic on Black Mountain</dc:description>
          <dc:format>Slide</dc:format>
          <dc:rights>https://library.osu.edu/statements/rights/post-1923/</dc:rights>
          <dc:source>139-074-8</dc:source>
          <dc:title>6_18_122a</dc:title>
          <dc:type>Image</dc:type>
        </oai_dc:dc>
      </metadata>
    </record>
    <record>
      <header>
        <identifier>oai:library.osu.edu:dc/g733fx38f</identifier>
        <datestamp>2016-10-05T11:13:35Z</datestamp>
        <setSpec>unit:ByrdPolarResearchCenterArchivalProgram</setSpec>
      </header>
      <metadata>
        <oai_dc:dc xmlns:oai_dc="http://www.openarchives.org/OAI/2.0/oai_dc/" xmlns:dc="http://purl.org/dc/elements/1.1/" xmlns:xsi="http://www.w3.org/2001/XMLSche
          <dc:creator>Mercer, J.</dc:creator>
          <dc:date>1965</dc:date>
          <dc:description>Erratic on Black Mountain</dc:description>
          <dc:format>Slide</dc:format>
          <dc:rights>https://library.osu.edu/statements/rights/post-1923/</dc:rights>
          <dc:source>139-074-8</dc:source>
          <dc:title>6_18_122b</dc:title>
          <dc:type>Image</dc:type>
        </oai_dc:dc>
      </metadata>
```

**FIGURE 5.3**

XML Display in OAI-PMH

common web protocols underlines some of the value found in moving metadata into well-known XML schemas. We will take a closer look at the OAI-PMH protocol in chapter 7, but the ability to provide XML-formatted data from one's digital repository provides a valuable access method. When making decisions regarding a digital platform, one should consider how the platform enables not just the creation, but the ability to share and remix data from the system. One should seek to answer the following questions:

1. Does the digital repository support XML-structured bibliographic and administrative metadata? Does the digital repository support structural metadata schema?

2. Can the metadata be harvested or extracted? And can the data be extracted in XML?

3. Does my digital platform support web standards-based APIs?

4. Can my digital repository support multiple metadata formats?

Individuals should be able to answer each of the questions above about a potential digital library platform. One must remember that an organization's

```xml
<?xml version="1.0" encoding="UTF-8" standalone="yes"?>
<bibs total_record_count="1">
  <bib link="/almaws/v1/bibs/99370648900561">
    <mms_id>99106548420001021</mms_id>
      <leader>00485cam-a2200145z--4500</leader>
      <controlfield tag="001">99370648900561</controlfield>
      <controlfield tag="005">20160803134623.0</controlfield>
      <controlfield tag="008">160829s2010    xx       o        eng d</controlfield>
      <datafield tag="020" ind1=" " ind2=" ">
        <subfield code="e">1-61519-110-0</subfield>
      </datafield>
      <datafield tag="020" ind1=" " ind2=" ">
        <subfield code="a">1-61519-006-6</subfield>
      </datafield>
      <datafield tag="035" ind1=" " ind2=" ">
        <subfield code="a">(CKB)2520000000009312</subfield>
      </datafield>
      <datafield tag="035" ind1=" " ind2=" ">
        <subfield code="a">(SSID)ssj0001533005</subfield>
      </datafield>
      <datafield tag="035" ind1=" " ind2=" ">
        <subfield code="a">(PQKBManifestationID)11892897</subfield>
      </datafield>
      <datafield tag="035" ind1=" " ind2=" ">
        <subfield code="a">(PQKBTitleCode)TC0001533005</subfield>
      </datafield>
      <datafield tag="035" ind1=" " ind2=" ">
        <subfield code="a">(PQKBWorkID)11477189</subfield>
      </datafield>
      <datafield tag="035" ind1=" " ind2=" ">
        <subfield code="a">(PQKB)10869221</subfield>
      </datafield>
      <datafield tag="035" ind1=" " ind2=" ">
        <subfield code="a">(EXLCZ)992520000000009312</subfield>
      </datafield>
      <datafield tag="040" ind1=" " ind2=" ">
        <subfield code="a">PQKB</subfield>
      </datafield>
      <datafield tag="041" ind1=" " ind2=" ">
        <subfield code="a">eng</subfield>
      </datafield>
      <datafield tag="050" ind1=" " ind2="0">
        <subfield code="a">BF721.S3425 2010</subfield>
```

**FIGURE 5.4**

Ex Libris Alma Bibliographic Object

digital repository will eventually be the storehouse for many important documents and research. As such, an organization must ensure that its repository will make the organization's metadata available to it in whatever format that it might need, both for the present and the future.

## Why Use XML-Based Metadata

A common question that comes up many times during the planning stages of many digital projects is: why should we utilize XML-based schemas at all for bibliographic description? Libraries have seemed to get along just fine with MARC for the last fifty years—why the sudden change? Why should an organization adopt a new way of doing bibliographic description when no one sees a problem with the current one? It's a fair question and one that an organization needs to be prepared to answer. This is especially true for organizations that may have no other projects utilizing a non-MARC markup format. From the perspective of building a digital repository, here are five reasons to support such a transition:

## XML Is Human-Readable

One of the primary benefits associated with XML is that the generated metadata is human-readable. This is very different from binary formats like PDF, MS Word, or even MARC21, which do not allow for easy inspection of data. Of course, many XML records are never meant to be natively read by an individual without the help of an XML reader—but this characteristic of XML makes data (1) more transparent, (2) makes the data less susceptible to data corruption, and (3) reduces the likelihood of data lockup.

1. Data transparency provides a number of immediate benefits. Within a closed binary system, the actual document schema, or the rules that give the document meaning, are hidden from the user. Within an XML-based metadata system, the document schema is always readily available. Users can inspect the data markup as well as any DTDs (document type definitions) or namespace files that are defined within the document schema. This is a powerful aspect of XML in that it opens one's data, making it easier for organizations or individuals to reuse the metadata within other systems. As noted, this is very different from other binary data formats—including MARC. Binary data formats, like MARC, are computer-generated formats, meaning that while they can be read with some difficulty by humans, they are not human-readable. Take the MARC record below:

04086cam 2200697 i
45000010010000000030006000100050017000160080041000330100001500074020001800089035001500107035002100122040000760014304200080021904300120022704900009002390500027002480500027002750660007003021000113003092450133004222460056005552500022006112640051000641006843360069007253370069007943380066008634900047009295040059510097654600040010276500005101067650005101118650004301169651004801212651010101012606500077013616510067014386500083015056500078015886500079016666500085017456550069018307870065018998300047019648800011702011880011202128880002202408800129022628800127023918800050025188800046025688800127026148800117027418800010502858880012502963880012303088880009903211880004603310925003203203356 948964079 OCoLC 20170501094141.0 160523s2016 ko a b 001 0 kor—a2016423183- a9791159050503- a.b79919881- a(OCoLC)948964079-aDLCbengerdacDLCdHMYdOCLCOdLOAdOSUdCNU-TOdRBNdEYMdOSUdU-tOrBLW- apcc- aa-kr—aOSUU-00aHJ1400.5b.C55476 2016-00aHJ1400.5b.C55476 2016- c$1-1 6880—01aCho, Yŏng-junc(Professor of Economics),eauthor.0http://id.loc.gov/authorities/names/n2014011732.-106880—02aChosŏn hugi wangsil chaejŏng kwa Sŏul sangŏp =bRoyal finance and procurement in late Choson Korea /cCho Yŏng-jun.-31aRoyal finance and procurement in late Chosun Korea.- 6880—03aCh'op'an.- 16880—04aSŏul-si :bSomyŏng Ch'ulp'an,c2016.- a365 pages :billustrations ;c23 cm.- atext2rdacontent0http://id.loc.gov/vocabulary/contentTypes/txt.- aunmediated2rdamedia0http://id.loc.gov/vocabulary/mediaTypes/n.- avolume2rdacarrier0http://id.loc.gov/vocabulary/carriers/nc. 1 6880—05aKyujanggak haksul ch'ongsŏ ;v11.- aIncludes bibliographical references and index.- aText in Korean and Koreanb(Hanmun)- 0aFinance, PubliczKoreaxHistoryy18th century.- 0aFinance, PubliczKoreaxHistoryy19th century.- 0aGovernment purchasingzKoreaxHistory.- 0aKoreaxKings and rulersxFinance, Personal.- 0aKoreaxPolitics and governmenty1637–1864.0http://id.loc.gov/authorities/subjects/sh2010009461.- 76880—06aFinance, Public.2fast-0http://id.worldcat.org/fast/fst00924477.- 76880—07aKorea.2fast0http://id.worldcat.org/fast/fst01206434.- 76880—08aGovernment purchasing.2fast-0http://id.worldcat.org/fast/fst00945538.- 76880—09aKings and rulers.2fast0http://id.worldcat.org/fast/fst00987694.- 76880—10aFinance, Personal.2fast-0http://id.worldcat.org/fast/fst00924449.- 76880—11aPolitics and government.2fast-0http://id.worldcat.org/fast/fst01919741.- 76880—12aHistory.2fast0http://id.worldcat.org/fast/fst01411628. 0 nOCLC Work Id-ohttp://worldcat.org/entity/work/id/3000468792.- 06880—13aKyujanggak haksul ch'ongsŏ ;v11.- 76650—00/$1-a조선(국명)[朝鮮]210cal/OSU-0http://lod.nl.go.kr/resource/KSH00058311 (조선(국명)[朝鮮] )-1 6100—01/$1a조 영준c(Professor of Economics),eauthor.-0http://id.loc.gov/authorities/names/n2014011732. 6250—03/$1a초판 106245—02/$1a조선 후기 왕실 재정 과 서울 상업 =bRoyal finance and procurement in late Choson Korea /c조 영준 7-6650—08/$1a정부 구매[政府購買]210cal/OSU-0http://lod.nl.go.kr/resource/KSH00597253 (정부 구매[政府購買] ) 16264—04/$1a서울시 :b소명 출판,c2016. 1 6490—05/$1a규장각 학술 총서 ;v11. 76650—06/$1a국가 재정[國家財政]210cal/OSU-0http://lod.nl.go.kr/resource/KSH00028603 (국가 재정[國家財政] ) 76651—07/$1a한국(국명)[韓國]¬210cal/OSU-0http://lod.nl.go.kr/resource/KSH00116553 (한국(국명)[韓國] ) 76650—09/$1a왕(국왕)[王]210cal/OSU-0http://lod.nl.go.kr/resource/KSH00021841 (왕(국왕)[王] ) 76650—10/$1a개인 금융[個人融]210cal/OSU-0http://lod.nl.go.kr/resource/KSH00011647 (개인 금융[個人融] ) 76650—11/$1a정부(행정부)[政府]210cal/OSU-0http://lod.nl.go.kr/resource/KSH00010204 (정부(행정부)[政府] ) 7¬655—12/$1a역사[史]210cal/OSU-0http://lod.nl.go.kr/resource/KSH00006486 (역사[史] ) 0-6830—13/$1a규장각 학술 총서 ;v11.- g1i0i32435087217568lthose

While much of this record can be read, it is itself not readable, since the information in the records directory and leader must be unscrambled to determine the meaning of each data element. Likewise, this record is in MARC21, meaning that only users who are literate in MARC21 will be able to understand the encoded data found within this record. Contrast this record with the following XML representation of the same record:

```xml
<?xml version="1.0" encoding="utf-8"?>
<modsCollection xsi:schemaLocation="http://www.loc.gov/mods/v3 http://www.loc.gov/standards/
mods/v3/mods-3-6.xsd" xmlns="http://www.loc.gov/mods/v3" xmlns:xsi="http://www.w3.org/2001/
XMLSchema-instance">
<mods version="3.6">
<titleInfo altRepGroup="02" script="Latn">
<title>Chosŏn hugi wangsil chaejŏng kwa Sŏul sangŏp =</title>
<subTitle>Royal finance and procurement in late Choson Korea</subTitle>
</titleInfo>
<titleInfo type="alternative">
<title>Royal finance and procurement in late Chosun Korea</title>
</titleInfo>
<name type="personal" usage="primary" altRepGroup="01" script="Latn">
<namePart>Cho, Yŏng-jun</namePart>
<namePart type="termsOfAddress">(Professor of Economics)</namePart>
<role>
<roleTerm type="text">author.</roleTerm>
</role>
<nameIdentifier>http://id.loc.gov/authorities/names/n2014011732.</nameIdentifier>
</name>
<typeOfResource>text</typeOfResource>
<genre authority="marcgt">bibliography</genre>
<genre authority="rdacontent">text</genre>
<genre authority="fast" altRepGroup="12" script="Latn">History.</genre>
<originInfo script="Latn" altRepGroup="03">
<place>
<placeTerm type="code" authority="marccountry">ko</placeTerm>
</place>
<dateIssued encoding="marc">2016</dateIssued>
<edition>Ch'op'an.</edition>
<issuance>monographic</issuance>
</originInfo>
<originInfo eventType="publication" altRepGroup="04" script="Latn">
<place>
<placeTerm type="text">Sŏul-si :</placeTerm>
</place>
<publisher>Somyŏng Ch'ulp'an,</publisher>
<dateIssued>2016.</dateIssued>
</originInfo>
<language>
<languageTerm authority="iso639-2b" type="code">kor</languageTerm>
</language>
<physicalDescription>
<form authority="marcform">print</form>
<extent>365 pages : illustrations ; 23 cm.</extent>
<form type="media" authority="rdamedia">unmediated</form>
<form type="carrier" authority="rdacarrier">volume</form>
</physicalDescription>
<note type="statement of responsibility" altRepGroup="00" script="Latn">Cho Yŏng-jun.</note>
<note type="bibliography">Includes bibliographical references and index.</note>
<note type="language">Text in Korean and Korean (Hanmun)</note>
<subject>
<geographicCode authority="marcgac">a-kr---</geographicCode>
</subject>
<subject authority="lcsh">
<topic>Finance, Public</topic>
<geographic>Korea</geographic>
<topic>History</topic>
<temporal>18th century</temporal>
</subject>
<subject authority="lcsh">
```

(Cont.)

```
<topic>Finance, Public</topic>
<geographic>Korea</geographic>
<topic>History</topic>
<temporal>19th century</temporal>
</subject>
<subject authority="lcsh">
<topic>Government purchasing</topic>
<geographic>Korea</geographic>
<topic>History</topic>
</subject>
<subject altRepGroup="06" script="Latn" authority="fast">
<topic>Finance, Public</topic>
</subject>
<subject altRepGroup="08" script="Latn" authority="fast">
<topic>Government purchasing</topic>
</subject>
<subject altRepGroup="09" script="Latn" authority="fast">
<topic>Kings and rulers</topic>
</subject>
<subject altRepGroup="10" script="Latn" authority="fast">
<topic>Finance, Personal</topic>
</subject>
<subject altRepGroup="11" script="Latn" authority="fast">
<topic>Politics and government</topic>
</subject>
<subject authority="lcsh">
<geographic>Korea</geographic>
<topic>Kings and rulers</topic>
<topic>Finance, Personal</topic>
</subject>
<subject authority="lcsh">
<geographic>Korea</geographic>
<topic>Politics and government</topic>
<temporal>1637-1864</temporal>
</subject>
<subject altRepGroup="07" script="Latn" authority="fast">
<geographic>Korea</geographic>
</subject>
<classification authority="lcc">HJ1400.5 .C55476 2016</classification>
<classification authority="lcc">HJ1400.5 .C55476 2016</classification>
<relatedItem type="series">
<titleInfo>
<title>Kyujanggak haksul ch'ongsŏ ; 11</title>
</titleInfo>
</relatedItem>
<subject altRepGroup="00" script="CJK" authority="local/OSU">
<topic>조선(국명) [朝鮮]</topic>
</subject>
<name type="personal" usage="primary" altRepGroup="01" script="CJK">
<namePart>조 영준</namePart>
<namePart type="termsOfAddress">(Professor of Economics)</namePart>
<role>
<roleTerm type="text">author.</roleTerm>
</role>
<nameIdentifier>http://id.loc.gov/authorities/names/n2014011732.</nameIdentifier>
</name>
<titleInfo altRepGroup="02" script="CJK">
<title>조선 후기 왕실 재정 과 서울 상업 =</title>
<subTitle>Royal finance and procurement in late Choson Korea</subTitle>
</titleInfo>
<note type="statement of responsibility" altRepGroup="00" script="CJK">조 영준</note>
```

```xml
<subject altRepGroup="08" script="CJK" authority="local/OSU">
<topic>정부 구매[政府購買]</topic>
</subject>
<relatedItem type="series" altRepGroup="05" script="CJK">
<titleInfo>
<title>규장각 학술 총서 ; 11</title>
</titleInfo>
</relatedItem>
<subject altRepGroup="06" script="CJK" authority="local/OSU">
<topic>국가 재정[國家財政]</topic>
</subject>
<subject altRepGroup="07" script="CJK" authority="local/OSU">
<geographic>한국(국명)[韓國]</geographic>
</subject>
<subject altRepGroup="09" script="CJK" authority="local/OSU">
<topic>왕(국왕)[王]</topic>
</subject>
<subject altRepGroup="10" script="CJK" authority="local/OSU">
<topic>개인 금융[個人融]</topic>
</subject>
<subject altRepGroup="11" script="CJK" authority="local/OSU">
<topic>정부(행정부)[政府]</topic>
</subject>
<genre authority="local/OSU" altRepGroup="12" script="CJK">역사[史]</genre>
<identifier type="isbn">9791159050503</identifier>
<identifier type="lccn">2016423183</identifier>
<identifier type="oclc">948964079</identifier>
<recordInfo>
<descriptionStandard>rda</descriptionStandard>
<recordContentSource authority="marcorg">DLC</recordContentSource>
<recordCreationDate encoding="marc">160523</recordCreationDate>
<recordChangeDate encoding="is08601">20170501094141.0</recordChangeDate>
<recordIdentifier source="OCoLC">948964079</recordIdentifier>
<recordOrigin>Converted from MARCXML to MODS version 3.6 using MARC21slim2MODS3-6.xsl
(Revision 1.117 2017/02/14)</recordOrigin>
<languageOfCataloging>
<languageTerm authority="is0639-2b" type="code">eng</languageTerm>
</languageOfCataloging>
</recordInfo>
</mods>
</modsCollection>
```

While the XML record is admittedly more verbose, its use of human-readable tagging and hierarchical structure allows this record to be easily read and parsed by human eyes. While one could perhaps guess the title of the document described in the MARC record, the XML document leaves no doubt about this, since the title of the document is actually found within an XML tag marked as "title." This level of data transparency is a big benefit of using non-binary data, since the data format, structure, and relationships can be easily inspected and understood by experts and novices alike.

2. With all binary data formats, data corruption is always a big concern. Even within a digital repository, one must have systems in place to protect against the corruption of any binary data loaded into the system. Why is this an issue? Within a binary document, each byte retains a special meaning. The loss or modification of one of these bytes will invalidate the entire binary document, making it unreadable. While XML documents are susceptible to data corruption, the ability to correct an XML document if data corruption does occur should give organizations much more confidence about storing their metadata in an open format. Consider how this relates to the above MARC sample. As described later in chapter 6, the MARC format utilizes fixed start positions and lengths to read field data within the record. This information is stored within the directory, that is, the first set of numerical bytes within the record. As a result, the modification of any of these bytes within the records directory, or the subtraction or addition of bytes within the record data itself (without the recalculation of the records directory), will result in an invalid or unreadable record. So, for example, by adding a single period to the following record (highlighted), I've made this MARC record unreadable, potentially losing the data stored in the record.

Within an XML-encoded record, this type of data corruption isn't an issue. Rather, so long as the data continues to follow the strict XML encoding rules, the record will always be readable.

04086cam 2200697 i
45000010010000000030006000100050017000160080041000330100001500074020001800089035001500107035002100210012204000076001430420008002190430012002270490009002390500002700248050000270027506600070030210001130030924501330042224600560055525000220061126400510063330000410068433600690072533700690079433800660086349000470092950400510097654600400102765000051010676500051011186500043011696510048012126510101012606500077013616510067014386500083015056500078015886500079016666500085017456550069018307870065018998300047019648800117020118800112021288800022024088001290226288001270239188000500025188800046025688800012702614880011702741880010502858880012502963880012303088880009903211880004603310925003203356 948964079 OCoLC 20170501094141.0 160523s2016 ko a b 001 0 kor—a2016423183- a9791159050503- a.b79919881- a(OCoLC)948964079-aDLCbengerdacDLCdHMYdOCLCOdLOAdOSUdCNU-TOdRBNdEYMdOSUdUtOrBLW-apcc- aa-kr—aOSUU-00aHJ1400.5b.C55476 2016-00aHJ1400.5b.C55476 2016- c$1-1 6880–01aCho, Yŏng-junc(Professor of Economics),eauthor.0http://id.loc.gov/authorities/names/n2014011732.-106880–02aChosŏn hugi wangsil chaejŏng kwa Sŏul sangŏp□ =bRoyal finance and procurement in late Choson Korea /cCho Yŏng-jun.-31aRoyal finance and procurement in late Chosun Korea.- 6880–03aCh'op'an.- 16880–04aSŏul-si :bSomyŏng Ch'ulp'an,c2016.- a365 pages :billustrations ;c23 cm.- atext2rdacontent0http://id.loc.gov/vocabulary/contentTypes/txt.- aunmediated2rdamedia0http://id.loc.gov/vocabulary/mediaTypes/n.- avolume2rdacarrier0http://id.loc.gov/vocabulary/carriers/nc. 1 6880–05aKyujanggak haksul ch'ongsŏ ;v11.- aIncludes bibliographical references and index.- aText in Korean and Koreanb(Hanmun)- 0aFinance, PubliczKoreaxHistoryy18th century.- 0aFinance, PubliczKoreaxHistoryy19th century. -0aGovernment purchasingzKoreaxHistory.- 0aKoreaxKings and rulersxFinance, Personal.- 0aKoreaxPolitics and governmenty1637–1864.0http://id.loc.gov/authorities/subjects/sh2010009461.- 76880–06aFinance, Public.2fast-0http://id.worldcat.org/fast/fst00924477.- 76880–07aKorea.2fast0http://id.worldcat.org/fast/fst01206434.- 76880–08aGovernment purchasing.2fast-0http://id.worldcat.org/fast/fst00945538.- 76880–09aKings and rulers.2fast0http://id.worldcat.org/fast/fst00987694.- 76880–10aFinance, Personal.2fast-0http://id.worldcat.org/fast/fst00924449.- 76880–11aPolitics and government.2fast-0http://id.worldcat.org/fast/fst01919741.- 76880–12aHistory.2fast0http://id.worldcat.org/fast/fst01411628. 0 nOCLC Work Id-ohttp://worldcat.org/entity/work/id/3000468792.- 06880–13aKyujanggak haksul ch'ongsŏ ;v11.- 76650–00/$1-a조선(국명)[朝鮮]210cal/OSU-0http://lod.nl.go.kr/resource/KSH00058311 (조선(국명)[朝鮮] )-1 6100–01/$1a조 영준c(Professor of Economics),eauthor.-0http://id.loc.gov/authorities/names/n2014011732. 6250–03/$1a초판 106245–02/$1a조선 후기 왕실 재정 과 서울 상업 =bRoyal finance and procurement in late Choson Korea /c조 영준 7-6650–08/$1a정부 구매[政府購買]210cal/OSU-0http://lod.nl.go.kr/resource/KSH00597253 (정부 구매[政府購買] ) 16264–04/$1a서울시 :b소명 출판,c2016. 1 6490–05/$1a규장각 학술 총서 ;v11. 76650–06/$1a국가 재정[國家財政]210cal/OSU-0http://lod.nl.go.kr/resource/KSH00028603 (국가 재정[國家財政] ) 76651–07/$1a한국(국명)[韓國]¬210cal/OSU-0http://lod.nl.go.kr/resource/KSH00116553 (한국(국명)[韓國] ) 76650–09/$1a왕(국왕)[王]210cal/OSU-0http://lod.nl.go.kr/resource/KSH00021841 (왕(국왕)[王] ) 76650–10/$1a개인 금융[個人融]210cal/OSU-0http://lod.nl.go.kr/resource/KSH00011647 (개인 금융[個人融] ) 76650–11/$1a정부(행정부)[政府]210cal/OSU-0http://lod.nl.go.kr/resource/KSH00010204 (정부(행정부)[政府] ) 7¬655–12/$1a역사[史]210cal/OSU-0http://lod.nl.go.kr/resource/KSH00006486 (역사[史] ) 0-6830–13/$1a규장각 학술 총서 ;v11.- g1i0i32435087217568lthose

3. Open-data XML formats ensure the long-term preservation of data, since it will always be readable by the current technology. By contrast, binary formats tend to change and become obsolete through time, essentially locking up the data that they contain. Outside the library community, the following question is being asked by a number of state governments interested in preserving access to their born-digital documents. Will documents produced in products

like MS Word or PDF be accessible into the future? Past experience tells us that they will not. Current versions of Adobe's PDF reader are not always compatible with its earliest formats, while MS Word struggles to open documents from much earlier versions. The difficulty with all binary documents is that their data formats will become stale and support for these older formats will disappear, "losing" the data. Open data formats like XML ensure that a document's data is always accessible—even if only through visual inspection—preserving long-term access to information.

The benefits of an open data structure cannot be overstated—particularly for an organization that may wish to customize or extend its digital repository software. The ability to read and understand the native metadata provides an invaluable tool for software and web developers, in addition to preventing data from being locked or lost in unsupported binary formats.

### XML Offers a Quicker Cataloging Strategy

While not everyone may consider this to be a benefit of many XML-based schemas, in many cases, XML-based metadata schemas will lower many of the barriers that organizations currently face when creating bibliographic metadata. One of the reasons why it lowers barriers is the separation of administrative, structural, and bibliographic metadata. Administrative metadata would include the technical information about the digital object being loaded into one's digital repository, while structural metadata stores a record of all digital objects, including metadata, that make up the "whole" record for the item. One of the benefits of many XML-based metadata schemas is that a number of specialized schemas exist for storing administrative metadata, separating this information from the descriptive metadata. Since many systems like DSpace and Fedora automatically generate administrative metadata for each object loaded into the repository system, the individual submitting material into a repository is only responsible for the actual description of their object. Moreover, unlike MARC, which is governed by RDA (Resource Description and Access), many XML-based systems provide few, if any, descriptive rules that will allow organizations to create custom metadata schemas and data dictionaries to best suit the metadata needs for a particular project. For example, at Oregon State University, the data dictionaries are used to define how Dublin Core elements for a particular project are to be defined and interpreted. So the following might be utilized as a data dictionary for a project:

| FIELD LABEL | DUBLIN CORE | DESCRIPTION |
|---|---|---|
| *Digital Collection Title* | Title | "Best of the Oregon State University Archives" |
| *Image Title* | Title | First sentence of caption provided by photographer or OSU Archives staff. |
| *Alternative Title* | Title-Alternative | Used like a 740 or a 246 in MARC, this gives the cataloger the ability to provide alternate access points to a title. Use AACR2 guidelines to add when appropriate. Will display in CONTENTdm only when data is present. |
| *Photographer/Studio* | Creator | Includes the photographer or photography studio when known. |
| *Date* | Date | Format should be [YYYY-MM-DD] so for items with just years, the format will be: 1910-00-00. Circa information should be added to the Time Period field. |
| *Time Period* | Coverage-Temporal | Selected from a control vocabulary, the Time Period will be used to represent the decade a particular image is from. |
| *Date Search* | NONE | This field will be used when constructing Date searches. This field will primarily be used to handle ca. dates, by including 2 years before and after the ca. date. This is a hidden field. |
| *Description/Notes* | Description | Includes complete caption information if not already contained in the Image Title field; and any additional interpretive information. |
| *Subject* | Subject | Use LC TGM I: subject terms; available within CONTENTdm and on Cataloger's Desktop. LCSH will be used when an appropriate heading is not available in LC TGM. |
| *Geographic Subject or Location Depicted* | Coverage-Spatial | Geographic region—LC Authority File. Oregon entries, for the time being, will be entered as (Ore.)<br><br>*Example:* Benton County (Ore.) |
| *Object Type* | Type | Genre—use LC TGM II. There will be several genre types for this project. |
| *Original Collection* | Source | Name of collection from which the image originated.<br><br>*Example:* Agriculture Photograph Collection (P 40). |
| *Item Number* | Identifier | Number of the image within its original collection. |
| *Other forms* | Type | Form of image other than what was scanned— print (if neg. scanned), enlarged print, copy negative. Use LC TGM II terms. |
| *Restrictions* | Rights | "Permission to use must be obtained from the OSU Archives." |
| *Transmission Data* | Format | Provides brief information regarding the creation of the digital image. For most of the images in this project, the text should read: "Master scanned with Epson 1640XL scanner at 600 or 800 dpi. Image manipulated with Adobe Photoshop ver. 7.0." |
| *File Name* | Identifier | File names will be constructed using a 10-digit identifier constructed using the Project and image numbers.<br><br>*Example:* P003_00012.tif |
| *Project Comments and Questions* | NONE | Internal note |

The data dictionary then defines for both the user and the submitter the necessary metadata fields, as well as the data that should be present. In the case of this sample collection, one can see that a number of Dublin Core elements have been repeated, but each element has a specific meaning within the data dictionary. Moreover, utilizing this data dictionary, a DTD can be created to give programmers within the library the ability to easily interpret the metadata from this collection.

## *Multi-Formatted and Embedded Documents*

One of XML's strengths is its ability to represent hierarchical data structures and relationships. An XML record could be generated that contains information on a single document that is available in multiple physical formats—with the unique features of each item captured within the XML data structure. Or, in the case of EAD (Encoded Archival Description), XML has the ability to capture structured relationships between items and the collections in which they are a part.

```
<dsc id="a23" type="combined">
        <c01 level="series">
        <did>
        <unitid encodinganalog="099">Series I</unitid>
        <unittitle encodinganalog="245$a">Scientific Reports</unittitle>
        <unitdate calendar="gregorian" era="ce" encodinganalog="245$f"
        normal="1977/1992">1977-1992</unitdate>
        <physdesc><extent encodinganalog="300$a">2.5 cubic
        feet</extent><extent encodinganalog="300$a">8 boxes</extent></physdesc>
        </did>
        <scopecontent>
        <p>Series I consists of published and unpublished scientific papers
        on spotted owls and aspects of spotted owl biology, including the Mexican
        spotted owl; annual reports from demographic studies in the Pacific Northwest;
        and reports prepared by industry biologists, consultants, and scientists.
        Reports from committee groups are found in Series VIII. Committee Efforts. </p>
        </scopecontent>
        <c02 level="item">
        <did>
        <container type="box">1</container>
        <unitid encodinganalog="099">0001</unitid>
        <origination>
        <persname encodinganalog="100" role="creator">Postovit,
        Howard</persname></origination>
        <unittitle encodinganalog="245$a">A Survey of the Spotted Owl
        in Northwestern Washington. Forest Industry Resource and Environment Program,
        Washington, D. C. 10 pages. (North Dakota State University)</unittitle>
        <unitdate era="ce" calendar="gregorian" encodinganalog="245$f"
        type="inclusive" normal="1977">1977</unitdate>
        </did>
        <scopecontent>
        <p>Surveys were conducted to locate spotted owls on public and
        private land in northwest Washington during April-August 1976.</p>
        <p>report from zoology department at North Dakota State
        University</p>
        <p>#SCIENTIFIC REPORT; STOC MONITORING; WASHINGTON STATE</p>
        </scopecontent>
        </c02>
```

In the above example, we see an EAD snippet in which a series and items have been defined. This allows an EAD record to capture the structural relationships that each child has with its parent. This offers EAD systems interesting opportunities in regard to the display and linking of elements within an EAD document, given the shared nature of the relationships. This gives the metadata object the ability to become an information object itself. This aspect allows XML metadata to exist outside of its parent systems and act almost as a surrogate for the object that it describes, making the data more meaningful to other organizations like libraries or search providers.

## Metadata Becomes "Smarter"

How exactly does metadata get smarter? As an XML document, metadata fields can have attributes and properties which can be acted upon. Moreover, by utilizing XSLT and XPath, data can be manipulated and reordered without having to rework the source XML document. XSLT commands like xsl:sort and position(), last(), xsl:for-each, xsl:for-each-group, xsl:if, and xsl:when offer users the ability to act upon data within the XML document by tag, attribute, or tag contents that separate the content from display. But this extends beyond simple data manipulation. The ability to illustrate relationships and interlinks between documents—the ability to store content or links to content within the metadata container—each of these options is available through XML or an XML-based system. As noted above, the document becomes an information object itself, having its own "metadata" and properties that can be leveraged both inside and outside its parent system. Systems like DSpace and Fedora that can use and produce object-oriented metadata objects like METS (Metadata Encoding and Transmission Standard) can be used outside their parent systems as surrogate items. Surrogates can then be utilized within a remote system to stand in for and link to the parent item. Most digital repository systems create a number of metadata objects for each document stored, creating metadata objects for structural, administrative, and bibliographic data. METS-based systems use the METS format to bind these individual objects together as a cohesive whole—but in doing so, they create "smart" metadata that are their own information objects.

## Metadata Becomes "Connected"

One of the most exciting developments related to metadata in libraries has been the move to understand how linked data concepts could improve and enhance existing metadata models and turn library metadata from a collection of strings into something that is much more actionable. Consider the current way in which libraries handle control vocabularies within their bibliographic data. Presently, libraries utilize a collection of strings—in most cases, from well-known libraries like the Library of Congress, or OCLC's FAST, and so on. These values provide important search points, as well as enabling systems to develop functionality like facets or filtering. Let's consider the following record snippet in MARC21XML

```
<marc:record>
<marc:datafield tag="100" ind1="1" ind2=" ">
<marc:subfield code="6">880-01</marc:subfield>
<marc:subfield code="a">Hu, Zongnan,</marc:subfield>
<marc:subfield code="d">1896-1962,</marc:subfield>
<marc:subfield code="e">author.</marc:subfield>
</marc:datafield>
<marc:datafield tag="600" ind1="1" ind2="0">
<marc:subfield code="6">880-06</marc:subfield>
<marc:subfield code="a">Hu, Zongnan,</marc:subfield>
<marc:subfield code="d">1896-1962</marc:subfield>
<marc:subfield code="v">Diaries.</marc:subfield>
</marc:datafield>
<marc:datafield tag="650" ind1=" " ind2="0">
<marc:subfield code="a">Generals</marc:subfield>
<marc:subfield code="z">China</marc:subfield>
<marc:subfield code="v">Biography.</marc:subfield>
</marc:datafield>
<marc:datafield tag="650" ind1=" " ind2="0">
<marc:subfield code="a">Generals</marc:subfield>
<marc:subfield code="z">Taiwan</marc:subfield>
<marc:subfield code="v">Biography.</marc:subfield>
</marc:datafield>
<marc:datafield tag="600" ind1="1" ind2="7">
<marc:subfield code="a">Hu, Zongnan,</marc:subfield>
<marc:subfield code="d">1896-1962.</marc:subfield>
<marc:subfield code="2">fast</marc:subfield>
<marc:subfield code="0">(OCoLC)fst00131171</marc:subfield>
</marc:datafield>
<marc:datafield tag="650" ind1=" " ind2="7">
<marc:subfield code="a">Generals.</marc:subfield>
<marc:subfield code="2">fast</marc:subfield>
<marc:subfield code="0">(OCoLC)fst00939841</marc:subfield>
</marc:datafield>
<marc:datafield tag="651" ind1=" " ind2="7">
<marc:subfield code="a">China.</marc:subfield>
<marc:subfield code="2">fast</marc:subfield>
<marc:subfield code="0">(OCoLC)fst01206073</marc:subfield>
</marc:datafield>
<marc:datafield tag="651" ind1=" " ind2="7">
<marc:subfield code="a">Taiwan.</marc:subfield>
<marc:subfield code="2">fast</marc:subfield>
<marc:subfield code="0">(OCoLC)fst01207854</marc:subfield>
</marc:datafield>
<marc:datafield tag="655" ind1=" " ind2="7">
```

```
<marc:subfield code="a">Diaries.</marc:subfield>
<marc:subfield code="2">lcgft</marc:subfield>
</marc:datafield>
<marc:datafield tag="655" ind1=" " ind2="7">
<marc:subfield code="a">Autobiographies.</marc:subfield>
<marc:subfield code="2">lcgft</marc:subfield>
</marc:datafield>
<marc:datafield tag="655" ind1=" " ind2="7">
<marc:subfield code="a">Biography.</marc:subfield>
<marc:subfield code="2">fast</marc:subfield>
<marc:subfield code="0">(OCoLC)fst01423686</marc:subfield>
</marc:datafield>
<marc:datafield tag="655" ind1=" " ind2="7">
<marc:subfield code="a">Diaries.</marc:subfield>
<marc:subfield code="2">fast</marc:subfield>
<marc:subfield code="0">(OCoLC)fst01423794</marc:subfield>
</marc:datafield>
<marc:datafield tag="700" ind1="1" ind2=" ">
<marc:subfield code="6">880-07</marc:subfield>
<marc:subfield code="a">Chen, Shiju,</marc:subfield>
<marc:subfield code="e">editor.</marc:subfield>
</marc:datafield>
<marc:datafield tag="700" ind1="1" ind2=" ">
<marc:subfield code="6">880-08</marc:subfield>
<marc:subfield code="a">Cai, Shengqi,</marc:subfield>
<marc:subfield code="e">editor.</marc:subfield>
</marc:datafield>
</marc:record>
```

This snippet of data includes just the controlled content found within the record. In this case, we have a mix of names and a wide range of subject vocabularies. This metadata would provide a rich set of content for a local system, but these are just strings within the system. The metadata doesn't enable the system to know anything about these values outside of the information embedded within the metadata. If these terms change, or need to be updated, this must be done manually within the system. If these vocabularies are related to other data or match other vocabularies, this information wouldn't be captured. So, while this snippet provides rich data for the system to utilize, it is "dumb" data, in that this information only exists as a string of data.

It is this notion of context and the interconnectivity of data that has pushed the cultural heritage community towards semantic data principles. Today, libraries are just experimenting with embedding linked data or URI[10] endpoints into their data in order to shift their metadata from simple strings to strings+. By simply adding URI endpoints to the example above, we get the following:

```
<marc:record>
<marc:datafield tag="100" ind1="1" ind2=" ">
<marc:subfield code="6">880-01</marc:subfield>
<marc:subfield code="a">Hu, Zongnan,</marc:subfield>
<marc:subfield code="d">1896-1962,</marc:subfield>
<marc:subfield code="e">author.</marc:subfield>
<marc:subfield code="0">http://id.loc.gov/authorities/names/n84029846</marc:subfield>
<marc:subfield code="1">http://viaf.org/viaf/70322743</marc:subfield>
</marc:datafield>
<marc:datafield tag="600" ind1="1" ind2="0">
<marc:subfield code="6">880-06</marc:subfield>
<marc:subfield code="a">Hu, Zongnan,</marc:subfield>
<marc:subfield code="d">1896-1962</marc:subfield>
<marc:subfield code="v">Diaries.</marc:subfield>
<marc:subfield code="0">http://id.loc.gov/authorities/names/n84029846</marc:subfield>
<marc:subfield code="1">http://viaf.org/viaf/70322743</marc:subfield>
</marc:datafield>
<marc:datafield tag="650" ind1=" " ind2="0">
<marc:subfield code="a">Generals</marc:subfield>
<marc:subfield code="z">China</marc:subfield>
<marc:subfield code="v">Biography.</marc:subfield>
<marc:subfield code="0">http://id.loc.gov/authorities/subjects/sh2008105087</marc:subfield>
</marc:datafield>
<marc:datafield tag="650" ind1=" " ind2="0">
<marc:subfield code="a">Generals</marc:subfield>
<marc:subfield code="z">Taiwan</marc:subfield>
<marc:subfield code="v">Biography.</marc:subfield>
<marc:subfield code="0">http://id.loc.gov/authorities/subjects/sh2008105117</marc:subfield>
</marc:datafield>
<marc:datafield tag="600" ind1="1" ind2="7">
<marc:subfield code="a">Hu, Zongnan,</marc:subfield>
<marc:subfield code="d">1896-1962.</marc:subfield>
<marc:subfield code="2">fast</marc:subfield>
<marc:subfield code="0">http://id.worldcat.org/fast/fst00131171</marc:subfield>
<marc:subfield code="1">http://viaf.org/viaf/70322743</marc:subfield>
</marc:datafield>
<marc:datafield tag="650" ind1=" " ind2="7">
<marc:subfield code="a">Generals.</marc:subfield>
<marc:subfield code="2">fast</marc:subfield>
<marc:subfield code="0">http://id.worldcat.org/fast/fst00939841</marc:subfield>
</marc:datafield>
<marc:datafield tag="651" ind1=" " ind2="7">
<marc:subfield code="a">China.</marc:subfield>
<marc:subfield code="2">fast</marc:subfield>
<marc:subfield code="0">http://id.worldcat.org/fast/fst01206073</marc:subfield>
</marc:datafield>
<marc:datafield tag="651" ind1=" " ind2="7">
<marc:subfield code="a">Taiwan.</marc:subfield>
<marc:subfield code="2">fast</marc:subfield>
<marc:subfield code="0">http://id.worldcat.org/fast/fst01207854</marc:subfield>
</marc:datafield>
<marc:datafield tag="655" ind1=" " ind2="7">
<marc:subfield code="a">Diaries.</marc:subfield>
<marc:subfield code="2">lcgft</marc:subfield>
<marc:subfield code="0">http://id.loc.gov/authorities/genreForms/gf2014026085</marc:subfield>
</marc:datafield>
<marc:datafield tag="655" ind1=" " ind2="7">
<marc:subfield code="a">Autobiographies.</marc:subfield>
<marc:subfield code="2">lcgft</marc:subfield>
<marc:subfield code="0">http://id.loc.gov/authorities/genreForms/gf2014026047</marc:subfield>
</marc:datafield>
```

```
<marc:datafield tag="655" ind1=" " ind2="7">
<marc:subfield code="a">Biography.</marc:subfield>
<marc:subfield code="2">fast</marc:subfield>
<marc:subfield code="0">http://id.worldcat.org/fast/fst01423686</marc:subfield>
</marc:datafield>
<marc:datafield tag="655" ind1=" " ind2="7">
<marc:subfield code="a">Diaries.</marc:subfield>
<marc:subfield code="2">fast</marc:subfield>
<marc:subfield code="0">http://id.worldcat.org/fast/fst01423794</marc:subfield>
</marc:datafield>
<marc:datafield tag="700" ind1="1" ind2=" ">
<marc:subfield code="6">880-07</marc:subfield>
<marc:subfield code="a">Chen, Shiju,</marc:subfield>
<marc:subfield code="e">editor.</marc:subfield>
<marc:subfield code="0">http://id.loc.gov/authorities/names/n02015103150</marc:subfield>
<marc:subfield code="1">http://viaf.org/viaf/311819060</marc:subfield>
</marc:datafield>
<marc:datafield tag="700" ind1="1" ind2=" ">
<marc:subfield code="6">880-08</marc:subfield>
<marc:subfield code="a">Cai, Shengqi,</marc:subfield>
<marc:subfield code="e">editor.</marc:subfield>
<marc:subfield code="0">http://id.loc.gov/authorities/names/n2009039850</marc:subfield>
<marc:subfield code="1">http://viaf.org/viaf/290899649</marc:subfield>
</marc:datafield>
<marc:datafield tag="830" ind1=" " ind2="0">
<marc:subfield code="6">880-09</marc:subfield>
<marc:subfield code="a">Minguo shi liao cong shu.</marc:subfield>
<marc:subfield code="0">http://id.loc.gov/authorities/names/nr94002254</marc:subfield>
</marc:datafield>
</marc:record>
```

The change in the records is subtle, but it is important because in each of the controlled vocabulary fields, a URI to the individual vocabulary element has been added. This URI has the potential to enable a local system to not only utilize the strings in the record, but interrogate the content at the URI for additional information related to the term. So, for example, if a system was to follow the VIAF[11] URI for Cai, Shengqi, the following data would be provided (truncated):

```
<?xml version="1.0" encoding="UTF-8"?>
<ns1:VIAFCluster xmlns:ns1="http://viaf.org/viaf/terms#" xmlns:void="http://rdfs.org/ns/void#"
xmlns:rdf="http://www.w3.org/1999/02/22-rdf-syntax-ns#" xmlns:owl="http://www.w3.org/2002/07/owl#"
xmlns:foaf="http://xmlns.com/foaf/0.1/" xmlns="http://viaf.org/viaf/terms#">
<ns1:viafID>290899649</ns1:viafID>
<ns1:Document about="http://viaf.org/viaf/290899649/">
<ns1:inDataset resource="http://viaf.org/viaf/data"/>
<ns1:primaryTopic resource="http://viaf.org/viaf/290899649"/>
</ns1:Document>
<ns1:nameType>Personal</ns1:nameType>
<ns1:sources>
<ns1:source nsid="0000000444674605">ISNI|0000000444674605</ns1:source>
<ns1:source nsid="n2009039850">LC|n 2009039850</ns1:source>
<ns1:source nsid="338995366">NTA|338995366</ns1:source>
</ns1:sources>
<ns1:length>121</ns1:length>
```

(Cont.)

```
<ns1:mainHeadings>
<ns1:data>
<ns1:text>Cai, Shengqi</ns1:text>
<ns1:sources>
<ns1:s>ISNI</ns1:s>
<ns1:sid>ISNI|0000000444674605</ns1:sid>
<ns1:s>LC</ns1:s>
<ns1:sid>LC|n 2009039850</ns1:sid>
<ns1:s>NTA</ns1:s>
<ns1:sid>NTA|338995366</ns1:sid>
</ns1:sources>
</ns1:data>
<ns1:mainHeadingEl>
<ns1:datafield tag="100" ind2=" " ind1="1" dtype="MARC21">
<ns1:subfield code="a">Cai, Shengqi</ns1:subfield>
</ns1:datafield>
<ns1:sources>
<ns1:s>LC</ns1:s>
<ns1:sid>LC|n 2009039850</ns1:sid>
</ns1:sources>
<ns1:id>LC|n 2009039850</ns1:id>
<ns1:links>
<ns1:link>
<ns1:match type="standard number"/>
NTA|338995366
</ns1:link>
<ns1:link>
<ns1:match type="joint author"/>
ISNI|0000000444674605
</ns1:link>
</ns1:links>
</ns1:mainHeadingEl>
<ns1:mainHeadingEl>
<ns1:datafield tag="100" ind2=" " ind1="1" dtype="MARC21">
<ns1:subfield code="a">Cai, Shengqi</ns1:subfield>
</ns1:datafield>
<ns1:sources>
<ns1:s>ISNI</ns1:s>
<ns1:sid>ISNI|0000000444674605</ns1:sid>
</ns1:sources>
<ns1:id>ISNI|0000000444674605</ns1:id>
<ns1:links>
<ns1:link>
<ns1:match type="joint author"/>
NTA|338995366
</ns1:link>
<ns1:link>
<ns1:match type="joint author"/>
LC|n 2009039850
</ns1:link>
</ns1:links>
</ns1:mainHeadingEl>
<ns1:mainHeadingEl>
<ns1:datafield tag="100" ind2=" " ind1="0" dtype="MARC21">
<ns1:subfield code="a">Cai, Shengqi</ns1:subfield>
</ns1:datafield>
<ns1:sources>
<ns1:s>NTA</ns1:s>
<ns1:sid>NTA|338995366</ns1:sid>
</ns1:sources>
<ns1:id>NTA|338995366</ns1:id>
<ns1:links>
```

```
<ns1:link>
<ns1:match type="joint author"/>
ISNI|0000000444674605
</ns1:link>
<ns1:link>
<ns1:match type="standard number"/>
LC|n 2009039850
</ns1:link>
</ns1:links>
</ns1:mainHeadingEl>
</ns1:mainHeadings>
<ns1:fixed>
<ns1:gender>u</ns1:gender>
</ns1:fixed>
<ns1:x400s>
<ns1:x400>
<ns1:datafield tag="400" ind2=" " ind1="0" dtype="MARC21">
<ns1:subfield code="a">蔡盛琦</ns1:subfield>
<ns1:normalized>蔡盛琦</ns1:normalized>
</ns1:datafield>
<ns1:sources>
<ns1:s>ISNI</ns1:s>
<ns1:sid>ISNI|0000000444674605</ns1:sid>
</ns1:sources>
</ns1:x400>
<ns1:x400>
<ns1:datafield tag="400" ind2=" " ind1="1" dtype="MARC21">
<ns1:subfield code="a">蔡盛琦</ns1:subfield>
<ns1:normalized>蔡盛琦</ns1:normalized>
</ns1:datafield>
<ns1:sources>
<ns1:s>NTA</ns1:s>
<ns1:sid>NTA|338995366</ns1:sid>
<ns1:s>LC</ns1:s>
<ns1:sid>LC|n 2009039850</ns1:sid>
</ns1:sources>
</ns1:x400>
<ns1:x400>
<ns1:datafield tag="400" ind2=" " ind1="1" dtype="MARC21">
<ns1:subfield code="a">蔡盛琦,</ns1:subfield>
<ns1:subfield code="d">editor.</ns1:subfield>
<ns1:normalized>蔡盛琦 editor</ns1:normalized>
</ns1:datafield>
<ns1:sources>
<ns1:s>LC</ns1:s>
<ns1:sid>LC|n 2009039850</ns1:sid>
</ns1:sources>
</ns1:x400>
</ns1:x400s>
<ns1:coauthors>
<ns1:data tag="950" count="8">
<ns1:text>Chen, Shiju</ns1:text>
<ns1:sources>
<ns1:s>ISNI</ns1:s>
<ns1:sid>ISNI|0000000444674605</ns1:sid>
<ns1:s>LC</ns1:s>
<ns1:sid>LC|n 2009039850</ns1:sid>
<ns1:s>NTA</ns1:s>
<ns1:sid>NTA|338995366</ns1:sid>
</ns1:sources>
</ns1:data>
<ns1:data tag="950" count="7">
```

(Cont.)

```
<ns1:text>陳世局.</ns1:text>
<ns1:sources>
<ns1:s>NTA</ns1:s>
<ns1:sid>NTA|338995366</ns1:sid>
<ns1:s>LC</ns1:s>
<ns1:sid>LC|n 2009039850</ns1:sid>
</ns1:sources>
</ns1:data>
<ns1:data tag="950" count="4">
<ns1:text>王紹堉, 1925-</ns1:text>
<ns1:sources>
<ns1:s>NTA</ns1:s>
<ns1:sid>NTA|338995366</ns1:sid>
<ns1:s>LC</ns1:s>
<ns1:sid>LC|n 2009039850</ns1:sid>
</ns1:sources>
</ns1:data>
<ns1:data tag="950" count="4">
<ns1:text>Wang, Shaoyu, 1925-</ns1:text>
<ns1:sources>
<ns1:s>NTA</ns1:s>
<ns1:sid>NTA|338995366</ns1:sid>
<ns1:s>LC</ns1:s>
<ns1:sid>LC|n 2009039850</ns1:sid>
</ns1:sources>
</ns1:data>
<ns1:data tag="950" count="3">
<ns1:text>Zhou, Xiuhuan</ns1:text>
<ns1:sources>
<ns1:s>ISNI</ns1:s>
<ns1:sid>ISNI|0000000444674605</ns1:sid>
<ns1:s>LC</ns1:s>
<ns1:sid>LC|n 2009039850</ns1:sid>
</ns1:sources>
</ns1:data>
<ns1:data tag="950" count="3">
<ns1:text>Shen, Changhuan 1913-</ns1:text>
<ns1:sources>
<ns1:s>ISNI</ns1:s>
<ns1:sid>ISNI|0000000444674605</ns1:sid>
<ns1:s>LC</ns1:s>
<ns1:sid>LC|n 2009039850</ns1:sid>
</ns1:sources>
</ns1:data>
<ns1:data tag="950" count="2">
<ns1:text>沈昌煥, 1913-</ns1:text>
<ns1:sources>
<ns1:s>LC</ns1:s>
<ns1:sid>LC|n 2009039850</ns1:sid>
</ns1:sources>
</ns1:data>
<ns1:data tag="950" count="2">
<ns1:text>張秀雲</ns1:text>
<ns1:sources>
<ns1:s>LC</ns1:s>
<ns1:sid>LC|n 2009039850</ns1:sid>
</ns1:sources>
</ns1:data>
<ns1:data tag="950" count="2">
<ns1:text>周琇環</ns1:text>
<ns1:sources>
<ns1:s>LC</ns1:s>
<ns1:sid>LC|n 2009039850</ns1:sid>
```

```
</ns1:sources>
</ns1:data>
<ns1:data tag="950" count="2">
<ns1:text>Hu, Jianguo.</ns1:text>
<ns1:sources>
<ns1:s>NTA</ns1:s>
<ns1:sid>NTA|338995366</ns1:sid>
</ns1:sources>
</ns1:data>
<ns1:data tag="950" count="1">
<ns1:text>陳世局</ns1:text>
<ns1:sources>
<ns1:s>ISNI</ns1:s>
<ns1:sid>ISNI|0000000444674605</ns1:sid>
</ns1:sources>
</ns1:data>
</ns1:coauthors>
<ns1:birthDate>0</ns1:birthDate>
<ns1:deathDate>0</ns1:deathDate>
<ns1:dateType>lived</ns1:dateType>
<ns1:dates min="200" max="200">
<ns1:date count="4" scaled="2.00">200</ns1:date>
</ns1:dates>
<ns1:RecFormats>
<ns1:data count="8">
<ns1:text>am</ns1:text>
<ns1:sources>
<ns1:s>NTA</ns1:s>
<ns1:sid>NTA|338995366</ns1:sid>
<ns1:s>LC</ns1:s>
<ns1:sid>LC|n 2009039850</ns1:sid>
</ns1:sources>
</ns1:data>
<ns1:data count="1">
<ns1:text>dm</ns1:text>
<ns1:sources>
<ns1:s>LC</ns1:s>
<ns1:sid>LC|n 2009039850</ns1:sid>
</ns1:sources>
</ns1:data>
</ns1:RecFormats>
<ns1:history>
<ns1:ht type="add" time="2017-03-13T16:14:09.483547+00:00" recid="ISNI|0000000444674605"/>
<ns1:ht type="add" time="2017-03-13T16:14:09.495794+00:00" recid="LC|n 2009039850"/>
<ns1:ht type="add" time="2017-03-13T16:14:09.508860+00:00" recid="NTA|338995366"/>
</ns1:history>
<ns1:creationtime>2017-06-25T15:18:42.211333+00:00</ns1:creationtime>
</ns1:VIAFCluster>
```

Within this VIAF cluster record, we find references to coauthors, works created, alternative authorized headings from different vocabularies and languages, and so on. By providing this URI, we've enabled our system to not only utilize the information that we've provided within the system, but we've enabled the system to reach beyond our system and learn about the particular concept. This ability has a wide range of potential ramifications for cultural heritage organizations, because it can enrich our existing metadata and potentially simplify some maintenance tasks, as well as enable the cultural heritage community to provide its own rich metadata as linked data and contribute to the web of knowledge about a term or item.

It's this development of a shared web, or knowledge graph, of information that continues to push cultural heritage organizations to explore ways to not only utilize but reconcile legacy metadata in order to take advantage of these semantic web concepts.

### Not Just a Library Standard

Traditionally, libraries have had very few vendor choices when it comes to software purchases or hiring outside consulting. The main reason for this difficulty has been the standards that libraries have become reliant on. MARC is a good example. No other profession utilizes MARC or RDA as a descriptive framework. As a result, only a handful of "library" vendors support the creation and use of legacy library data. Libraries inevitably have few ILS choices—and larger organizations essentially have to choose from only two or three larger vendors. So while these "library" standards have served libraries well for many years, they have also perpetuated a retarding of software development within the library community. Today, library "innovation" is essentially pushed by a handful of large vendors providing large, monolithic systems. To a large degree, the library community's continued reliance on MARC and RDA has stagnated library development over the current generation. Non-MARC metadata schemas (either in XML, JSON, etc.) have the potential to unyoke the library community from traditional "library" vendors and enable the information sciences community to use the technology and innovations developed for web-native standards and best practices. While the library and information sciences community has created XML-based schemas like MODS, METS, and Dublin Core, and non-XML schemas like IIIF, the fact that these schemas are in open and well-understood "languages" allows libraries to look outside the traditional library vendors to a broader development community. For the first time, libraries can truly start to leverage the larger open-source community, and not simply the handful of open source developers that happen to work for libraries.

## JSON

While library metadata formats and data models are primarily reflected in XML and XML Schema documents, the use of XML as a communication format between applications has become less and less common. To some degree, this is probably why library communication standards like SRU/W have failed to gain significant traction as a replacement for older standards like Z39.50. Though XML provides a technology-neutral method of transferring data between systems, the processing of XML documents carries with it significant overhead. Additionally, the technology needed to transfer XML content on the client side (when used in web browsers) has largely remained stagnant. The current XSLT and XQuery standards may continue to be developed, but as of this writing, support on the client side remains frozen at version 1.0 for XSLT, and XQuery support remains completely absent. These limitations have caused developers to look at other standards for communication data packets between systems, and in most cases, the standard that is being utilized is JSON.

JSON[12] (JavaScript Object Notation) is a data exchange format for passing structured and unstructured data between applications. Of course, one can express these same relationships in XML—which might make one wonder why developers are gravitating to JSON; and the answer would be grounded in the support that most current-generation programming languages provide for JSON-based content. When working with XML documents, developers must work with the data using one of two processing methods: DOM (Document Object Model) processing or SAX (Simple API for XML) processing. Each of these models has its benefits and drawbacks. DOM processing, for example, allows developers to interact with XML documents as objects; that is, as elements that can have properties and attributes. DOM also enables developers to approach the processing of documents using XPath or accessing the data using complex data structures like dictionaries or hashes. The challenge with DOM processing, however, is that in order to achieve this functionality, the entire document must be loaded and validated by the XML parser. This overhead is costly, and small errors in the XML document will corrupt the entire data packet, rendering it unusable. For very large XML documents, this model simply isn't an efficient means of processing data. And what's more, most programming languages provide limited DOM processing support, farming out that functionality to external XML-parsing libraries. This means that XML support within specific programming languages can vary greatly. SAX processing, on the other hand, is designed for large document processing, but to achieve this level of performance, a number of tradeoffs are made. The most significant is that XML documents are read element by element. This means that documents cannot be processed via XPath—and that all processing of the document must be done by the developer. This also means that the documents hierarchy is not retained, since SAX processing is event-based; that is, operations occur when specific tags are encountered.

So how is JSON different? The JSON file format was created to ensure that developers could pass complex, hierarchical data to the client (web browser), and have a standard-based, high-performance method of processing the information. But it's become so much more. For many web-based languages like Python, Ruby, and PHP, the JSON format has become the primary currency by which data is sent and consumed. These languages natively consume JSON data, and in consuming it, they create rich data objects that can then be acted upon within the application. This richness makes JSON an ideal language to consume many of the rich metadata types that one will find in a digital library, and given the native support for JSON in most web-based programming languages, can be automatically generated through a couple of simple commands. This has led to the reimaging of many library XML formats as JSON serializations. MARC is a notable example. Take the following record output in MARCXML:

```
<?xml version="1.0" encoding="UTF-8" ?>
<marc:collection xmlns:marc="http://www.loc.gov/MARC21/slim" xmlns:xsi="http://www.w3.org/2001/
XMLSchema-instance" xsi:schemaLocation="http://www.loc.gov/MARC21/slim http://www.loc.gov/standards/
marcxml/schema/MARC21slim.xsd">
<marc:record>
<marc:leader>01365cem a22003491 4500</marc:leader>
<marc:controlfield tag="001">5572119</marc:controlfield>
<marc:controlfield tag="005">20021214203517.0</marc:controlfield>
<marc:controlfield tag="007">cr||||</marc:controlfield>
<marc:controlfield tag="007">aj|canzn</marc:controlfield>
<marc:controlfield tag="008">980520t18541851nyu a 0 eng </marc:controlfield>
<marc:datafield tag="035" ind1=" " ind2=" ">
<marc:subfield code="9">(DLC) 98688538</marc:subfield>
</marc:datafield>
<marc:datafield tag="906" ind1=" " ind2=" ">
<marc:subfield code="a">7</marc:subfield>
<marc:subfield code="b">cbc</marc:subfield>
<marc:subfield code="c">orignew</marc:subfield>
<marc:subfield code="d">u</marc:subfield>
<marc:subfield code="e">ncip</marc:subfield>
<marc:subfield code="f">19</marc:subfield>
<marc:subfield code="g">y-geogmaps</marc:subfield>
</marc:datafield>
<marc:datafield tag="010" ind1=" " ind2=" ">
<marc:subfield code="a"> 98688538 </marc:subfield>
</marc:datafield>
<marc:datafield tag="040" ind1=" " ind2=" ">
<marc:subfield code="a">DLC</marc:subfield>
<marc:subfield code="c">DLC</marc:subfield>
<marc:subfield code="d">DLC</marc:subfield>
</marc:datafield>
<marc:datafield tag="050" ind1="0" ind2="0">
<marc:subfield code="a">G4081.P3 1851</marc:subfield>
<marc:subfield code="b">.E5</marc:subfield>
<marc:subfield code="u">RR 280</marc:subfield>
</marc:datafield>
<marc:datafield tag="052" ind1=" " ind2=" ">
<marc:subfield code="a">4081</marc:subfield>
</marc:datafield>
<marc:datafield tag="072" ind1=" " ind2="7">
<marc:subfield code="a">P3</marc:subfield>
<marc:subfield code="2">lcg</marc:subfield>
</marc:datafield>
<marc:datafield tag="110" ind1="2" ind2=" ">
<marc:subfield code="a">Ensign, Bridgman &amp; Fanning.</marc:subfield>
</marc:datafield>
<marc:datafield tag="245" ind1="1" ind2="0">
<marc:subfield code="a">Railroad &amp; township map of Ohio.</marc:subfield>
</marc:datafield>
<marc:datafield tag="260" ind1=" " ind2=" ">
<marc:subfield code="a">New York,</marc:subfield>
<marc:subfield code="c">1854, c1851.</marc:subfield>
</marc:datafield>
<marc:datafield tag="300" ind1=" " ind2=" ">
<marc:subfield code="a">col. map</marc:subfield>
<marc:subfield code="c">81 x 71 cm.</marc:subfield>
</marc:datafield>
<marc:datafield tag="507" ind1=" " ind2=" ">
<marc:subfield code="a">Scale ca. 1:580,000.</marc:subfield>
</marc:datafield>
<marc:datafield tag="500" ind1=" " ind2=" ">
```

```xml
<marc:subfield code="a">LC also has 1879 edition measuring 92 x 84 cm., which includes a list of
railroad stations and distances.</marc:subfield>
</marc:datafield>
<marc:datafield tag="510" ind1="4" ind2=" ">
<marc:subfield code="a">LC Railroad maps,</marc:subfield>
<marc:subfield code="c">280</marc:subfield>
</marc:datafield>
<marc:datafield tag="500" ind1=" " ind2=" ">
<marc:subfield code="a">Description derived from published bibliography.</marc:subfield>
</marc:datafield>
<marc:datafield tag="520" ind1=" " ind2=" ">
<marc:subfield code="a">Detailed township map showing drainage, cities and towns, county and town-
ship boundaries, roads, and railroads.</marc:subfield>
</marc:datafield>
<marc:datafield tag="500" ind1=" " ind2=" ">
<marc:subfield code="a">County population in upper left.</marc:subfield>
</marc:datafield>
<marc:datafield tag="530" ind1=" " ind2=" ">
<marc:subfield code="a">Available also through the Library of Congress Web site as a raster image.</
marc:subfield>
</marc:datafield>
<marc:datafield tag="650" ind1=" " ind2="0">
<marc:subfield code="a">Railroads</marc:subfield>
<marc:subfield code="z">Ohio</marc:subfield>
<marc:subfield code="v">Maps.</marc:subfield>
</marc:datafield>
<marc:datafield tag="752" ind1=" " ind2=" ">
<marc:subfield code="a">United States</marc:subfield>
<marc:subfield code="b">Ohio.</marc:subfield>
</marc:datafield>
<marc:datafield tag="852" ind1="0" ind2=" ">
<marc:subfield code="a">Library of Congress</marc:subfield>
<marc:subfield code="b">Geography and Map Division</marc:subfield>
<marc:subfield code="e">Washington, D.C. 20540-4650 USA</marc:subfield>
<marc:subfield code="n">dcu</marc:subfield>
</marc:datafield>
<marc:datafield tag="856" ind1="4" ind2="1">
<marc:subfield code="d">g4081p</marc:subfield>
<marc:subfield code="f">rr002800</marc:subfield>
<marc:subfield code="u">http://hdl.loc.gov/loc.gmd/g4081p.rr002800</marc:subfield>
<marc:subfield code="q">c</marc:subfield>
</marc:datafield>
</marc:record>
</marc:collection>
```

While the above record is well structured, and would be easy to process, the ability to process this document efficiently and quickly generally isn't directly supported within most web-based programming languages. For this reason, communication of this data between most applications would occur in JSON. We can re-serialize the above record into JSON:

{"leader":"01365cem a22003491 4500,"
"fields":[{"001":"5572119"},
{"005":"20021214203517.0"},
{"007":"cr||||"},
{"007":"aj|canzn"},
{"008":"980520t18541851nyu\\\\\\\\\\\\\\\\a\\\\\\\\\\0\\\\\\eng\\\\"},
{"035":{"ind1":"\\,"
"ind2":"\\,"
"subfields":[{"9":"(DLC) 98688538"}]}},
{"906":{"ind1":"\\,"
"ind2":"\\,"
"subfields":[{"a":"7"},
{"b":"cbc"},
{"c":"orignew"},
{"d":"u"},
{"e":"ncip"},
{"f":"19"},
{"g":"y-geogmaps"}]}},
{"010":{"ind1":"\\,"
"ind2":"\\,"
"subfields":[{"a":" 98688538 "}]}},
{"040":{"ind1":"\\,"
"ind2":"\\,"
"subfields":[{"a":"DLC"},
{"c":"DLC"},
{"d":"DLC"}]}},
{"050":{"ind1":"0,"
"ind2":"0,"
"subfields":[{"a":"G4081.P3 1851"},
{"b":".E5"},
{"u":"RR 280"}]}},
{"052":{"ind1":"\\,"
"ind2":"\\,"
"subfields":[{"a":"4081"}]}},
{"072":{"ind1":"\\,"
"ind2":"7,"
"subfields":[{"a":"P3"},
{"2":"lcg"}]}},
{"110":{"ind1":"2,"
"ind2":"\\,"
"subfields":[{"a":"Ensign, Bridgman & Fanning."}]}},
{"245":{"ind1":"1,"
"ind2":"0,"
"subfields":[{"a":"Railroad & township map of Ohio."}]}},
{"260":{"ind1":"\\,"
"ind2":"\\,"
"subfields":[{"a":"New York,"},
{"c":"1854, c1851."}]}},
{"300":{"ind1":"\\,"
"ind2":"\\,"
"subfields":[{"a":"col. map"},
{"c":"81 x 71 cm."}]}},
{"507":{"ind1":"\\,"
"ind2":"\\,"
"subfields":[{"a":"Scale ca. 1:580,000."}]}},
{"500":{"ind1":"\\,"
"ind2":"\\,"
"subfields":[{"a":"LC also has 1879 edition measuring 92 x 84 cm., which includes a list of railroad stations and distances."}]}},
{"510":{"ind1":"4,"
"ind2":"\\,"
"subfields":[{"a":"LC Railroad maps,"},

```
{"c":"280"}]}},
{"500":{"ind1":"\\,"
"ind2":"\\,"
"subfields":[{"a":"Description derived from published bibliography."}]}},
{"520":{"ind1":"\\,"
"ind2":"\\,"
"subfields":[{"a":"Detailed township map showing drainage, cities and towns, county and township
boundaries, roads, and railroads."}]}},
{"500":{"ind1":"\\,"
"ind2":"\\,"
"subfields":[{"a":"County population in upper left."}]}},
{"530":{"ind1":"\\,"
"ind2":"\\,"
"subfields":[{"a":"Available also through the Library of Congress Web site as a raster
image."}]}},
{"650":{"ind1":"\\,"
"ind2":"0,"
"subfields":[{"a":"Railroads"},
{"z":"Ohio"},
{"v":"Maps."}]}},
{"752":{"ind1":"\\,"
"ind2":"\\,"
"subfields":[{"a":"United States"},
{"b":"Ohio."}]}},
{"852":{"ind1":"0,"
"ind2":"\\,"
"subfields":[{"a":"Library of Congress"},
{"b":"Geography and Map Division"},
{"e":"Washington, D.C. 20540-4650 USA"},
{"n":"dcu"}]}},
{"856":{"ind1":"4,"
"ind2":"1,"
"subfields":[{"d":"g4081p"},
{"f":"rr002800"},
{"u":"http:\/\/hdl.loc.gov\/loc.gmd\/g4081p.rr002800"},
{"q":"c"}]}}]}
```

Again, the data above is well structured, but when consumed by a browser or a language as a JSON file, the elements within the field become actionable objects. Unlike the XML document, which would require decisions related to processing type, technologies, and so on, loading this record into a JSON parser would immediately allow the developer to process the data as a set of objects, an array of objects, or as a hash. For example, I would easily count the number of times a field appeared by simply asking a count of the object: json_object["856"].count. This changes the relationship that developers are able to have with the data, and adds a level of richness that XML simply doesn't provide when interacting with the information as a programmer.

So, what does this mean for digital libraries? If you are a metadata creator or an individual exporting metadata to share with another organization or individual, it is very likely that you will only be working with XML data, and technologies like XSLT or XQuery will be the primary method that will be used to process the information. For this use case, XML's portability and ability to embed the schema documents within the XML data packet are extremely valuable because they give other individuals the ability to validate not just the structure, but the content of the data provided. However, for individuals working as developers of library systems, JSON will likely be the primary currency that they will use to move data between various parts of the application. This doesn't mean that the XML won't be visible or utilized; it just means that XML won't be the standard currency by which data is transferred within an application. And this transition at the developer level from XML to JSON will be welcome, since it follows the predominant patterns for application development outside of the library community, expanding the potential pool of tools and expertise that can be called upon as cultural heritage institutions develop new applications and platforms.

## Data Manipulation

It would be impossible to write about the full breadth of topics surrounding data manipulation. When working with metadata, transferring data between systems, and upgrading digital platforms, data manipulation will always be required. Even when restricted to digital libraries, the topic covers so many different formats, technologies, and languages that it is easy to be overwhelmed. It's a big topic, and there are books[13] specially dedicated to the topics and techniques that are required to efficiently move data between formats and systems, as well as to identify and understand the challenges associated with the manipulation of data.

Given the breadth of the topic of data manipulation, how does one even prepare for the future to meet this inevitable challenge? The best advice is to build up a data toolkit; that is, to identify a set of languages, tools, and strategies that one might use to perform specific data manipulation tasks, and become familiar with them. The truth is that many developers, metadata specialists, and others will have specific tools and languages that they cannot live without. And just like operating systems and browsers, the advocacy for one tool or language can take on a kind of religious fervor. But the reality is that data manipulation, like any task, can be done in a wide variety of ways and through a wide range of workflows. There really isn't a best way or tool to do it. There are certainly many wrong ways, but no one best way; this means that for the most part, the tools or languages that one chooses to learn are often less important than one's ability to understand and master the resource. The following subsections describe just a small selection of potential tools and services that libraries should consider evaluating as they develop their own personalized toolkits.

### *Programming Languages*

Programming language selection often comes down to one of two things: personal choice or organizational support. By and large, most programming languages provide the same toolkits and functionalities. Differences primarily show up in the form of syntax, object structure, and language performance.

> *Ruby, Python, PHP, PERL:* For the sake of brevity, these four languages are being placed together in the same category. While each is different, they all are interpreted languages, that is, these are languages that don't require the use of a compiler. Within the library community, PHP and Ruby are currently the most widely utilized languages. For the purposes of data manipulation, Python and PERL are the two most widely used languages, and they have significant communities outside the cultural heritage community that can provide support and feedback.

> *Java, C#, C++, Object-C, Swift:* These are compiler-dependent programming languages. Unlike interpreted languages, these languages are compiled into binary files that can then be run as stand-alone applications. These languages are often more difficult to learn because they require a mastery of concepts like garbage collection, advanced memory management, and so on, but they also provide significant performance and functional advantages over current interpreted languages. These languages are often used in the development of core digital library components. For example, Fedora is written in Java, as is DSpace, while many XML processing tools like nokogiri (for Ruby) and libxml are written in C++. For the purposes of data manipulation, these languages are best used when large data processing is required.

## Programming Tools

A sizeable number of programming tools have been created to aid the manipulation and creation of the data that are commonly found in cultural heritage institutions. This section will highlight a few of them.

> *MARC4J* (https://github.com/marc4j/marc4j): MARC4J is a Java library developed to enable the creation, manipulation, and processing of MARC and MARCXML data. The tool is widely used and actively supported.

> *MARC::Record* (http://search.cpan.org/perldoc?MARC%3A%3A Record): MARC::Record is a popular PERL module developed to enable the creation, manipulation, and processing of MARC and MARCXML data. The module is used in many popular library applications, like Koha (https://koha-community.org/), with an active development and support community.

> *pymarc* (https://github.com/edsu/pymarc): pymarc is a popular Python library that was developed to enable the creation, manipulation, and processing of MARC21 records.

*rubymarc* (https://github.com/ruby-marc/ruby-marc/): rubymarc is a pure ruby library developed to support the creation, manipulation, and processing of MARC21 and MARCXML data.

*Saxon* (https://sourceforge.net/projects/saxon/): Saxon is a high-performance XSLT/XQuery-processing toolkit that can be run as a library or stand-alone application. Many would argue that it is the gold standard of XML/XSLT/XQuery processing tools, since the creator, Michael Kay, plays a key role on the advisory committee overseeing the development of the XSLT and XQuery standards.

*nokogiri* (www.nokogiri.org/): nokogiri is a high-performance ruby library created to provide XML functionality to the language. While Ruby does provide a core set of XML functionality, the overall performance of its built-in language tools makes it nearly unusable for data manipulation purposes. Nokogiri fills this niche and is used throughout the digital library community, particularly in projects like the Samvera project.

*Catmandu* (http://librecat.org/): Catmandu is a set of command-line and PERL tools that provide a wide range of data manipulation functionality for dealing with many of the data formats found in libraries.

## Software Tools

While the formal tool development for the cultural heritage community is fairly sparse, there are a handful of tools that are nearly universally part of every metadata or digital library manager's toolkit.

*OpenRefine* (http://openrefine.org/): It's hard to describe just how powerful OpenRefine can be as a data manipulation tool. When a user first comes across it, OpenRefine looks like a spreadsheet program, on steroids. But in reality, it's much more than that. OpenRefine excels in providing structure and meaning to unstructured data. It includes its own macro language and robust regular expression language; and it has a wide range of plug-ins and flavors that add additional support for data reconciliation with linked data services.

*Oxygen XML Editor* (www.oxygenxml.com/): There are a lot of XML editors available for download and use, but none are better than Oxygen. Unlike the other tools on this list, Oxygen isn't free to use; it is a proprietary application that carries a relatively high price tag, but its ability to create, test, and model data and data transformations makes it worth noting.

*Yaz* (www.indexdata.com/yaz): The Yaz toolkit is ubiquitous; it powers nearly all of the available Z39.50 servers on the Internet and is available as programming libraries for nearly all of the major development languages (both compiler-based and interpreted). Additionally, the Yaz toolkit comes with a number of stand-alone command-line tools that provide light-weight data manipulation, character conversion, and format manipulation.

*MarcEdit* (http://marcedit.reeset.net): MarcEdit is a free library metadata software suite that provides support for working with nearly all of the metadata formats currently used by cultural heritage institutions. It provides both built-in transformation tools and wizards to create dynamic transformations, as well as editors and global tools for the batch processing of information. The resource also provides a wide range of functions for doing data reconciliation with linked data services.

# Application Development

Digital libraries often form the initial foundation of a cultural heritage organization's digital platform, and they represent a significant reorientation of the role and services provided by the organization. In a traditional environment, analog services are easy to define; they are visible and tangible, and are often tied to people or places. Digital library applications tend to not be viewed the same way. Digital services are often viewed through the lens of their function or application. This difference silos applications and functions, making it difficult to see these as parts of a larger whole. But it doesn't have to be like that. Through thoughtful and careful planning and development, an organization's infrastructure can be re-formed from a group of distinct applications to a more cohesive platform of services . . . though in the case of a digital platform, these services would be represented as a set of APIs. These programming interfaces offer windows into the library platform to enable access to actions, data, and services. As one considers the development of these services and programming interfaces, a handful of technologies, protocols, and standards will be important.

## REST (Representational State Transfer)

Communication online is actually a somewhat messy process with lots of competing protocols. In the cultural heritage communities, we have traditionally complicated this process through the use of domain-specific communication protocols such as Z39.50, SRU, and OAI-PMH. These technologies are built on top of rather than utilizing traditional established patterns related to standard web-based communication protocols. The library community is hardly alone in pursuing such practices. In 2006, it looked like the business community was shifting its online communications services away from traditional HTTP-based communications, but to message-based communication formats like WSDL and SOAP. Even in the library community, momentum was developing around SOAP-based processing with the development of the SRW specification . . . and then, it just stopped. While these message-based communication formats still exist and are utilized, they are now the exception when developing web-based services and programming interfaces.

Instead, both the library and larger development communities shifted to the utilization and creation of RESTful-based services. And this made a lot of sense. While most people would find it difficult to describe what REST is, they interact with RESTful-based services all the time. HTTP(S) is the most common example of a REST-based protocol, which is a stateless protocol designed to use URIs to perform a set of predefined actions. When using HTTP(S), this would be one of four defined actions: GET, POST, DELETE, and PUT—with response to these actions defined by a predefined set of HTTP status codes. These codes and actions form the foundation of the Internet and the communication between web browsers and Internet service providers. Today, most web services are developed to take advantage of the HTTP(S) model, utilizing RESTful services and leveraging predefined HTTP status codes to denote the success or failure of each operation. By utilizing this process, developers can leverage all of the existing tools on the Web and be confident that their resources and services will be widely supported.

## SPARQL (SPARQL Protocol and RDF Query Language)

Very simply, SPARQL is a query language that was developed to support the semantic web. SPARQL uses the RDF triple concepts of subject, object, and predicate to perform SQL-like searches against a semantic data store. Presently, SPARQL is primarily used by large organizations like the Getty Research Institute or national libraries (like the Japanese Diet Library) to provide an interface with their linked data infrastructures.

## SRU (Search and Retrieval via URL)

SRU represents an XML-based search protocol. SRU was paired with the development of SRW (Search and Retrieval via Webservice), and was created to take the place of Z39.50 as the primary method for searching and transferring data between library systems. While this format is used within the library community, the protocol has never enjoyed the broad use and adoption that Z39.50 has had and still maintains.

## Code Management

Not too long ago, it was very difficult to imagine cultural heritage organizations as engines for software development. While these organizations have always had "developers" that have created local projects and systems, these tools were rarely shared and maintained outside of the organization. This has been one of the transformational changes that have occurred in the library and larger cultural heritage community: the coordinated development of digital library software and platforms. But this change has brought with it a new set of questions that digital library managers need to consider. When working with or contributing to an open source or coordinated application development effort, there needs to be a reliable way of sharing and managing code contributions. While the cultural heritage community has definitely gravitated to a specific code management environment, a number of options are available:

> *GitHub* (http://github.com): GitHub is a popular distributed code management system that is used by a large number of library and cultural heritage development projects. In fact, it is probably the most popular of the available code management options. Whether one's library or organization decides that it will use a public or private instance of GitHub to manage its application development, proficiency with GitHub will be required to participate in nearly any outside software development effort.

> *Subversion* (https://subversion.apache.org/): Subversion is a centrally managed document/code management system. Prior to GitHub, Subversion was popular as an organizational code management solution, since it enabled organizations to centrally manage all changes. It's still used at many organizations for local code/document management.

Today, the use of a code management system should be a requirement for any organization with individuals developing code. These systems enable organizations to preserve historical memory, protect against code breakage, and share projects either outside or inside the organization. These systems are, essentially, how software code is preserved because these tools manage version control, contribution records, and provide snapshots of major releases. These tools protect an organization, as people move on and change jobs.

## Future of Software Development

The future of software development is always difficult to predict because the changes happen so rapidly. Few saw the ubiquity of mobile application development until Apple shifted the paradigm with the iPhone. Software development within the cultural heritage space is equally difficult to predict because so much of this community is reliant on open source development and grant funding. With that said, a couple of trends are worth noting.

## Mobile Application Development

Libraries have largely stayed out of the mobile development space, choosing instead to purchase programs that can turn application websites into stand-alone mobile applications. But we think that this space is too big to ignore. As of the time of this writing, more people access the Internet through their mobile devices than through a traditional desktop environment. And in developing countries, mobile services are the only method of Internet access. As mobile systems continue the trend of creating increasingly walled gardens for their users, cultural heritage organizations will be forced to make decisions around mobile development. And this will be hard, since the mobile development of services, at least in the current paradigm, is very local.

## Applications Continue to Become More Micro

By now, individuals in the digital library space should be very familiar with the microservices development model. Since 2010, a number of papers and services have been created utilizing these concepts, in an effort to reduce an application's complexity and footprint. We believe that this process will continue, as library software developers shift away from developing domain-specific solutions and move to leverage existing solutions created outside of the library community in order to solve large problems. This development model is illustrated in the Fedora 4.x development. Fedora 3.x was a large, monolithic object store that was designed for the long-term preservation of digital objects. When the community began development on Fedora 4.x, the decision was made to shift much of the core architecture outside of the library community. This meant that Fedora 4.x development would entail the development of a framework and messaging system around other open source projects and technologies to achieve the same goal as Fedora 3.x. The benefit of this was that the cultural heritage community would no longer need to maintain the entire application stack, but only those parts that were unique to the Fedora application. This type of development carries with it certain risks, since it makes tools dependent on a much wider array of dependencies, but it also shares the larger cost of development.

## Deeper Reliance on Interpreted Languages and JavaScript

Digital library development has always been separated into two camps: system work that was primarily coded in Java, and process work that was created in a range of interpreted languages (such as PHP, Ruby, PERL, or Python). This is still true for much of the core software used in digital libraries, but it is coming to an end. The cultural heritage development community has been slowly shifting away from using Java as a development language. Some of this might be due to the change in ownership of the language, though much of the change is due to the improved performance found in interpreted languages. The availability of high-performance interpreted languages, and frameworks like Angular, React, or Node.js, for development-responsive applications completely in JavaScript has changed the way applications are created. We see this outside of the library community, and believe that it is only a matter of time before most digital library development adopts these development concepts as well.

## Sharing Your Services

Given the relatively low barriers for the development of RESTful-base web services, the question really comes down to how much control an organization is willing to give up as it relates to content. Organizations considering a digital repository need to ask the following questions when considering whether or not to offer web-services access to their systems:

1. Is your organization comfortable giving up some control over how content is utilized? This is a big question to consider, since users occasionally have a quirky way of doing unexpected things. The Hamster sudoku game is a benign example of a user repurposing images in a way that was never intended by the content owners. However, these images could just as easily show up on a website in a way that the content owners would find inappropriate. Is this something your organization can live with? If not, then the organization will need to carefully consider what types of access it is comfortable providing.

2. Can we support it? In the case of providing web-services access to one's digital repository, support will need to be twofold. First, the organization needs to be willing to provide infrastructure support. Where a digital collection to build a popular web service—how would the additional traffic affect the quality of the service? And second, the organization needs to be willing to provide users with support through the creation of documentation, and so on. Could your organization provide support for these types of API usage? What kind of programming staff is currently available in your organization?

3. Can your digital repository exist outside your organization's existing information infrastructure? If the answer to this question is no, then you likely will need API access to the digital repository. At this point, one would just need to decide whether to make that access public or private.

Each of these questions should be carefully considered and weighed against the potential pitfalls and benefits for outside users. Of the three questions, the ability to give up some control over the content in one's digital repository is likely the most difficult one. Given the care and thought that often goes into the creation of a digital repository, it's understandable for an organization to want to "protect" its brand and its content. Digital repository builders should consider, however, that this ability to provide remove-access mechanisms is what the current Web 2.0 and future Web 3.0 frameworks are built on. The ability to dynamically query and repurpose content is a powerful tool for all users of a digital repository. What's more, information organizations can set an example to their commercial vendors in regard to open access for digital information. As a whole, the information access community continues to work with their vendors, which are data aggregators with traditionally closed publishing models like LexisNexis or Elsevier, to provide an unmediated form of access to their content. Some vendors like OCLC are actively undertaking projects to provide content available through RESTful-based APIs, while other vendors still need some gentle nudging. The information community can be a role model of sorts, by making their own data available with as few access restrictions as possible.

## Summary

When building or considering one's digital repository platform, careful thought should be taken regarding all aspects of the platform's implementation. As previous chapters have stated, a digital repository will require new workflows, new acquisition models, and new responsibilities from your organization's information technology departments. And while it might be tempting to simply let the repository platform guide your decisions relating to metadata and metadata access, one must resist this. Aside from the content, the metadata entered into a digital repository is the single most important part of the digital repository. And in many cases, it's likely the most valuable component of the digital repository, given the large investments that go into creating metadata and the value that outside users and data harvesters place on that metadata. As such, digital repository builders should weigh their available options, selecting from the myriad of metadata schemas currently available the schema that best suits the needs of their organization, its users, and the bibliographic description of the repository's content.

Additionally, digital repository builders need to consider how much access and how truly available they wish the content of their repositories to be. Opening one's digital repository beyond the walls of the application platform allows other services like search engines or users to search, harvest, or integrate data from one's digital repository into a different context or workflow. It can enable content users to create new and exciting services or "virtual collections" that a repository owner would be happy to be associated with, or it could result in materials being used in more unsavory contexts. Repositories that support open sharing of data should consider how important information context is within their organization. At the same time, these same web services that support open sharing of data provide opportunities for one's own organization to better integrate its digital repository content into their own existing information architecture, enabling better findability and collection development. Ultimately, it comes down to the organization's ability to support open access and their long-term values related to the accessibility of content. How many different access points does an organization wish to provide, and what metadata schemas will be needed to support these points of access?

## Notes

1. W3C XHTML2 Working Group, "A Vocabulary and Associated APIs for HTML and XHTML," www.w3.org/TR/htm15/.

2. OCLC, "WorldCat.org," www.worldcat.org.

3. W3C XML Working Group, "XML Path Language," www.w3.org/TR/xpath.

4. W3C XForms Working Group, "XForms 1.0 (2nd Ed.)," www.w3.org/TR/xforms/.

5. W3C XSLT Working Group, "XSL Transformations (XSLT)," www.w3.org/TR/xslt.

6. W3C XLink Working Group, "XML Linking Language (XLink) Version 1.0," www.w3.org/TR/xlink/.

7. W3C XQuery Working Group, "XQuery 1.0: An XML Query Language," www.w3.org/TR/xquery/.

8. W3C XPointer Working Group, "XML Pointer Language (XPointer)," www.w3.org/TR/xptr/.

9. W3C Schema Working Group, "W3C XML Schema," www.w3.org/XML/Schema.

10. Wikipedia, "Uniform Resource Identifier," https://en.wikipedia.org/wiki/Uniform_Resource_Identifier.

11. OCLC's VIAF, www.viaf.org.

12. Wikipedia, "JSON," https://en.wikipedia.org/wiki/JSON.

13. Kyle Banerjee and Bonnie Parks, *Migrating Library Data: A Practical Manual* (Chicago: American Library Association, 2017).

# Metadata Formats

**When digital library** platforms first started emerging, users had few options when it came to metadata frameworks for their bibliographic description. Systems tended to support a single descriptive schema like Unqualified Dublin Core or the system's own closed internal metadata schema. This meant that one of the first and most important decisions that a digital repository implementer would need to make was the selection of a bibliographic data model and metadata schema that would be sufficient for use in describing the various materials that might be eventually loaded into the digital repository system. And once selected, all metadata decisions would be left to the digital repository platform, giving the implementer few options for customization or expansion. While this approach would lead to a universal descriptive format on the digital repository platform (in many respects, emulating the ubiquity of MARC in integrated library systems), its net effect was to create metadata that was in many cases tied too closely to a specific software product, or was too broad to be meaningful outside of a particular system.

Today, digital repository software has become much more flexible in terms of how metadata is shared and created. This allows implementers to store bibliographic data using one of many current metadata schemas, and to create metadata storehouses that are heterogeneous in nature and which can interoperate with a greater variety of systems. This flexibility allows organizations to take a much closer look at how they describe different types of materials, as well as control the granularity of description for each item appearing in the digital repository. While this chapter will not provide a comprehensive guide for any one metadata schema, it examines a handful of metadata schemas that are currently being used by digital repository implementers, looking at how and when specific schemas may be utilized.

# Metadata Primitives

Considering the significant investment that organizations make towards metadata creation, it seems fitting to start this chapter by looking at why the ability to use a heterogeneous metadata system is important. The most obvious reason for this is that libraries function within a very homogenous environment. Since 1969, when the Library of Congress first released the specifications for the MARC framework, libraries have optimized their workflows and systems to support MARC record creation. Even when utilizing non-MARC formats, libraries still tend to rely on the traditional AACR2 or Resource and Descriptive Access (RDA) guidelines when dealing with metadata creation. In general, librarians want to maintain the homogenous nature of their bibliographic content, while experimenting with non-MARC formats. However, no single metadata element set accommodates the functional requirements of all applications, and as the Web dissolves boundaries, it becomes increasingly important to be able to also cross discovery boundaries.[1] For many organizations, the digital repository represents the first significant foray into the world of non-MARC, semantic web-centric, metadata. And while many may find themselves wishing that the American Library Association or the Library of Congress would step up and create a single, universal XML metadata schema that adopts current cataloging rules (AACR2, RDA),[2] we find ourselves in a place where multiple standard formats have been developed to allow description to happen in the schema that is best suited for a particular type of material.

In 2002, Roy Tennant[3] wrote his now famous (or infamous, depending on your perspective) column calling for the death of the MARC metadata format. He argued that libraries would be unable to move forward so long as MARC was being used as the primary descriptive metadata schema, and he thus provoked an ongoing debate about whether libraries should use MARC or XML. However, different schema serve different purposes, so it is normally not productive to think in terms of using only MARC or only XML. Much of Tennant's dismissal of MARC relates to the general rules that govern MARC record creation.

In part, it was this question that spurred the development of RDA. For years, libraries labored under AACR2, a set of rules created during a period when libraries largely dealt with analog materials and still printed and maintained card catalogs. While these rules were updated, and improved to provide support for the burgeoning web environment, AACR2's inability to provide the flexibility needed to rapidly shift and support non-analog description and discovery required libraries to develop an alternative: RDA (Resource Description and Access).

The development of RDA was ambitious. Given the need to create a standard set of best practices for bibliographic description beyond the library community, RDA was developed as a first attempt to harmonize the various bibliographic description data models and practices and bring them together. The ultimate hope was that RDA would be used not just to replace AACR2, but to eventually become the dominant set of practices for describing all bibliographic metadata. RDA attempted to shed the MARC-isms, and focus on modeling questions to allow the concepts to be applied outside of traditional MARC, but into other library schemas (like EAD, TEI, MODS), but outside of the library community to support archive and museum cataloging, as well as the emerging digital library space. Additionally, it was hoped that RDA would provide the foundation upon which a new bibliographic model could be developed: one that went beyond MARC and that would usher libraries into the world of semantic web description. And while one could certainly argue whether these goals were achieved, RDA has successfully supplanted AACR2 as the primary data model for describing MARC data, and it has had a tremendous impact on the Library of Congress's semantic web efforts, including the continued development of BIBFRAME.

A better question to ask is whether RDA is still relevant within today's digital environment—particularly given the fact that AACR2 was created for a print-centric world where the only catalogs contained printed cards. In fact, Tennant seems to make this argument in a later article[4] where he steps back from calling for the death of MARC, and argues for a new way of thinking about bibliographic infrastructure. Today organizations like the Library of Congress question the need for traditional controlled access points[5] and the future of metadata creation,[6] leaving libraries to struggle with how digital materials should be described and be accessed within local and remote systems. This does not mean that much cannot be taken from the current descriptive rules and utilized as an organization begins its digital repository efforts, but an organization must recognize that using only the current bibliographic descriptive rules will be insufficient. However, before taking a closer look at some of the common XML metadata formats that are supported using today's digital repository software, a very brief look at the MARC metadata schema is in order.

Finally, one of the significant changes in digital repository development over the past ten years has been the increasing support for semantic data, and the ability to model bibliographic data utilizing RDF (Resource Description Framework). In the early and mid-2000s, libraries primarily selected a single metadata framework, and utilizing that framework, all content would need to be captured. Admittedly, some tools like DSpace provided the ability to create custom fields for local use, but ultimately, at the system level, all data was mapped into a single metadata format. Today, this is no longer true. Systems like Fedora 4 and Ex Libris's Rosetta software have been developed using linked data and semantic web concepts as their foundations. This means that data is no longer limited to a single metadata schema or data model; instead, through the use of multiple schemas and data namespaces, materials can utilize multiple metadata schemas through RDF. In this section, I will detail a handful of the common metadata primitives that are still utilized within digital repositories, but I will also discuss the emerging presence of linked and RDF data, and how this is changing the way that we both interact with and describe materials in the new and emerging digital repository environments.

## *MARC*

As previously noted, MARC was originally developed in 1969 by the Library of Congress as a standard method for transferring bibliographic data between systems on electromagnetic tapes. Today, MARC is the lingua franca for transmitting data between ILS systems within the library community. And while very few digital repositories handle MARC records directly, a handful can export their bibliographic metadata in MARC or provide an easy path to the creation of MARC records for stored content.

Within the library community, MARC itself is often misunderstood. When many think MARC, they are often thinking of the fields and tags defined by the physical rules governing the input of data, like RDA. Figure 6.1 shows a representation of a MARC21 record of an electronic thesis from Ohio State University.

These rules define what data elements can be placed within a particular MARC field, creating specific "flavors" of MARC. For example, one could find flavors for MARC21 (a merging of USMARC, CANMARC and UKMARC), CHMARC, FINMARC, UNIMARC, and so on. Currently, the Library of Congress recognizes approximately forty[7] different MARC flavors that are actively utilized around the world.

Technically, MARC is nothing more than a binary data format made up of three distinct parts: (1) the leader, (2) the directory, and (3) the bibliographic data. The leader makes up the first twenty-four bytes and contains information about the MARC record itself. The leader will include the total length of the record, note the start position of the field data, the character encoding, the record type, and the encoding level of the record. However, it is within the leader that one of MARC's most glaring limitations becomes visible. A MARC record reserves just five bytes to define the total length of

z3950_1.mrc - Notepad

File Edit Format View Help

01821ctm a2200325la
45000010013000000003000600013005001700019008004100036040002500077035002000102050002300122100002100145245008200166260001200248300004700260 3360
0260030733700280033333800270036150000140038850200400040250400560044252006720049853000420117065000480121265000510126065000470131185600830 1358
994001201441948004201453ocm63527152 OCoLC20170731160137.0060207s2005 xx a bm 000 0 eng d aOREbengcOREdOCLCQ a(OCoLC)63527152 4aLD4330
2006b.S6561 aSorte, Shraddha.10aEnd user software engineering features for both genders /cShraddha R. Sorte. c©2005. a92 leaves, bound :billustrations ;c29 cm
atextbtxt2rdacontent aunmediatedbn2rdamedia avolumebnc2rdacarrier aPrintout. bM.S.cOregon State Universityd2006 aIncludes bibliographical references (leaves
51-55). aPrevious research has revealed gender differences that impact females? willingness to adopt software features in end users? programming environments. Since
these features have separately been shown to help end users problem solve, it is important to female end users? productivity that we find ways to make these features
more acceptable to females. This thesis draws from our ongoing work with users to help inform our design of theory-based methods for encouraging effective feature
usage by both genders. This design effort is the first to begin addressing the gender differences in the ways that people go about problem solving in end-user
programming situations. aAlso available on the World Wide Web. 0aComputers and womenxPsychological aspects. 0aWomenxEffect of technological innovations on.
0aEnd-user computingxPsychological aspects.41uhttp://hdl.handle.net/1957/510zConnect to this title online.qapplication/pdf aZ0bOSU hNO HOLDINGS IN OSU - 1
OTHER HOLDINGS

**FIGURE 6.1**

MARC21 Example

the record. This means that the length of a valid MARC record can never exceed a total length, including directory and field data, of 99,999 bytes. And it should also be noted that the length is indeed calculated against bytes, not characters—a distinction that has become more important as more library software transitions to UTF-8. For example, while an e with an acute (é) is represented as a single UTF-8 character, it is deconstructed as two distinct bytes. Within the MARC record leader and directory, this single character would need to be represented as two bytes for the record/field lengths to be valid. What's more, the introduction of UTF-8 support into MARC records has raised other issues—specifically ones related to the indexing of data elements, and to compatibility with legacy MARC-8 systems.

### Indexing Issues

Indexing issues can be particularly tricky when working with data that originates from MARC records. This is largely due to the fact that UTF-8 MARC records preserve compatibility with MARC-8 data. To do this, UTF-8 MARC data is coded utilizing a compatibility normalization of the UTF-8 language. What does this mean? Well, let's think about that e with an acute accent again (é). When represented in MARC-8, this value would be created utilizing two distinct characters. These would be the "e" and the modifier {acute}. Together, the system would recognize the e{acute} characters and render them as a single value. In order to preserve the ability to move between UTF-8 and MARC-8, the Library of Congress has specified that data be coded utilizing the UTF-8 compatibility normalization. This normalization retains the MARC-8 construction, utilizing two distinct characters to represent the e with an acute accent (é), rather than a single code point. This means that in UTF-8 MARC records, the (é) is represented as an {acute} and an e ({acute}e). Again, a computer will recognize the presence of the modifier, and render the data correctly. However, this introduces indexing issues, because the modifier, not the (é), is what tends to be indexed. For systems that utilize legacy MARC data, or that utilize recommended MARC data-encoding rules when coding data into UTF-8, these character normalization rules lead to significant indexing issues, making it difficult to support search and discovery for non-English scripts.

However, in recent years, this problem has gotten progressively more difficult and complicated as many systems are no longer requiring UTF-8 data to be presented in the recommended UTF-8 normalization, resulting in records that contain mixed normalization rules. At the operating system level, these normalization rules have little impact on search and discovery of content. These rules only come into play when making changes to data, as data changes tend to happen using ordinal (or binary) case. So, while I may have a file that represents an é using both composed and decomposed characters, the system will generally render these items so that they look identical. It's only when these items are edited that it becomes clear that the mixed normalization is present. In prior years, this tended not to be a concern, as major bibliographic entities like OCLC normalized UTF-8.

This changed around 2017 when OCLC allowed all valid UTF-8 data to be entered into cataloging records. At that point, data was no longer normalized, and records placed into the bibliographic repository could have multiple normalizations represented in a record. This has had significant impacts for both indexing and display within library catalogs, as some systems assume very specific normalization rules, and are unable to process data logically when mixed normalizations are present within a record. In those cases, users will need to utilize a third-party tool, like MarcEdit, to ensure that data conforms to a single normalized form, or develop the scripts and workflows themselves to normalize their data prior to ingest.

## Compatibility Issues

While UTF-8 expands the support for a wider range of characters, most MARC systems only support a very limited set of characters. This means that when moving data between legacy and UTF-8-encoded systems, a method of representing data outside of the traditional MARC-8 encoding schema needed to be developed. Again, the Library of Congress provides a set of best practices, and in this case, the NCR (numerical character reference) scheme is utilized to support the lossless conversion between legacy and UTF-8 systems. Unfortunately, while this has been the best practice since the early 2000s, many legacy library systems still fail to recognize NCR encodings in bibliographic data, causing display and indexing issues. What's more, most digital repository software fails to decode NCR-encoded data into the proper UTF-8 equivalents, again affecting indexing (though not display).

While the move to UTF-8 has created some issues for libraries that are intent on utilizing their legacy data streams or wish to move data between data streams, the benefit of the increased number of characters that the language supports has largely outweighed these issues. What's more, well-established workflows and tools exist that support the conversion of character data not only between character encoding (UTF-8 and MARC-8) but between character normalizations (compatibility versus canonical), enabling libraries to reuse copious amounts of legacy data with very little data loss.

## MARC Dictionary

The MARC dictionary, which starts at byte 25, is made up of numerous 12-byte blocks where each block is representative of a single bibliographic field. Each block then contains a field label (bytes 0–2), the field length (bytes 3–6), and the position relative to the bibliographic data (bytes 7–11). Field data is limited to 9,999 bytes, given that the field length can only be expressed as a 4-byte value. In figure 6.1, we can look at the following example from the directory: 245008200162. Here, we can break this block down into the following sections:

- Field label: 245
- Field length: 0082
- Start position: 00162

This information tells a MARC parser how to extract the 245 field data from the MARC record.

So, if we look at this record broken into a text view (figure 6.2), we can see how a MARC parser treats this information. In figure 6.2, we see the same record as in figure 6.1, only in this case, a MARC parser has read the leader and directory and has extracted the MARC data into a more visually friendly format.

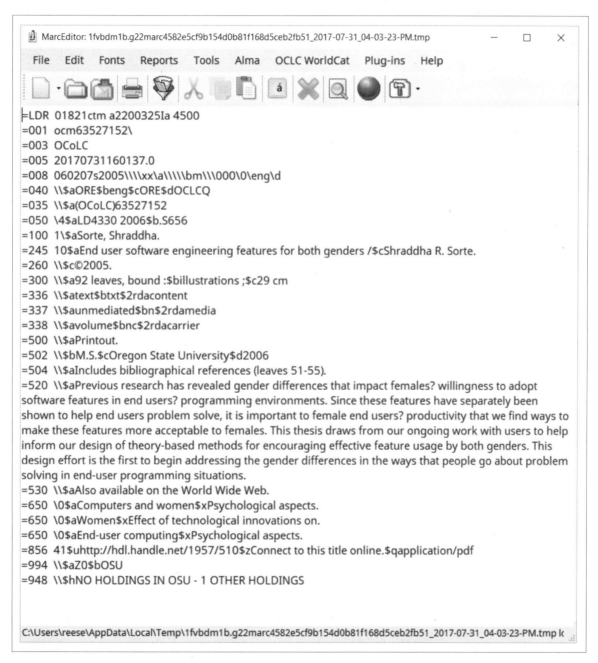

**FIGURE 6.2**

Plain-Text View of MARC Record

Many technical limitations exist that make MARC a poor choice for a digital repository. First and foremost, as a metadata schema, MARC is virtually unknown outside of the library community. This fact limits the number of available partners or vendors that can be used to create or support systems utilizing the record format. Moreover, it limits data-sharing to primarily the library community. Second, the record-size restrictions limit the amount and type of bibliographic content that can be provided. This is generally quite obvious when one is looking at a MARC record derived from a more robust XML language; the fields dealing with descriptions and abstracts are often truncated or broken into multiple related fields in order to overcome the field length limits. Within the XML formats to be described later in this chapter, records can be created containing a much richer set of data, including large data elements like tables of contents, abstracts, summaries, or even the full text of an item. In addition, within XML formats, rich content like images and documents can be embedded into the metadata themselves, turning the metadata records into information objects.

## MARC21XML

As one might guess, MARC21XML is a lossless XML representation of MARC, with one notable exception. Unlike MARC, which supports the MARC-8 character set, MARC21XML exclusively supports the UTF-8 character set, meaning that character data in MARC-8 must be rectified to UTF-8. MARC21XML was first proposed by the Library of Congress in 1994 as one potential method for migrating MARC data into an XML schema. However, MARC21XML has found only sparse use within the library community—and primarily as a data crosswalking mechanism for MARC between other metadata schemas. For example, MarcEdit,[8] a free application written by Terry Reese, utilizes MARC21XML as the control metadata schema when moving data between differing library metadata schema. Figure 6.3, for example, is a MARC21XML representation of the sample record found in figure 6.1. This representative record was generated using MarcEdit.

Looking at figure 6.3, one can see that MARC21XML is an XML-based metadata format; because of this, few of the technical restrictions relevant to MARC are inherently present with MARC21XML. For example, MARC21XML has no predefined record size limit, meaning that users can embed large data elements into the XML record. Moreover, like all XML-based metadata schemas, MARC21XML can have data-like images or documents embedded directly into the metadata.

While MARC21XML does not contain the same limitations of MARC at the technical level, these limitations do exist. However, they are limitations imposed due to the requirement that MARC21XML be a lossless representation of MARC. For MARC21XML to be utilized as initially conceived, it must inherit the same technical limitations as the MARC framework if compatibility between the two formats is to remain.

```
▼<marc:collection xmlns:marc="http://www.loc.gov/MARC21/slim" xmlns:xsi="http://www.w3.org/2001/XMLSchema-instance" xsi:schemaLocation="http://www.loc.gov/MARC21/slim
  http://www.loc.gov/standards/marcxml/schema/MARC21slim.xsd">
  ▼<marc:record>
    <marc:leader>01821ctm a2200325Ia 4500</marc:leader>
    <marc:controlfield tag="001">ocm63527152</marc:controlfield>
    <marc:controlfield tag="003">OCoLC</marc:controlfield>
    <marc:controlfield tag="005">20170731160137.0</marc:controlfield>
    <marc:controlfield tag="008">060207s2005 xx a bm 000 0 eng d</marc:controlfield>
    ▼<marc:datafield tag="040" ind1=" " ind2=" ">
      <marc:subfield code="a">ORE</marc:subfield>
      <marc:subfield code="b">eng</marc:subfield>
      <marc:subfield code="c">ORE</marc:subfield>
      <marc:subfield code="d">OCLCQ</marc:subfield>
    </marc:datafield>
    ▼<marc:datafield tag="035" ind1=" " ind2=" ">
      <marc:subfield code="a">(OCoLC)63527152</marc:subfield>
    </marc:datafield>
    ▼<marc:datafield tag="050" ind1=" " ind2="4">
      <marc:subfield code="a">LD4330 2006</marc:subfield>
      <marc:subfield code="b">.S656</marc:subfield>
    </marc:datafield>
    ▼<marc:datafield tag="100" ind1="1" ind2=" ">
      <marc:subfield code="a">Sorte, Shraddha.</marc:subfield>
    </marc:datafield>
    ▼<marc:datafield tag="245" ind1="1" ind2="0">
      ▼<marc:subfield code="a">
        End user software engineering features for both genders /
      </marc:subfield>
      <marc:subfield code="c">Shraddha R. Sorte.</marc:subfield>
    </marc:datafield>
    ▼<marc:datafield tag="260" ind1=" " ind2=" ">
      <marc:subfield code="c">©2005.</marc:subfield>
    </marc:datafield>
    ▼<marc:datafield tag="300" ind1=" " ind2=" ">
      <marc:subfield code="a">92 leaves, bound :</marc:subfield>
      <marc:subfield code="b">illustrations ;</marc:subfield>
      <marc:subfield code="c">29 cm</marc:subfield>
    </marc:datafield>
    ▼<marc:datafield tag="336" ind1=" " ind2=" ">
      <marc:subfield code="a">text</marc:subfield>
      <marc:subfield code="b">txt</marc:subfield>
      <marc:subfield code="2">rdacontent</marc:subfield>
    </marc:datafield>
    ▼<marc:datafield tag="337" ind1=" " ind2=" ">
      <marc:subfield code="a">unmediated</marc:subfield>
      <marc:subfield code="b">n</marc:subfield>
      <marc:subfield code="2">rdamedia</marc:subfield>
    </marc:datafield>
    ▼<marc:datafield tag="338" ind1=" " ind2=" ">
```

**FIGURE 6.3**

MARC21XML Record

## *Dublin Core*

Serendipity can be a funny thing, since small decisions or discussions can have a lasting effect on the world around us. For example, in 1980–81, David J. Bradley, a computer engineer at IBM, wrote a few lines of code that would forever change the way that people interact with present-day computers. Bradley introduced the three-key sequence combination "CTRL+ALT+DEL." In what he would later describe in an interview[9] as "not a memorable event," Bradley's few lines of code were designed specifically to give developers a set of escape sequences to do administrative functions before powering down a computer; the lines were never meant to be seen by the general public. However, this three-key sequence has become one of the primary methods that are used today to perform the actions of logging on/off, locking, and powering down one's computer. In much the same serendipitous way, Dublin Core has surprisingly become one of the most important metadata frameworks within the library community and beyond.

## History

The history of Dublin Core traces back to the 2nd International WWW Conference in 1994. During the conference, Yuri Rubinsky (of SoftQuad), Stuart Weibel, Eric Miller, and Terry Noreault (of OCLC), and Joseph Hardin of the NCSA (National Center for Supercomputing Applications) had a hallway conversation focusing on the current difficulties of finding materials on the Internet.[10] Because of that conversation, OCLC and the NCSA decided to team up and collectively look for a solution to this growing problem. In 1995, at Dublin, Ohio, OCLC and the NCSA led a joint workshop called the OCLC/NCSA Metadata Workshop. The workshop was to focus on three primary goals:

1. Deciding what descriptive elements would be needed to promote the findability of all documents on the Web

2. Exploring how to create a solution that would be flexible for past, present, and future online publication on the Web

3. Exploring how to promote the usage of such a solution if it exists

After this meeting, the participants were able to produce an agreed-upon set of descriptive elements; these were fifteen general descriptive terms that could be universally applied to virtually any resource currently available on the Web at the time. From these initial fifteen elements, the Dublin Core Initiative was born.

Originally, the Dublin Core schema was defined primarily as a method for describing web documents, like websites, through the use of meta tags within a documents header. These tags would then provide a reliable mechanism for search engines to harvest and index materials, since metadata elements like titles, descriptions, authors, and even subject access points could be easily identifiable. A number of tools[11] were created to help users who wished to mark up their web documents.

Figure 6.4 provides a simple illustration of how Dublin Core was to be used on the Web. Prior to the Dublin Core specification, web page developers had few options when it came to tagging documents for indexing by search systems. Dublin Core's syntax made this possible, giving web developers a standard set of tags that could be used to create uniform metadata for documents published on the Web—while at the same time, giving search providers a standard set of metadata from which to harvest and index. However, in general, this concept wasn't very successful, since search engines tended to ignore meta tagging due to tag abuse. Approved by ANSI (American National Standards Institute) in 2001,[12] the Dublin Core Initiative schema has since been accepted as an ANSI standard (Z39.85 2001) and an ISO (International Organization for Standardization) standard (15836) and has been adopted for formal use by several national governments (Australia, United Kingdom, Canada, etc.).

The Dublin Core itself is made up of fifteen central, unqualified elements known as Unqualified Dublin Core. These elements represent the

```
<link rel="schema.DC" href="http://purl.org/dc/elements/1.1/">
<meta name="DC.title" lang="en" content="Dublin Core Meta tags - Test Document">
<meta name="DC.creator" content="Terry Reese">
<meta name="DC.subject" lang="en" content="DCMI; Dublin Core Metadata Initiative; DC META Tags">
<meta name="DC.description" lang="en" content="Examples of Dublin Core META Tags.">
<meta name="DC.publisher" content="Terry Reese">
<meta name="DC.contributor" content="DCMI Dublin Core Metadata Initiative">
<meta name="DC.date" scheme="W3CDTF" content="2004-01-01">
<meta name="DC.type" scheme="DCMIType" content="Text">
<meta name="DC.format" scheme="IMT" content="text/html">
<meta name="DC.identifier" content="http://library.osu.edu/meta-tags/dublin/">
<meta name="DC.language" scheme="RFC1766" content="en">
<meta name="DC.coverage" content="World">
<meta name="DC.rights" content="https://library.osu.edu/about/policies-procedures/
copyright-information/">
```

**FIGURE 6.4**

Dublin Core Meta Tag Example

fifteen agreed-upon core descriptive elements shared by all published documents. These core elements provide document publishers with a known set of metadata values that can be applied to create minimal-level metadata records that can then be utilized by any system that is Dublin Core-aware. However, this comes at a cost, because Unqualified Dublin Core metadata suffers from a low level of granularity—that is, much of the contextual information about the data within a record is retained only at the most basic level.

In figure 6.5, the Dublin Core equivalent of the MARC record found in figure 6.1 has been provided. Initially, it should be easy to see how the record has been flattened, since information relating to subjects and classification

Show simple item record

| dc.contributor.advisor | Burnett, Margaret |
| --- | --- |
| dc.creator | Sorte, Shraddha |
| dc.date.accessioned | 2005-10-17T14:19:21Z |
| dc.date.available | 2005-10-17T14:19:21Z |
| dc.date.copyright | 2005-09-26 |
| dc.date.issued | 2005-10-17T14:19:21Z |
| dc.identifier.uri | http://hdl.handle.net/1957/510 |
| dc.description | Graduation date: 2006 |
| dc.description.abstract | Previous research has revealed gender differences that impact females' willingness to adopt software features in end users' programming environments. Since these features have separately been shown to help end users problem solve, it is important to female end users' productivity that we find ways to make these features more acceptable to females. This thesis draws from our ongoing work with users to help inform our design of theory-based methods for encouraging effective feature usage by both genders. This design effort is the first to begin addressing the gender differences in the ways that people go about problem solving in end-user programming situations. | en |

**FIGURE 6.5**

Unqualified Dublin Core

was removed from the sample record. At present, Unqualified Dublin Core defines the following fifteen elements:[13]

| ELEMENT | DESCRIPTION |
| --- | --- |
| Title | Stores all title information about a piece. When working with Unqualified Dublin Core, the title field can store the primary title as well as alternate titles. |
| Creator | Notes all individuals or organizations responsible for the creation of a document. |
| Contributor | Notes individuals, organizations, etc. that contributed to the publication of a document. This could include editors and sponsoring organizations. For individuals with a background in AACR2, the contributor field is often a difficult one, since it has no clear equivalent in MARC. For this reason, the contributor field is often ignored when crosswalking Dublin Core data into MARC. |
| Description | Stores information about an item. This includes information like notes, abstracts, table of contents, summaries, etc. For all practical purposes, the description element is a free text element where any information about an item can be stored. |
| Date | Stores temporal information relating to the life cycle of the document. This includes information related to the publication, creation, or modification of the document. |
| Subject | Stores topical information about a document. This includes information like keywords, phrases, controlled vocabularies, or classification codes. |
| Coverage | Stores contextual information about a document as it relates to spatial and temporal information. For example, coverage could be utilized to store the time period that a document's content covers, or note the spatial area of a document's study area. |
| Publisher | Notes the individual, organization, or entity responsible for the publication of the described resource. |
| Rights | Identifies any licenses, restrictions, or copyright statements covering the described resource or relating to the accessibility of the described resource. |
| Format | Identifies the physical or digital aspects of the described resource. This includes the dimensions and material type for a physical item or a description of the digital resources type. |
| Language | Notes the language or languages used within the described resource. |
| Relation | Notes any materials related to the described resource. |
| Source | Used primarily for reproductions or for resources created from a larger work—the source element notes the parent document from which the described resource was derived. |
| Type | Primarily utilized to note the document's type. This field traditionally references a controlled vocabulary like DCMITYPE to provide a known list of available document types. For example, the DCMITYPE list defines resource types like moving images, image, text, etc. |
| Identifier | Specifies a unique identifier like a URI, control number, or classification number that can be used to uniquely identify the resource. |

Within many of these elements, the Dublin Core has made available a set of refinements—attributes that can be used to refine the meaning of a specific element and to provide additional context. This is known as Qualified Dublin Core. For example, a qualifier exists for title, allowing one to note if a title is an alternative title or not. Likewise, a few qualifiers exist for the date element, allowing one to note the creation and modification date. The qualifiers give metadata creators the ability to create documents with a greater level of metadata granularity than would be found within an Unqualified Dublin Core record without breaking compatibility with most Dublin Core data parsers.

## Strengths

Today, Dublin Core is one of the most ubiquitous metadata schemas within the library community. Many digital repository platforms, like DSpace and CONTENTdm, utilize Dublin Core as their primary metadata language. The reason why Dublin Core has been so successful is its greatest strength, its

```
▼<rdf:RDF xmlns:rdf="http://www.w3.org/1999/02/22-rdf-syntax-ns#" xmlns:dc="http://purl.org/dc/elements/1.1/">
  ▼<rdf:Description>
    ▼<dc:title>
        End user software engineering features for both genders /
      </dc:title>
      <dc:creator>Sorte, Shraddha.</dc:creator>
      <dc:type manuscript="yes">text</dc:type>
      <dc:publisher/>
      <dc:date>©2005.</dc:date>
      <dc:language>eng</dc:language>
      <dc:format>application/pdf</dc:format>
    ▼<dc:description>
        Previous research has revealed gender differences that impact females? willingness to adopt software features in
        end users? programming environments. Since these features have separately been shown to help end users problem
        solve, it is important to female end users? productivity that we find ways to make these features more
        acceptable to females. This thesis draws from our ongoing work with users to help inform our design of theory-
        based methods for encouraging effective feature usage by both genders. This design effort is the first to begin
        addressing the gender differences in the ways that people go about problem solving in end-user programming
        situations.
      </dc:description>
      <dc:description>Printout.</dc:description>
      <dc:description/>
    ▼<dc:description>
        Includes bibliographical references (leaves 51-55).
      </dc:description>
    ▼<dc:description>
        Previous research has revealed gender differences that impact females? willingness to adopt software features in
        end users? programming environments. Since these features have separately been shown to help end users problem
        solve, it is important to female end users? productivity that we find ways to make these features more
        acceptable to females. This thesis draws from our ongoing work with users to help inform our design of theory-
        based methods for encouraging effective feature usage by both genders. This design effort is the first to begin
        addressing the gender differences in the ways that people go about problem solving in end-user programming
        situations.
      </dc:description>
      <dc:subject>Computers and women</dc:subject>
      <dc:subject>Women</dc:subject>
      <dc:subject>End-user computing</dc:subject>
      <dc:relation type="original">Also available on the World Wide Web.</dc:relation>
      <dc:identifier>http://hdl.handle.net/1957/510</dc:identifier>
  </rdf:Description>
</rdf:RDF>
```

**FIGURE 6.6**

DSpace Dublin Core Display

flexibility. Dublin Core recognizes that it does not cover the potential needs of all users and is not sufficient for purposes other than simple resource discovery—so the metadata schema itself has been designed to allow for the creation of local extensions to meet local needs. However, unlike many other metadata schemas, the addition of these local extensions does not cause compatibility problems for Dublin Core, since metadata elements can always be reduced down to the core fifteen unqualified elements. This allows metadata implementers to customize the Dublin Core schema for their own local usage without sacrificing the ability to share metadata with other systems. For example, within DSpace, Qualified Dublin Core is utilized when doing metadata creation so that information can be captured at the highest level of granularity that Dublin Core provides.

Figure 6.6 provides a screenshot of a record within the Ohio State University DSpace repository. Within the metadata, one can see how elements, like date, are being utilized with refinements to provide additional contextual information about the metadata located within the attribute. For example, "dc.date.created" indicates to the user when the item was created. Moreover, within DSpace, a number of local refinements have been defined to provide additional context to controlled vocabularies like water basins or Ohio State University departments. However, since many of these refinements would have little value outside of the Ohio State University digital repository, they are removed when metadata is provided for public consumption through OAI (Open Archives Initiative), allowing users to harvest metadata in Unqualified Dublin Core.

It's difficult to overstate the importance of the Dublin Core community itself. The Dublin Core community is a large international body that is helping to evolve the Dublin Core by worldwide consensus. This has allowed the Dublin Core schema to tackle areas such as semantic interpretability and multilingualism on a global scale. Likewise, the community provides strong leadership in the form of the Dublin Core Initiative and promotes Dublin Core as an extensible standard both within the library community and beyond.

Additionally, the simple but comprehensive nature of Dublin Core has allowed for quick adoption by a number of digital library providers, as well as by standards providers from various fields and disciplines. Within the library community, protocols like OAI, SRU (Search and Retrieval URL), and Z39.50 all provide standard methods for utilizing Dublin Core as a metadata capture language—which makes sense, given that a Dublin Core element will mean the same thing across disciplines. Metadata creation can also be greatly simplified utilizing Dublin Core, since metadata can be created at varying levels of granularity and the use of automated metadata creation methods is encouraged.

## Challenges

Ironically, Dublin Core's simplicity is also its greatest weakness. Unqualified Dublin Core was purposefully designed as a lowest common denominator language in order to preserve the highest level of semantic interoperability—but this has come at a high cost. Dublin Core simply isn't as granular as many other specialty metadata formats, like MARC. This means that a great deal of data, both real and contextual, is lost when data needs to be moved between metadata formats. Given the low costs related to the implementation of Unqualified Dublin Core, many early digital repository systems did just that—they implemented systems that supported only Unqualified Dublin Core, causing many to loathe the overly simplistic nature of the metadata produced.

In this same vein, librarians tend to view Dublin Core's lack of formalized input standards as a cause for great concern. Given the rigid set of rules utilized in traditional library metadata creation (RDA), the lack of such standardization for entering information like controlled names, keywords, subjects, and so on has been seen as one of the major deficiencies relating to Dublin Core's use within the library community. Groups such as the Greater Western States Metadata Group have sought to fill this void for libraries through the creation of more formal standards to govern the input of data into Dublin Core,[14] but this level of flexibility is still viewed as a fundamental weakness within the schema.

## MODS

Given the large quantity of metadata, workflows, and knowledge tied up in the development of bibliographic data such as MARC, the question of how these legacy records and systems will be moved towards a more XML-centric metadata schema is an important one. In the mid-1990s, the Library of Congress took an important first step by offering an XML version of MARC in MARC21XML. As noted above, MARC21XML was developed to be MARC, but also in XML. It represented a lossless XML format for MARC data, with many of the benefits of XML while at the same time being inhibited by the technical limitations of MARC.

### History

Unfortunately, MARC21XML has had little uptake from the metadata community. While benefits exist to using MARC21XML over traditional MARC, few library systems have made the move to support MARC21XML as an ingestible metadata format. Given this fact, the usage of MARC21XML has been primarily by library developers creating custom applications for their own local use.

In part, MARC21XML likely didn't catch on as a popular library metadata format precisely because it was so tied to traditional MARC. For many, MARC and the rules governing it had simply become too archaic. MARC was developed for a time when bibliographic data was printed on catalog cards, and the move to an XML-based metadata schema represented a chance to break away from that bibliographic model.

For its part, the Library of Congress recognized the need within the library community for a metadata schema that would be compatible with the library community's legacy MARC data, while providing a new way of representing and grouping bibliographic data. These efforts led to the development of the MODS (Metadata Object Description Schema) metadata format. MODS represents the next natural step in the evolution of MARC into XML. MODS represents a much simpler alternative that retains its compatibility with MARC. Developed as a subset of the current MARC21 specification, MODS was created as a richer alternative to other metadata schemas like Dublin Core. However, unlike MARC21XML, which faithfully transferred MARC structures into XML, the structure of MODS allowed for metadata elements to be regrouped and reorganized within a metadata record.

As seen in figure 6.7, another major difference between MODS and MARC and MARC21XML is the use of textual field labels rather than numeric fields. This change allows MODS records to be more readable than a traditional MARC/MARC21XML record, and it allows for element descriptions that can be reused throughout the metadata schema. A number

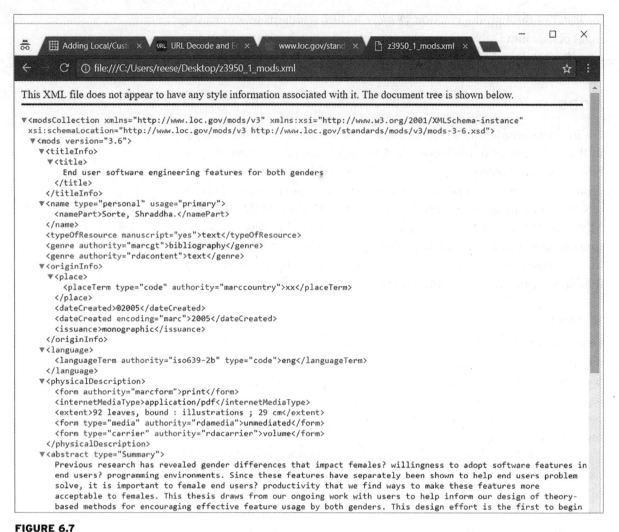

**FIGURE 6.7**

MODS Record Example

of digital library efforts have begun to try to formalize MODS support to either replace or augment previously Dublin Core-only metadata systems. Likewise, groups like the Digital Library Federation have started recommending that organizations and software designers provide a MODS-based OAI harvesting capability to allow for a higher level of metadata granularity. E-print systems like DSpace have looked at ways of utilizing MODS either as an internal storage format or as a supported OAI protocol, while digital repositories like Fedora currently utilize a MODS-like metadata schema as the internal storage schema. What's more, interest has grown in using MODS for ILS development, due in large part to the open-source development work being done by the Georgia Public Library System on Evergreen, and the open-source ILS building around MODS.

Finally, MODS was not developed in a vacuum or as a one-off alternative to MARC. MODS was developed as a subset of a number of larger ongoing metadata initiatives at the Library of Congress. While MODS offered the library community many potential benefits, it was developed in part as an extension format to METS, in order to provide a MARC-like bibliographic metadata component for METS-generated records. Likewise, the MODS schema was tapped as one of the registered metadata formats for SRU/SRW, the next-generation communication format designed as a replacement for Z39.50. So, while MODS was created to work as a stand-alone metadata format that could be used for original record creation, translating MARC data into XML, and facilitating the harvesting of library materials, it was also created as part of a larger ongoing strategy at the Library of Congress to create a set of more diverse, lightweight XML formats that would have the ability to work with the library community's current legacy data.

## Strengths

As mentioned earlier in the chapter, MODS has a number of advantages over other general-purpose metadata schemas like Dublin Core when one considers the current environment within the library community. While applications like digital repositories tend to avoid using MARC for bibliographic description, the reality is that MARC still dominates the metadata landscape within the library community. Nearly all major ILS vendors currently support MARC as their de facto metadata schema, leading to thousands of MARC-filled databases. The ability of MODS to provide an element set that is already compatible with the existing bibliographic descriptions within these large MARC databases provides a clear migration path for users to an XML-based schema. This is very different from other schemas like Dublin Core, which lacks the granularity of elements needed to provide a clear migration path away from something like MARC. By providing this compatibility, MODS can provide a bridge as the metadata continues to evolve. This increased granularity also allows MODS records to provide richer descriptions than those found within a Dublin Core record. MODS utilizes an expanded element set (about twenty high-level elements, coupled with multiple refinements) to encourage richer bibliographic description, and as a result, it is well-suited for the hierarchical nature of the METS framework.

MODS introduces the ability to utilize hierarchies within the bibliographic description of an item. This is very different from MARC and even Dublin Core, which are flat metadata schemas, meaning that their descriptions are limited to the item that they are describing. MODS provides the capability for users to describe an idea, as well as the parts that make up that item, arranging the bibliographic description hierarchically within the record. This allows MODS objects to create "actions" around the various levels of the hierarchy, and it encourages software designers to utilize these hierarchical elements in displaying relationships within, to, and from an individual resource.

## Challenges

Like Dublin Core, MODS's biggest challenge is a result of its biggest asset. While MODS does not prescribe any set of input rules upon the metadata framework, its close relationship to MARC emphasizes the type of data that is best suited for this format. The Library of Congress has attempted to position

MODS as a general metadata format, but its need to maintain compatibility with the library community's MARC legacy data does raise barriers to the general mainstream adoption of MODS outside the library community.

Moreover, unlike Dublin Core, MODS is an internal metadata schema created for the Library of Congress. While the Library of Congress has accepted a leadership role within the library community and has committed to growing MODS to meet the needs of that community, it lacks the large-scale community input and oversight that are found with Dublin Core. While a large community is currently working with and providing feedback to the Library of Congress regarding the MODS implementation, the schema lacks the support of a multi-organizational maintenance body. Rather, MODS is developed primarily by the Network Development and MARC Standards Office at the Library of Congress, which may ultimately limit the growth and scope of the MODS framework as it goes forward. Obviously, within today's global environment, a more multinational metadata schema like Dublin Core presents a number of distinct advantages over a schema developed primarily for the purposes of a single nation or organization.

## METS

Unlike earlier metadata formats discussed within this chapter, METS (Metadata Encoding and Transmission Standard) is not a metadata format utilized for the bibliographic description of objects. Dublin Core, MODS, and even MARC/MARC21XML all share the same primary purpose of providing a vehicle for the description of bibliographic data. While each metadata format has its own advantages and disadvantages that may help a digital repository developer select one metadata format over another, they all still share the same goal. Ultimately, each of the metadata formats discussed previously functions to provide various levels of bibliographic description of a digital object. The same, however, cannot be said of METS. METS is a very different animal, in that it acts as a container object for the many pieces of metadata needed to describe a single digital object. Within a digital repository, a number of pieces of metadata are attached to each digital object. While the individual who submitted the digital object may only be responsible for adding information to the bibliographic metadata, the digital repository itself is generating metadata related to the structural information of the digital object—that is, assembling information about the files that make up the entire digital object (metadata, attached items, etc). METS provides a method for binding these objects together, so that they can be transferred to other systems or utilized within the local digital repository system as part of a larger application profile.

### History

The history of METS is closely tied to the history of MODS. In the late 1990s, the Library of Congress began exploring avenues for moving locally created digital collections to an XML-based platform. During this period of exploration, only two general-purpose XML metadata formats existed—MARC21XML and Dublin Core. Each of these two formats would prove to be undesirable for several reasons: Dublin Core due to its inability to capture metadata at a fine enough level of granularity, and MARC21XML due to its reliance on MARC structures and rules. This caused the Library of Congress to develop MODS, a simpler subset of MARC that could produce rich descriptions at the desired level of granularity. However, lost in this development was the release of a complementary technology, METS. While MODS provided a robust format for bibliographic metadata description, a method still needed to be developed that would bind together the administrative, structural, and bibliographic metadata of a digital object. Moreover, loading and exporting digital objects from a digital repository would need to include this information as well—meaning that the digital object must be able to retain its metadata, in all its forms, to be useful outside of the host system. So, in essence, METS was created to be this glue for digital objects, binding together all relevant metadata relating to item structure, description, and administration.

The Library of Congress started experimenting with the mixing of METS and MODS almost immediately after releasing the specifications in 2002. Later that year, the Library of Congress started work on the Digital Audio-Visual Preservation Prototyping project,[15] which combined the use of MODS as the bibliographic description framework with METS as the digital object framework. Since then, the Library of Congress has produced a wide variety of projects utilizing the MODS/METS combination.

## METS at a Glance

Before looking at how METS is being used within current digital repository efforts, we need to quickly take a look at what makes up a METS document. Obviously, this is by no means comprehensive, since the current METS documentation spans hundreds of pages and examples, but it should provide an adequate overview of what makes up a METS document, and how those elements tie the various pieces of a digital object together. There are currently seven sections to a METS document.[16] These sections are:

| ELEMENT | DESCRIPTION |
|---|---|
| metsHdr | METS Header: tag group stores information about the METS document itself, not the digital object which it describes. |
| dmdSec | Descriptive Metadata Section: tag group stores all the descriptive metadata for all items referenced by the METS document. |
| amdSec | Administrative Metadata Section: tag group stores all the administrative metadata for all items referenced by the METS document. |
| fileSec | Content File Section: tag group stores information on all files referenced by the METS document. |
| structMap | Structural Map: tag group stores the hierarchical arrangement of items referenced by the digital object. |
| structLink | Structural Map Linking: tag group stores linking information between referenced items in the structural map section. |
| behaviorSec | Behavior Section: tag group defines behaviors associated with the referenced items in a METS document (i.e., executable behaviors, etc.). |

```
<?xml version="1.0" standalone="no" ?>
- <mets:mets xmlns:mets="http://www.loc.gov/METS/" xmlns:dc="http://purl.org/dc/elements/1.1/" xmlns:xlink="http://www.w3.org/TR/xlink"
   xmlns:xsi="http://www.w3.org/2001/XMLSchema-instance" xmlns="http://www.loc.gov/METS/" xsi:schemaLocation="http://www.loc.gov/METS/
   http://www.loc.gov/standards/mets/mets.xsd" OBJID="osudpu:/b1331737/9/28/2005 6:44:31 PM" LABEL="Willamette River :river lands and river
   boundaries /thesis prepared by Eugene Arthur Hoerauf.">
  - <mets:metsHdr CREATEDATE="9/28/2005 6:44:31 PM" LASTMODDATE="9/28/2005 6:44:31 PM">
    - <mets:agent ROLE="CREATOR">
       <mets:name>Oregon State University Libraries</mets:name>
      </mets:agent>
    </mets:metsHdr>
  - <mets:dmdSec ID="DM1">
      <mets:mdRef LOCTYPE="URL" MDTYPE="MARC" xlink:href="http://oasis.oregonstate.edu/record=b1331737" LABEL="Catalog Record" />
    </mets:dmdSec>
  - <mets:dmdSec ID="DM2">
      <mets:mdRef LOCTYPE="URL" MDTYPE="OTHER" xlink:href="http://hdl.handle.net/1957/277" LABEL="Dspace Catalog Record" />
    </mets:dmdSec>
  - <mets:dmdSec ID="DM3">
    - <mets:mdWrap MDTYPE="DUBLIN CORE">
      - <mets:xmlData>
         <dc:title>Willamette River :river lands and river boundaries /thesis prepared by Eugene Arthur Hoerauf.</dc:title>
         <dc:creator>Hoerauf, Eugene Arthur,1939-</dc:creator>
         <dc:publisher>Corvallis, Or. :Water Resources Research Institute, Oregon State University,1970.</dc:publisher>
         <dc:date>1970.</dc:date>
         <dc:description />
        </mets:xmlData>
      </mets:mdWrap>
    </mets:dmdSec>
  - <mets:fileSec>
    - <mets:fileGrp USE="archive">
      - <mets:file ID="WRRI-1ocr.pdf" MIMETYPE="application/pdf" SEQ="0" CREATED="8/15/2005 9:08:56 PM">
         <mets:FLocat LOCTYPE="OTHER" OTHERLOCTYPE="UNIX FILESYSTEM" xlink:href="/var/dspace/WRRI/WRRI-1WRRI-1ocr.pdf" />
        </mets:file>
      - <mets:file ID="WRRI-1Gray600NoneFron0001.tif" MIMETYPE="image/tif" SEQ="1" CREATED="8/15/2005 8:26:49 PM">
         <mets:FLocat LOCTYPE="OTHER" OTHERLOCTYPE="UNIX FILESYSTEM" xlink:href="/var/dspace/WRRI/WRRI-1WRRI-1Gray600NoneFron0001.tif" />
        </mets:file>
      - <mets:file ID="WRRI-1Gray600NoneFron0002.tif" MIMETYPE="image/tif" SEQ="2" CREATED="8/15/2005 8:27:24 PM">
```

**FIGURE 6.8**

METS with Dublin Core Example

Figure 6.8 illustrates a very basic METS document that is used at Oregon State University (OSU) for archiving structural information about digitized text. In this example, one can see that OSU has chosen to utilize Dublin Core, rather than MODS, for embedding its bibliographic descriptive data. This decision was made primarily due to the fact that OSU utilizes DSpace, which stores metadata in Dublin Core. In the interest of repurposing metadata, Dublin Core was chosen as the descriptive metadata language. However, this example demonstrates the flexibility of the METS container. While METS was developed in concert with MODS, its greatest strength lies in its ability to accommodate a descriptive metadata format—allowing users to take advantage of the METS framework while still utilizing the metadata schema best suited for their materials or infrastructure. The Library of Congress provides access to a number of additional METS example documents at its METS home page (www.loc.gov/mets).

## Importing Digital Objects

As a transmission format, METS has provided digital repository designers with a simple structure that can be supported to facilitate the batch import of digital objects. For systems that do not natively support METS, batch importing tends to be done using simple tab-delimited files for flat objects or the file system to preserve document hierarchy. However, this type of importing tends to be problematic because it assumes that metadata is clean, has been delineated correctly, and is laid out in the file system in a very specific structure. Digital library systems like DSpace and Fedora that provide native support for METS objects greatly simplify the import process by utilizing a highly structured metadata framework in which all metadata about the object is self-contained.

## METS Today

There was a time when METS was the gold standard for encoding structural data within a digital repository, but that sentiment is quickly changing. While METS still has a place within the digital library landscape, and likely will for some time, a transition has begun to move to more lightweight, semantically relevant data. While METS provides a good deal of flexibility and structure, as an XML language, it is very expensive to develop against. Just as systems have moved to embrace linked data and semantic web principles, a shift is occurring within the computer science landscape, moving away from XML processing to more lightweight languages—particularly JSON. We can see this shift occurring within the digital library and digital humanities communities, as more and more systems move away from directly supporting METS and instead support formats like IIIF. Like METS, IIIF provides methods for creating and defining the structure of an object, but it does so utilizing JSON, a lightweight format that can be used by developers, and can be easily manipulated with most mainstream programming tools. This allows data to be unlocked and easily consumed by those outside of the library, making it an attractive data format.

## *IIIF*

The International Image Interoperability Framework (IIIF) is a grassroots community standard that was originally developed to provide a set of best practices for sharing and interacting with images. Today, IIIF currently provides multiple "metadata" streams, including the original specification for image display and manipulation, but it has expanded to include specifications for defining the presentation of an option, authentication methodology, search, and annotation. When compared to the other primitives highlighted in this chapter, IIIF is a bit of an outlier. Like METS, it's a structure that is largely machine-generated—in that the development and utilization of IIIF is largely system-generated in order to support the sharing of works.

## History

The history of IIIF is tied up in the complicated history of displaying images within digital library systems. Digital library systems have traditionally developed their own internal image viewers, utilizing proprietary formats (like MR.SID) or readers to interact with content. While JPEG2000 (an open-wavelet image format designed to support advanced image interaction) was developed and largely adopted in the early 2000s, the implementations of the readers, the APIs utilized to render and call images, were largely proprietary. This made it very difficult for scholars to utilize content from disparate systems, and stunted the ability of digital humanities scholars who were interested in comparing, searching, or analyzing large swaths of image data. IIIF was developed to solve this issue. IIIF's image protocol defined a common set of parameters, allowing systems to represent their images as JSON objects. This allowed the library community and those external to the library community to develop common methods of consuming image content, leading to the development of tools like Mirador or the Universal Browser, which co-opt the OpenSeadragon project to provide an open-source, easy-to-use image-rendering and manipulation viewer. The development of the IIIF standard, and the viewers that could utilize the standard, opened new veins of research. Archivists now had ways to re-create long-lost manuscripts digitally by leveraging the IIIF framework to create their own digital editions, and humanities scholars were able to develop tools that could mine and interact with digital library systems supporting IIIF easily. Below, I'd like to specifically highlight the IIIF image and presentation schemas.

### IIIF Image Schema

The IIIF Image schema is the oldest and best-established IIIF format. The Image schema provides a JSON representation of an image object, which can then be used by an image viewer to render and interact with the object on the system—enabling libraries to encourage the embedding of digital content, while still maintaining control of the digital asset.

Figure 6.9 demonstrates how an image may be represented utilizing the IIIF Image schema. In addition to defining how an image object might be represented, the schema provides a common language for requesting data from IIIF-enabled image servers. This allows repositories to respond to a common set of instructions, and it allows users to request full or scaled images, as well as full or specific regions. The protocol standardizes image rendering and manipulation, providing interoperability between a wide range of images being served via IIIF-enabled servers.

### IIIF Presentation Schema

The IIIF Presentation schema provides a method for digital library systems to define the structure of a digital object. Whether this structure is represented as a monograph (with a table of contents) or a collection, or a set of digital objects, the IIIF Presentation schema provides systems with a method to represent the physical structure and relationships of a set of objects. If this sounds familiar, it should, since the IIIF Presentation schema's goals mirror the same goals found with METS. Unlike METS, however, IIIF's Presentation schema is very lightweight and is developed to be actionable. Utilizing JSON, the IIIF Presentation schema can be consumed and processed by most current-generation programming languages and tool

```
{
  "@id":"http://manifest.reeset.net/normal",
  "@type":"sc:Sequence",
  "label":"Current Page Order",
  "canvases": [
    {
      "@id":"http://manifest.reeset.net/canvas-1",
      "@type":"sc:Canvas",
      "label":"Image 1",
      "height":1000,
      "width":750,
      "images": [
        {
          "@id":"http://manifest.reeset.net/canvas-1/annotation/p0001-image",
          "@type":"oa:Annotation",
          "motivation":"sc:painting",
          "resource":{
            "@id":"https://library.osu.edu/loris/v9%2F79%2Fxw%2F02%2Fv979xw021-version1-low_resolution/full/400,/0/default.jpg",
            "@type":"dctypes:Image",
            "format":"image/jpeg",
            "service": {
              "@context": "http://iiif.io/api/image/2/context.json",
              "@id": "https://library.osu.edu/loris/v9%2F79%2Fxw%2F02%2Fv979xw021-version1-low_resolution",
              "profile":"http://iiif.io/api/image/2/level1.json"
            },
            "height":2000,
            "width":1500
          },
          "on":"http://manifest.reeset.net/canvas-1"
        }
      ],
      "otherContent": [
        {
          "@id":"http://manifest.reeset.net/canvas-1/list/p1",
          "@type":"sc:AnnotationList"
        }
      ]
    },
```

**FIGURE 6.9**

IIIF Image API Response

sets—providing obvious advantages over a library-only data structure like
METS. Additionally, the schema's flexibility, semantic web roots, and agile
grassroots community make it a good fit for digital library development.
As of this writing, most digital repository systems (CONTENTdm, DSpace,
BePress, the Samvera project) are actively working to implement the IIIF
Presentation protocol in order to enable digital humanities research and to
create interoperability between digital repositories. If this support comes
to fruition, it is likely that IIIF will replace METS as the dominant format
for defining structure within a digital repository.

```
{"sequences": [{
"@type": "sc:Sequence,"
"canvases": [
{
"@id": "http://manifest.reeset.net/newspaper/wooster/issue/64245/canvas/64240,"
"@type": "sc:Canvas,"
"label": "Page 1,"
```

(Cont.)

```
"metadata": [
{
"label": "Page Title,"
"@language": "eng,"
"value": "Page 1"
},
{
"label": "Page Identifier,"
"value": "64240"
}
],
"height": 5000,
"width": 7000,
"images": [{
"@id": "http://manifest.reeset.net/newspaper/wooster/issue/64245/annotation/64240-image,"
"@type": "oa:Annotation,"
"motivation": "sc:painting,"
"resource": {
"@id": "http://cdm15963.contentdm.oclc.org/digital/iiif/p15963c0119/64240/full/full/0/default.jpg,"
"@type": "dctypes:Image,"
"format": "image/jpeg,"
"service": {
"@context": "http://iiif.io/api/image/2/context.json,"
"@id": "http://cdm15963.contentdm.oclc.org/digital/iiif/p15963c0119/64240,"
"profile": "http://iiif.io/api/image/2/level1.json,"
"height": 5000,
"width": 7000
},
"height": 5000,
"width": 7000
},
"on": "http://manifest.reeset.net/newspaper/wooster/issue/64245/canvas/64240"
}]
},
{
"@id": "http://manifest.reeset.net/newspaper/wooster/issue/64245/canvas/64241,"
"@type": "sc:Canvas,"
"label": "Page 2,"
"metadata": [
{
"label": "Page Title,"
"@language": "eng,"
"value": "Page 2"
},
{
"label": "Page Identifier,"
"value": "64241"
}
],
"height": 5000,
"width": 7000,
"images": [{
"@id": "http://manifest.reeset.net/newspaper/wooster/issue/64245/annotation/64241-image,"
"@type": "oa:Annotation,"
"motivation": "sc:painting,"
"resource": {
"@id": "http://cdm15963.contentdm.oclc.org/digital/iiif/p15963c0119/64241/full/full/0/default.jpg,"
"@type": "dctypes:Image,"
"format": "image/jpeg,"
"service": {
"@context": "http://iiif.io/api/image/2/context.json,"
```

```
"@id": "http://cdm15963.contentdm.oclc.org/digital/iiif/p15963c0119/64241,"
"profile": "http://iiif.io/api/image/2/level1.json,"
"height": 5000,
"width": 7000
},
"height": 5000,
"width": 7000
},
"on": "http://manifest.reeset.net/newspaper/wooster/issue/64245/canvas/64241"
}]
},
{
"@id": "http://manifest.reeset.net/newspaper/wooster/issue/64245/canvas/64242,"
"@type": "sc:Canvas,"
"label": "Page 3,"
"metadata": [
{
"label": "Page Title,"
"@language": "eng,"
"value": "Page 3"
},
{
"label": "Page Identifier,"
"value": "64242"
}
],
"height": 5000,
"width": 7000,
"images": [{
"@id": "http://manifest.reeset.net/newspaper/wooster/issue/64245/annotation/64242-image,"
"@type": "oa:Annotation,"
"motivation": "sc:painting,"
"resource": {
"@id": "http://cdm15963.contentdm.oclc.org/digital/iiif/p15963c0119/64242/full/full/0/default.jpg,"
"@type": "dctypes:Image,"
"format": "image/jpeg,"
"service": {
"@context": "http://iiif.io/api/image/2/context.json,"
"@id": "http://cdm15963.contentdm.oclc.org/digital/iiif/p15963c0119/64242,"
"profile": "http://iiif.io/api/image/2/level1.json,"
"height": 5000,
"width": 7000
},
"height": 5000,
"width": 7000
},
"on": "http://manifest.reeset.net/newspaper/wooster/issue/64245/canvas/64242"
}]
}
]
}]}
```

The example above provides a simple representation of an IIIF Presentation object. This object defines an issue of a newspaper. While not nearly as verbose as METS, the IIIF Presentation API provides information related to the structure, images, and metadata of a particular set of objects. While this is also true of METS, again, data represented in the IIIF format becomes immediately actionable, since any tool that can utilize JSON can make use of this data. Moreover, given that all modern browsers support JSON on the client side, and well-documented tools like node.js provide a rich set of JavaScript processing libraries on the server side, repositories that make use of this format immediately enable greater interoperability opportunities, simply due to the ubiquitous nature of the data structure and the wide range of tools and developers that are familiar with JSON and its processing libraries.

## BIBFRAME

The final data primitive that I wish to highlight is the Library of Congress's BIBFRAME initiative. However, unlike the other metadata formats discussed above, BIBFRAME is still largely an in-development format that is not yet used within digital repository software. At the same time, the BIBFRAME development has been incredibly important and influential, because it has pushed linked data and semantic web concepts to the foreground of library metadata discussion—so it is worth highlighting here.

### History

The BIBFRAME[17] initiative started as a project to develop a new data model for library bibliographic metadata. Essentially, BIBFRAME would be developed to replace MARC, and it would enable libraries to move beyond some of MARC's inherent limitations. At the same time, BIBFRAME was very much a test bed for investigating how linked data and semantic web concepts could be leveraged within library data. As of this writing, the Library of Congress has released two drafts of the BIBFRAME schema, BIBFRAME1 and BIBFRAME2. BIBFRAME2 fills in many of the gaps found in the initial implementation, presenting a more complete set of concepts and data model, but offers some challenges for libraries because the BIBFRAME2 model made some substantial breaks from current RDA practice.

Has BIBFRAME been successful? From a practical perspective, it might be difficult to argue that the BIBFRAME initiative has met its goals. Started in mid-2000 and developed to utilize RDA concepts, BIBFRAME was ambitiously scheduled to become the predominant metadata framework found within the library community by 2010. This goal has yet to be met, however. In fact, outside of some very targeted research initiatives, very few systems utilize any BIBFRAME concepts though we are starting to see projects in Europe and within the LD4L (Linked Data 4 Libraries) community implement projects that utilize the BIBFRAME vocabularies. More interesting, libraries are also looking at a wide range of other efforts, specifically within the schema.org community, to evaluate different ways in which bibliographic data could be modeled for use in a modern bibliographic system. While efforts are ongoing to look at ways in which efforts in the schema .org and BIBFRAME communities could be harmonized, as of this writing, harmonization is still a goal that is yet to be achieved. So, where does that leave BIBFRAME and the library community? This is still an open question. Much like the development and implementation of RDA, many in the community see the implementation of systems utilizing a BIBFRAME model as simply a matter of time. While the MARC standard is still being maintained and grown, the bulk of the development work within the standards community appears to be focused on BIBFRAME and RDA. At the same time, libraries have a significant amount of legacy data and infrastructures, resources that simply cannot be left behind. And in this, there is the challenge. While BIBFRAME development continues within the community, practical development and implementation have yet to move outside of the research and development phase.

While BIBFRAME may never replace the MARC format, it has been hugely successful in underlining the importance of linked data to the future of libraries. BIBFRAME was developed as a semantic language, and the need for linked data infrastructure and URIs has highlighted a glaring omission in the library community's current infrastructure. This has led to the rapid development of semantic endpoints by organizations opening up their controlled vocabularies for machine-readable processing. Organizations like the Library of Congress, the Japanese Diet Library, OCLC, and the Getty Research Institute have made tremendous strides over the past few years in developing an infrastructure to support the rich linking of string data to semantic resources.

As this infrastructure has developed, the library metadata community has moved to enable linked data support within legacy data formats like MARC in order to help ease the transition to a new data model, and hopefully spur innovation within current library systems. Tools like MarcEdit, Catmandu, and OpenRefine have developed special tool sets to support the reconciliation of library data with these new linked-data services.

As of this writing, the jury on BIBFRAME's success as a format is still out. Will it become a predominant data format like MARC? Will it replace MARC? BIBFRAME's primary success and greatest long-term benefit to the library community will be as an experimental format that pushed semantic and linked-data concepts into the forefront of library metadata discussion. Through these discussions, libraries are now taking the development of semantic web infrastructure seriously, and are actively looking at how they can support the enhancement of legacy data to enable future innovation. In the long term, I think that these successes will be the lasting legacy of the BIBFRAME development, and may ultimately be what spurs libraries to ensure that their digital repository systems natively support the semantic web, allowing for their repositories' interoperability with systems and tools well beyond the traditional library community.

### Domain-Specific Metadata Formats

Unfortunately, this chapter just scratches the surface when it comes to the metadata formats that are currently in use within the digital library community. While Dublin Core, MODs, and METS are likely the most widely used today, these represent general-purpose formats. Within the various disciplines within the cultural heritage community, domain-specific or format-specific metadata formats exist to provide a richer descriptive experience. Additionally, administrative and preservation metadata (discussed in chapter 4) add to this already expanding metadata universe. Below, we've tried to highlight some of the most important domain-specific metadata formats.

### PBCore (Public Broadcasting Metadata Dictionary)

URL: http://pbcore.org/

The PBCore is a metadata schema that is designed to richly describe sound and moving images. Its primary usage community is museums and cultural heritage organizations that manage film and media archives.

### VRA Core (Visual Resources Association Metadata Dictionary)

URL: http://loc.gov/standards/vracore/

The VRA Core was developed by the Visual Resources Association, in cooperation with the Library of Congress, to develop a metadata schema for richly describing images and works of art.

### EAD (Encoded Archival Description)

URL: https://www.loc.gov/ead/

The EAD schema was developed by the archives community to describe collection finding aids in an electronic environment.

### TEI (Text Encoding Initiative)

URL: www.tei-c.org/index.xml

The TEI schema is an international metadata format that was created to support the markup of manuscripts and other document materials.

### Darwin Core

URL: http://rs.tdwg.org/dwc/

Darwin Core is a format that was developed specifically for the description and categorization of biological diversity information.

### CSDGM (Content Standard for Digital Geospatial Metadata)

URL: https://www.fgdc.gov/metadata/csdgm-standard

The CSDGM is a metadata standard that was developed specifically for the documenting, describing, and sharing of geospatial data.

## ONIX

URL: www.editeur.org/

> ONIX is a metadata specification that was developed for use by the book trade, specifically publishers and booksellers.

## IPTC (International Press Telecommunications Council)

URL: https://iptc.org/

> The IPTC provides a number of metadata standards that are used by the press to structure information related to a wide range of topics. For example, for images, the IPTC Photo metadata defines properties and structures noting subject, captions, dates, and so on. Likewise, the IPTC has metadata formats covering rights statements, press articles, and so on. IPTC can be embedded within objects and has widespread industry support.

## *Embedded Metadata Formats*

In addition to descriptive metadata, many file formats include embedded metadata that can be used for a variety of purposes within a digital library system. Three of the most common formats are noted below:

## Exif

URL: www.exif.org/

> Exif is a metadata format used by digital camera manufacturers to store technical metadata about an image. The format is embedded into the image file, providing technical information about the recording device and its settings.

## XMP (eXtensible Metadata Platform):

URL: www.adobe.com/products/xmp.html

> XMP is a metadata format created by Adobe and the IPTC to provide a format for embedding technical and brief descriptive metadata about an item (generally an image). This enables the metadata to be embedded with the object, so that it can be read and used by any system capable of understanding XMP-encoded data.

## *PCDM (Portland Common Data Model)*

The Portland Common Data Model (PCDM)[18] isn't necessarily a metadata format, but it is a data model that may have significant impact on how digital libraries, or more specifically digital repositories, are developed in the future. The PCDM was developed out of a number of conversations between developers from the Samvera (then Hydra) project and developers from the Islandora project. As these two projects developed, many began to question the need for highly customized data models for representing digital library, or more specific, digital repository, content. Within the early Fedora community, data modeling of content was one of the primary activities that repository owners and developers would need to complete, and the local nature of these models made compatibility between various Fedora repositories difficult to achieve. The goal, in creating the PCDM, was to create a shared data model that could be implemented at the repository level. This would enable repositories to have, at least in a limited sense, a basic level of compatibility. This would mean that potentially, an organization could more easily move between different repository software, because the use of a common data model would ease the migration process between systems. An image in one system would be able to be recognized as an image in another system, which would also allow for the development of a shared set of properties and methods.

Presently, the PCDM data model is in active development and is in constant flux. It is currently used by the members of the Samvera project to model data into Fedora 4.x, and it is being implemented by the Islandora community. However, outside of these two groups, there appears to be little interest in this standard . . . but it's hard to gauge if this will change. The promise of a common data model between repository platforms is a powerful one. If the Samvera and Islandora communities can demonstrate that data interoperability can be achieved through the utilization of the PCDM data structure, we believe that its use will increase. If it does not, then this may remain primarily a data structure used within these two specific projects, but it could serve as a template for other projects or organizations developing their own data models. It's really hard to say today.

### Semantic Web

What becomes very apparent when one starts working with digital repositories and their content is the wide range of metadata choices that one must choose from. This chapter merely discusses the most widely utilized general metadata frameworks, but other frameworks like FGDC (Federal Geographic Data Committee) for GIS data, VRC (Visual Resource Core) for visual items, EAD (Encoded Archival Description) for finding aids, MADS (Metadata Authority Description Schema) for authority data, ONIX for publishers' data, and so on all provide specialized metadata forms that a digital library program may find it needs to integrate within its digital and metadata architecture. In the past, the need to select the correct metadata format was incredibly important, since the decision could potentially limit the ability to fully represent diverse types of objects or formats within one's system. In some ways, I think this is why many organizations utilized multiple digital repositories within their infrastructures. It wouldn't be uncommon for a library to maintain a documents repository like DSpace or BePress, and a repository for other digital content, like images and videos—since the metadata decisions made to support one type of content often didn't translate well to the others. But this is changing and changing quickly. Tools like Fedora, and communities like the Samvera community, are shifting the bibliographic data model from one where users must select a single metadata framework, to one where we can utilize semantic web principles and make use of multiple metadata namespaces to provide the best support for our digital objects. This flexibility is allowing libraries to think more holistically about the type of metadata frameworks that they utilize, and choose elements from a wider range of communities that best support the data model for their content. In addition, libraries may find that digital repositories which support semantic principles may have easier paths when considering discovery, data interoperability, and migrations. But can we see this today?

The answer, at least as it relates to data interoperability, is that we largely can't. Data interoperability between formats and communities continues to be governed primarily through the use of data crosswalks to normalize the metadata from one community into a format that can be understood by another. With that said, the use of semantic principles or formats like the schema.org are moving quickly to provide a set of "common language" elements that can be used to allow communities to cross barriers. Will these common languages be as robust as older data crosswalks? Likely not. Most data crosswalks provide one-to-one translations of a system, but in many cases, data interoperability doesn't require strict data mapping, but rather mapping that is good enough to provide enough context to support search and discovery, creating a framework that will allow machines to understand the relationships between interconnected data.

Browsing the Web has become second nature for most individuals—but even new users with very little experience working on the Web are able to quickly view and make decisions regarding the content found there. When browsing web content, human beings are easily able to understand the difference between advertisements and content—giving people the ability to unconsciously filter the advertisement out of their mind's eye. Likewise, when one considers library metadata, a cataloger with any experience can quickly determine the primary control number found within a MARC record, allowing the cataloger to interpret not only the metadata record, but the rules necessary to place that metadata into alternative formats. Machines simply do not have this ability at this point in time. Automated machine processes require the presence of rules and schemas to identify for the software application the relationships that exist between data. Considering these two examples, a machine would have a very difficult time distinguishing an advertisement from content simply by examining the content. In part, this is why the pop-up blockers and advertisement scrubbers that can be found in web browsers today work primarily through the use of blacklists and known advertising content providers to determine how the elements of a document may relate to it. In reality, automated advertisement-blocking software is primarily making its best guess regarding the nature of the examined content. For catalogers, the problem is the same. Automated bibliographic creation/editing processes still require a great deal of human intervention to create the necessary rules for a machine to interpret a metadata set. Without these rules, a machine could certainly parse a metadata set, but it would have no way of building or interpreting the relationships of this bibliographic data to other metadata content.

The semantic web, then, is about connecting these dots to give machine processes the ability to determine and infer relationships and meaning about the data that it describes. If this sounds a lot like metadata for one's metadata, you would be essentially right. RDF, the Resource Description Framework, is one of the cornerstones of the semantic web initiative. RDF, and similar serializations, provide the Web with a common descriptive language. In theory, RDF provides a common descriptive framework that can be used to "wrap" an existing set of metadata/data to provide the missing information needed to give machine processes the ability to draw relationships between heterogeneous datasets. RDF, coupled with OWL (Web Ontology Language), make up two major components of the semantic web framework that is designed to bring out the relationships between data on the Web.

So, what does this look like? Well, it depends on the serialization and the namespaces being used. The Dublin Core community has a long history of utilizing RDF as part of its metadata description language. As early as 2007, the Dublin Core Metadata Initiative produced a draft document entitled "Expressing Dublin Core Metadata Using the Resource Description Framework (RDF)."[19] This was its most detailed document to date discussing how Dublin Core metadata could be expressed within the RDF metadata framework. The document illustrates how Dublin Core can be encoded to ensure that nonhuman processes can understand the important concepts related to the metadata record—for example, details relating to classification, ontologies, and relationships (both hierarchical and relational) to other items. At its simplest, the RDF encoding of Dublin Core data can look something like the following:

```
<?xml version="1.0" encoding="utf-8"?>
<rdf:RDF xmlns:rdf="http://www.w3.org/1999/02/22-rdf-syntax-ns#" xmlns:dc="http://purl.org/dc/elements/1.1/">
<rdf:Description>
<dc:title>Report of the exploring expedition to the Rocky Mountains in the year 1842 : and to Oregon and north California in the years 1843-44 /</dc:title>
<dc:creator rdf:resource="http://authorities.loc.gov/" />Frémont, John Charles,1813-1890.</dc:creator>
<dc:creator rdf:resource="http://authorities.loc.gov/" />Torrey, John,1796-1873.</dc:creator>
<dc:creator rdf:resource="http://authorities.loc.gov/" />Hall, James,1811-1898.</dc:creator>
<dc:creator rdf:resource="http://authorities.loc.gov/" />United States.Army.Corps of Engineers.</dc:creator>
<dc:type>text</dc:type>
<dc:publisher>Washington : Blair and Rives, Printers,</dc:publisher>
```

```
<dc:date>1845.</dc:date>
<dc:language>eng</dc:language>
<dc:description>The Astronomical and Meteorological observations of the 1842 expedition,
which form p. 585-693 of the Senate edition (Senate ex. doc. 174) are not included in this.</
dc:description>
<dc:subject rdf:resource="http://www.loc.gov" />Discoveries in geography</dc:subject>
<dc:subject rdf:resource="http://www.loc.gov" />Paleontology</dc:subject>
<dc:subject rdf:resource="http://www.loc.gov" />Botany</dc:subject>
</rdf:Description>
</rdf:RDF>
```

In the above example, RDF elements are used to define the ontologies utilized by the controlled terms found within the record. In this case, I've placed representative URIs (Universal Resource Identifiers) identifying the creator and subject elements. So while the URIs provided will not resolve to anything meaningful, this does capture the idea behind the RDF markup. Ideally, the rdf:resource URIs would resolve to the ontology, which could then be parsed to build relationships between the terms utilized in this record and the terms found within the ontology. Of course, this is just a simple example of how RDF could be utilized to represent a Dublin Core record. The draft formalized in 2008 provides much more detail illustrating the many different levels of RDF encoding that can be supported and recommended for use and has been used as a jumping off point for additional specification development, specifically the LRMI Community (http://lrmi. dublincore.org/) efforts to develop new classes to expand schema.org's description of learning resources. But we can go further. We can incorporate multiple schemas using various serializations to represent wide ranges of data. For example, let's use the example above, but incorporate multiple metadata schemas.

```
<?xml version="1.0" encoding="utf-8"?>
<rdf:RDF xmlns:rdf="http://www.w3.org/1999/02/22-rdf-syntax-ns#" xmlns:dc="http://purl.org/dc/
elements/1.1/"
xmlns:dcterms= "http://purl.org/dc/terms/"
xmlns:relators="http://id.loc.gov/vocabulary/relators/">
<rdf:Description>
<dc:title>Report of the exploring expedition to the Rocky Mountains in the year 1842 : and to
Oregon and north California in the years 1843-44 /</dc:title>
<dc:creator rdf:about="http://id.loc.gov/authorities/names/n50025411">
Frémont, John Charles,1813-1890
<relators:aut rdf:about="http://id.loc.gov/vocabulary/relators/aut">author</relators:aut>
</dc:creator>
<dc:contributor rdf:about="http://id.loc.gov/authorities/names/n84075762">
Torrey, John,1796-1873
<relators:ctb rdf:about="http://id.loc.gov/vocabulary/relators/ctb">contributor</relators:ctb>
</dc:contributor>
<dc:contributor rdf:about="http://id.loc.gov/authorities/">
Hall, James,1811-1898
<relators:ctb rdf:about="http://id.loc.gov/vocabulary/relators/ctb">contributor</relators:ctb>
</dc:contributor>
<dc:contributor rdf:about="http://id.loc.gov/authorities/names/n79069640">
United States. Army Corps of Engineers
```

(Cont.)

```
<relators:pma rdf:about="http://id.loc.gov/vocabulary/relators/pma">Permitting Agency</
relators:pma>
</dc:contributor>
<dc:type>text</dc:type>
<dc:publisher>Washington : Blair and Rives, Printers,</dc:publisher>
<dc:date>1845.</dc:date>
<dc:language>eng</dc:language>
<dc:description>The Astronomical and Meteorological observations of the 1842 expedition,
which form p. 585-693 of the Senate edition (Senate ex. doc. 174) are not included in this.</
dc:description>
<dc:subject rdf:about="http://id.loc.gov/authorities/subjects/sh85038366">
Discoveries in geography
</dc:subject>
<dc:subject rdf:about="http://id.loc.gov/authorities/subjects/sh85097123">
Paleontology
</dc:subject>
<dc:subject rdf:about="http://id.loc.gov/authorities/subjects/sh85015976">
Botany
</dc:subject>
<dcterms:spatial rdf:about="http://id.loc.gov/authorities/names/n79021953">
Oregon
</dcterms:spatial>
</rdf:Description>
</rdf:RDF>
```

Utilizing semantic concepts, we can begin to construct smarter data that begins to support the self-description of the data. In this case, we utilize URIs to embed actionable data into our metadata. This shifts our metadata from a collection of strings to a collection of strings paired with their objects, and these objects provide information that can be acted upon to not only keep data fresh and valid, but to build additional relationships to additional vocabularies and concepts. By utilizing semantic data principles in our own metadata and in the systems that we build, we enable the data to be meaningful beyond our repositories, ultimately supporting better discovery for our users.

### Schema.org

With the ability to embed semantic metadata directly into one's metadata and create deep links between systems online, libraries can immediately begin to take advantage of a lightweight method of embedding existing data into a semantic format that web browsers currently understand and are using in building their own linked knowledge bases: schema.org.[20] Schema .org is a structured markup language that was developed by large search engine providers to replace the traditional meta-tagging syntax with more structured data. Within the format, schemas are used to define different types of things, like people, places, events, and so on. Within these schemas, there have been extensions like the bibliographic extension, which improve on the core schema entry. The bib extension, for example, extends the core books schema. The format allows organizations to utilize this "micro language" to better describe the content on their websites, and to allow search engines like Google to provide "cards" about specific topics. For example, when you search for a public library, it might return information about specific hours or related library branches.

Within the library community, schema.org has generated strong interest due to OCLC's use of the language. While the library metadata community has looked to the Library of Congress and the BIBFRAME development, OCLC has quietly created the largest set of linked library data[21] through the generation of schema.org data within WorldCat.org.

Figure 6.10 illustrates how OCLC has integrated linked data into World-Cat.org. Utilizing the schema.org namespaces, OCLC has been able to

---

**Linked Data**

More info about Linked Data

Primary Entity
<http://www.worldcat.org/oclc/861827187> # How to teach quantum physics to your dog
　　a schema:CreativeWork, schema:Book ;
　library:oclcnum "861827187" ;
　library:placeOfPublication <http://experiment.worldcat.org/entity/work/data/3875659024#Place/oneworld> ; # Oneworld
　schema:about <http://dewey.info/class/530.12/> ;
　schema:about <http://experiment.worldcat.org/entity/work/data/3875659024#Topic/quantum_theory_popular_works> ; # Quantum theory Popular works
　schema:bookFormat bgn:PrintBook ;
　schema:copyrightYear "2010" ;
　schema:creator <http://experiment.worldcat.org/entity/work/data/3875659024#Person/orzel_chad> ; # Chad Orzel
　schema:datePublished "2010" ;
　schema:exampleOfWork <http://worldcat.org/entity/work/id/3875659024> ;
　schema:genre "Fiction"@en ;
　schema:inLanguage "en" ;
　schema:name "How to teach quantum physics to your dog"@en ;
　schema:productID "861827187" ;
　schema:publication <http://www.worldcat.org/title/-/oclc/861827187#PublicationEvent/oneworld_oxford_2010> ;
　schema:publisher <http://experiment.worldcat.org/entity/work/data/3875659024#Agent/oxford> ; # Oxford
　schema:workExample <http://worldcat.org/isbn/9781851687794> ;
　wdrs:describedby <http://www.worldcat.org/title/-/oclc/861827187> ;

---

Related Entities
<http://dewey.info/class/530.12/>
　　a schema:Intangible ;


<http://experiment.worldcat.org/entity/work/data/3875659024#Agent/oxford> # Oxford
　　a bgn:Agent ;
　schema:name "Oxford" ;


<http://experiment.worldcat.org/entity/work/data/3875659024#Person/orzel_chad> # Chad Orzel
　　a schema:Person ;
　schema:familyName "Orzel" ;
　schema:givenName "Chad" ;
　schema:name "Chad Orzel" ;


<http://experiment.worldcat.org/entity/work/data/3875659024#Place/oneworld> # Oneworld
　　a schema:Place ;
　schema:name "Oneworld" ;


<http://experiment.worldcat.org/entity/work/data/3875659024#Topic/quantum_theory_popular_works> # Quantum theory Popular works
　　a schema:Intangible ;
　schema:name "Quantum theory Popular works"@en ;


<http://worldcat.org/isbn/9781851687794>
　　a schema:ProductModel ;
　schema:isbn "1851687793" ;

---

**FIGURE 6.10**

Linked Data in OCLC WorldCat.org

leverage markup syntax to enable search engines to reach into, and index, the data in WorldCat.org. More interesting to libraries, however, is that this data can be mined using XPath and Sax, since this marked-up data is also embedded within the results page as XHTML. This makes WorldCat .org a powerful linking service, since the results page can now be utilized to retrieve URIs to a Works page, to VIAF information about the author, as well as to a whole host of other information about the record. OCLC has been out in front of the library community in demonstrating how semantic data can be made manifest within library catalogs and websites today, with minimal effort.

### Moving Forward

So, what can you do today? Libraries are sitting on a precipice. On the one hand, our community understands the work that needs to be done, and in many cases, we have systems that support the ability to begin moving library data into semantically aware systems. At the same time, we have mountains of legacy data that need to be reconciled, and currently we lack the widespread library infrastructure to enable large-production reconciliation projects. It's a tough place to be. How do we start?

> Begin encoding your data now. Libraries and metadata specialists must stop thinking about their metadata as a collection of strings, and must start encoding their data. For a time, this will be slow going while library infrastructure develops, but we cannot have a future in which libraries utilize linked data and linked-data concepts at scale until our metadata shifts from a series of strings to encoded objects.

> Use systems that support heterogenous data profiles. While MARC may remain the lingua franca for our traditional library catalogs, the community has an opportunity to move beyond this and expand our bibliographic data model within the digital repository space. Libraries should be adopting systems that allow them to support and utilize a wide range of data schemas. Developing models, like the Portland Common Data Model, embrace this approach, and as library systems continue to develop, this type of heterogeneous data modeling should become more of the rule—as libraries are able to use existing ontologies from a wide range of communities to not only enable better description and discovery, but to provide more actionable data that supports self-description.

## Summary

Sadly, this chapter can only cover a small number of the metadata frameworks that are currently available to digital library designers. As such, this chapter focused on the three metadata frameworks that currently are most widely used on today's digital repository platforms, but many more exist. Frameworks targeting geographic content (FGDC),[22] images (VRA),[23] textual documents (TEI),[24] and archival finding aids (EAD)[25] all provide metadata frameworks for the rich description of specific material types. When choosing a digital repository, implementers should take stock of the types of materials that will likely be stored within the resource and ask some of the following questions:

- Who will be creating metadata within my digital repository?
- What level of granularity will I require?
- Should my system support the batch importing and exporting of its digital objects?
- What role will legacy metadata play in my digital library programs?
- Will my organization use a single monolithic system or will my digital repository system be made up of many heterogeneous components?

Obviously, how one answers these questions will impact what metadata framework would likely be best suited for one's digital library system. For example, will materials be entered by technical services staff, or will metadata be submitted by faculty and students? If it's the latter, utilizing a metadata framework like Dublin Core, which provides a set of generally understandable elements, would likely reduce the chances of metadata creation becoming a barrier for submission. However, each of these choices must be weighed by the individual institution—factoring in current workflows, expertise, and system infrastructure.

# Notes

1. Bruce Johnson, "XML and MARC: Which Is 'Right?'" *Cataloging & Classification Quarterly 32,* no. 1 (2001): 81–90.

2. Ibid., 86.

3. Roy Tennant, "MARC Must Die," *Library Journal* 127, no. 17 (2002): 26–28.

4. Roy Tennant, "Building a New Bibliographic Infrastructure," *Library Journal* 129, no. 1 (2004): 38.

5. Karen Calhoun, "The Changing Nature of the Catalog and Its Integration with Other Discovery Tools," Library of Congress, March 2006, www.loc.gov/catdir/calhoun-report-final.pdf.

6. Deanna B. Marcum, "Future of Cataloging," address to the EBSCO leadership seminar, Library of Congress, January 16, 2004, www.loc.gov/library/reports/CatalogingSpeech.pdf.

7. Library of Congress, "MARC Code List: Part V: Format Sources," www.loc.gov/marc/relators/relaform.html.

8. Terry Reese, "MarcEdit," Oregon State University, http://oregonstate.edu/~reeset/marcedit/.

9. David Bradley, unattributed interview, www.youtube.com/watch?v=TVRMrxF9BkQ.

10. Priscilla Caplan, *Metadata Fundamentals for All Librarians* (Chicago: American Library Association, 2003).

11. Andy Powell, "Dublin Core Metadata Editor," www.ukoln.ac.uk/metadata/dcdot/.

12. National Information Standards Organization, "The Dublin Core Metadata Element Set," 2001, www.niso.org/standards/resources/Z39–85.pdf.

13. Dublin Core Metadata Initiative, "DCMI Metadata Terms," www.dublincore.org/documents/dcmi-terms/.

14. Collaborative Digitization Program, "CDP Dublin Core Best Practices," www.cdpheritage.org/cdp/documents/CDPDCMBP.pdf.

15. Morgan Cundiff, "Using METS and MODS to Create an XML Standards-Based Digital Library Application," Library of Congress, www.loc.gov/standards/mets/presentations/Digital_Future_Cundiff.ppt#7.

16. Library of Congress, "METS Schema 1.11 Schema," www.loc.gov/standards/mets/version111/mets.xsd.

17. Library of Congress, "Bibliographic Framework Initiative," http://loc.gov/bibframe/.

18. "Portland Common Data Model," https://github.com/duraspace/pcdm/wiki.

19. Dublin Core Metadata Initative, "Expressing Dublin Core Metadata Using the Resource Description Framework (RDF)," 2007, www.dublincore.org/documents/2007/04/02/dc-rdf/.

20. Schema.org, "Schema.org," http://schema.org/.

21. OCLC, "OCLC Adds Linked Data to WorldCat," www.oclc.org/en/news/releases/2012/201238.html.

22. Federal Geographic Data Committee, www.fgdc.gov/.

23. Visual Resources Association Data Standards, www.vraweb.org/vracore3.htm.

24. Text Encoding Initiative, www.tei-c.org/.

25. Library of Congress, "Encoding Archival Description," www.loc.gov/ead/.

# Sharing Data
## Harvesting, Linking, and Distribution

**The collecting, sharing,** and curating of information is one of the bedrock values of the library community. We see this practice all the time. From the creation of a global consortium like OCLC to promote the shared maintenance of the written bibliographic record, to the creation of more local cooperatives like OhioLINK, the Orbis-Cascade Alliance, or the Midwest Collaborative for Library Services—these groups enable local collaboration and the sharing of practices and resources. This value can also be seen reflected in the standards that the library community embraces. Standards like Z39.50, OAI-PMH, SRU, and others are used to provide a standard method for individuals and organizations to share metadata. Throughout the cultural heritage community, at conferences, and in the literature, one will hear it said that "information wants to be free."[1] This is a refrain that many within the library community fervently believe as settled fact. And yet, within the digital library community, this statement, this belief, seems to have little basis in reality. While the community has been very active in developing methods to share metadata, many libraries put up barriers to prevent the sharing of content or metadata. So, while most would agree that "information wants to be free," it would appear that this value begins to dissipate as the information becomes a greater asset to the organization.

However, it doesn't have to be this way. Libraries have the opportunity to not only preserve the cultural record, but to actively promote and provide democratic access to the information. They have the ability to push the boundaries of copyright and fair use, and leverage their repositories of information to enrich not only their own organizations and campus communities, but, through the adoption of linked data and a liberal open-data policy, support interdisciplinary and emerging digital humanities researchers. It is with this future in mind that this chapter will focus on how libraries can work to enable the sharing, linking, and greater distribution of their content.

## The Evolving Role of Libraries

The members of the library community have traditionally been early technology adopters when it comes to the world of information distribution. But as the current information ecosystem has evolved, so too has the library community's role within that ecosystem. In the not too distant past, the library community was the information ecosystem, representing the central location for trusted content within its user community. The library was the warehouse of information, and its physical materials were its single largest tangible asset. How valuable this asset was, however, depended on the size of the library—meaning that user communities were served unequally depending on the size and scope of the community's library. Interlibrary loan changed this paradigm, as libraries made materials available for inter-institutional borrowing. Interlibrary loan effectively made every small library a giant, by providing its users with access to various research collections around the country. Moreover, as new digital capture technologies developed, libraries have been able to integrate these new processes in order to speed document delivery and provide new and exciting levels of access. And throughout each of these changes, the library remained its users' central repository for information.

This changed with the Internet, and the trend has accelerated with the availability of low-cost mobile data access. The Internet has expanded the researcher's universe. No longer is access to primary resources limited to one's physical proximity to an object. What's more, information companies like Facebook and Google have developed a new form of currency around the exchange of personal information, obscuring the true cost of information access. Libraries have struggled to engage in this environment, given the high value that their community places on the patron's right to privacy. Ironically, though, it has been this value and the community's cautious engagement with this new information ecosystem that have greatly contributed to the library's shift away from the center of the user's information universe.

But is this evolution a negative one for users? It doesn't have to be. Users today have access to a much wider breadth of information and opportunities to collaborate, as well as to access and remix data in ways that would have been hard to imagine even a few years ago. These new methods of access have opened new research opportunities and have democratized access to primary data. For the first time, access to primary resources housed in locations that restrict access are being viewed by new eyes. Additionally, these changes have forced libraries to look at how they interact with the larger information communities. As cultural heritage organizations, libraries and museums cannot remain on the sidelines, and so they have looked for areas of collaboration and ways that they can participate within this new information infrastructure without compromising the library community's core values.

For the library community, this means learning a new language and new rules. How much should libraries engage in social networks or work with these toolkits? What is the price in information currency that they are willing to pay to aggregate statistics or enable integration with common social media authentication platforms? What's more, how much information should the library share? Should one's digital library be largely transparent, encouraging tools like Google and Bing to index content, or should the community support a more walled-off model that focuses on supporting access through larger aggregators like the HathiTrust or the Digital Public Library of America? These are key questions for the community, but ones that we believe have significant historical precedent, if one looks closely at the development of OCLC and other similar initiatives. Libraries have always been strongest and most effective when they reduce the number of barriers and actively work to promote the sharing and integration of their content. To this end, digital library developers and managers need to come to an understanding that library services need to be transparent. This means that services need to be not only open, but documented. Unlike commercial information providers, the library is most successful when it gets users to information in the most unobtrusive way possible. Digital library developers and managers should work to do a better job of not tripping over their own technology, and work to find ways to provide more direct paths to information. In some cases, this may mean looking outside the library community for usable or compatible technologies, or engaging with standards bodies outside the library community to develop pathways for libraries to more easily interact in the new information environment. And we see this happening with Schema.org and the larger Dublin Core community . . . communities that don't primarily serve the library community, but which have encouraged and made space for members of the library community to serve and contribute.

## Metadata Doesn't Want to Be Free . . . If It Did, It Would Be Easy

Concepts can develop into mythologies that take on a life of their own. "Information wants to be free" has morphed into "metadata wants to be free," and within the library community, I believe that it does. Libraries have invested significant capital and energy to develop protocols and standards that enable the sharing of bibliographic information. This is why MARC was developed:[2] so the Library of Congress could share its metadata. And this is what spurred on the development of Z39.50—a need to provide a remote protocol to share bibliographic data. Since libraries first started creating electronic bibliographic records in the early 1970s, they have worked to develop technologies that would simplify the process of sharing metadata.

And we share metadata . . . but only within our community. The library metadata community has historically been wary of openly sharing bibliographic metadata, in part to prevent a third party from capitalizing on and commercializing the profession's investments. So, while libraries have worked hard to develop protocols to enable the sharing of metadata and information within their own community, traditional library bibliographic systems have actively prevented this information from being shared outside of the community . . . and libraries' users have been worse off because of this. By preventing the open sharing of library data, the community has stunted the growth of new research and innovation, and has inadvertently become a barrier to researchers who are interested in digital humanities research, data mining, or image and document analysis. Consider the following questions, and try to honestly answer how easy it would be for your own institution to:

1. Provide all of your bibliographic metadata to a researcher for publication

2. Provide access to your local control vocabularies and how these vocabularies map to other content in use

3. Provide an automated method to evaluate copyright for digital content

4. Provide full text of one's repository or collection for the purposes of data mining

The reality is that most digital library providers couldn't easily answer many of these requests, and in many cases, the barrier would not be a technical one. Just as libraries have had to navigate the many technology challenges that have occurred within this new information ecosystem, so too have they had to address the changing user expectations related to the rise of digital humanities researchers. As humanities researchers have embraced computational research, libraries have been forced to confront the technical and policy barriers that they have erected around their own digital content.

But what happens when we lower these barriers? Innovation happens. When libraries shift resources from barring or gatekeeping access to collections and make a commitment to actively promote shared access and use, history has shown that opportunities have emerged to break down traditional barriers related to organization, collection, and access. Consider these two examples:

### Digital Public Library of America (DPLA)
http://dp.la

> The DPLA is an ambitious project that has set out to surface a digital public commons of cultural heritage information related to the United States. Patterned after a similar project in Europe,[3] the DPLA is made possible by the availability and use of open communication standards and a willingness to place one's metadata into the public domain. And the results have been impressive. As a portal for content, the DPLA provides access to nearly

17 million digital objects from cultural heritage institutions around the United States, exposing millions of users to collections and primary resources that would have previously been unknown. But what is more, the DPLA is creating services and exposing its aggregated metadata to the research community, and in the course of utilizing these services, researchers have exposed new ways of searching, evaluating, and imagining the DPLA collections. The DPLA applications page[4] illustrates what can happen when a cultural heritage organization makes a commitment to not only access, but to exposing the underlying metadata.

### *Biblissima, Grandes Chroniques de France, ca. 1460*
http://demos.biblissima-condorcet.fr/chateauroux/demo/

This project by the Biblissima and the Bibliothèque Nationale de France illustrates how open data, coupled with open standards, can be utilized to reclaim the historical record. In the world of rare books and illuminated manuscripts, it is not uncommon to have a manuscript or manuscript pages where the text is intact, but the illuminations are missing. Throughout time, illuminated manuscripts have been pulled apart, with pieces ending up at organizations around the world. As organizations digitize this content, cultural heritage organizations have an opportunity to reclaim these manuscripts and restore them, at least digitally, to their original form. This collaboration between the Biblissima and the Bibliothèque Nationale de France demonstrates just such a project. Using IIIF, these two organizations have been able to reclaim the initial manuscripts for future generations.

These are just two of the thousands of examples of digital projects, exhibits, and innovative research projects that are being developed by organizations committed to providing open data and services. Libraries, and especially digital library managers, need to shift their primary focus from primarily an access mindset to an open data mindset. To be sure, access in any form is better than no access, or to extremely restricted access to content. But as the digital humanities and new fields of interdisciplinary research continue to emerge, it will be access to the aggregated underlying data that will likely drive future discoveries and innovation.

## Linked Data

While some libraries still struggle to make their digital metadata and collections openly available, the larger information community continues to move forward. Outside the library community, the need for interoperability and some level of data-sharing are settled arguments, and work has largely

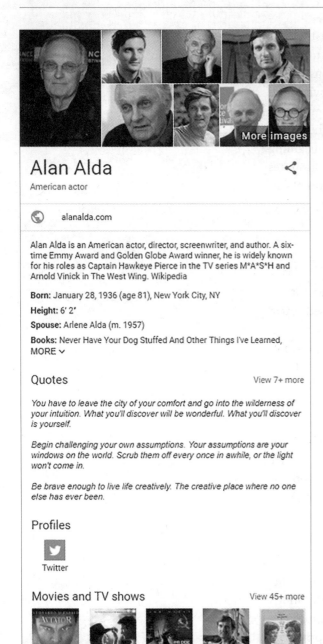

### Alan Alda

American actor

alanalda.com

Alan Alda is an American actor, director, screenwriter, and author. A six-time Emmy Award and Golden Globe Award winner, he is widely known for his roles as Captain Hawkeye Pierce in the TV series M*A*S*H and Arnold Vinick in The West Wing. Wikipedia

**Born:** January 28, 1936 (age 81), New York City, NY

**Height:** 6' 2"

**Spouse:** Arlene Alda (m. 1957)

**Books:** Never Have Your Dog Stuffed And Other Things I've Learned, MORE ⌄

Quotes                                    View 7+ more

*You have to leave the city of your comfort and go into the wilderness of your intuition. What you'll discover will be wonderful. What you'll discover is yourself.*

*Begin challenging your own assumptions. Your assumptions are your windows on the world. Scrub them off every once in a while, or the light won't come in.*

*Be brave enough to live life creatively. The creative place where no one else has ever been.*

Profiles

Twitter

Movies and TV shows                       View 45+ more

| The Aviator 2004 | The Longest Ride 2015 | Bridge of Spies 2015 | M*A*S*H 1972 – 1983 | The Four Seasons 1981 |

People also search for                     View 15+ more

**FIGURE 7.1**

Google Knowledge-Graph Example

shifted to the development and support for linked data and other semantic principles. So, what is linked data? Very broadly, the driving principle behind linked data is to use the Web to build connections and relationships to other information. These relationships create linking points, and this interlinked data begins to form what is called a knowledge graph about a concept, topic, person, or thing.

This is vague, I know—but we see the evidence of these knowledge graphs and "linked" data all around us. One of the most visible examples of linked data in action is seen on Google thousands of times a day. . . . the visual placecard Google generates around people, places, or things. For example, if one does a search for "Alan Alda," Google generates the following content (see figure 7.1):

One probably sees these kinds of placecards many times each day, but taking a closer look, one can see how this simple visual element not only provides simple biographical information about the topic, but that a graph starts to surface about the topic—linking to people, places, and things that are closely related or have relationships to the topic. In this case, the graph for Alan Alda not only includes information about the movies and TV shows that he's been in, but it creates relationships to other actors and directors that are related to him in some way . . . that are linked to him.

Libraries have these same needs. Cultural heritage organizations invest significant resources in developing metadata for resources. This metadata often includes links to subjects, people, and places. These access points represent potential relationships, data that could be mined to develop the same kinds of graphs that we see being created by Google. And in some places, this is happening. OCLC, as the largest aggregator of library bibliographic and authority data, has been leading these efforts, creating services and projects that demonstrate the potential that creating these kinds of relationships can have for improving both the findability and access to content. This effort is probably best illustrated by OCLC's VIAF (Virtual International Authority File) project and web service.

OCLC's VIAF project started out as an effort to understand how the various national controlled vocabularies are related to each other. When you think about it, it's a basic findability problem. National libraries around the world maintain their own national authorized vocabularies—meaning that the same individual is likely represented in many different forms across the various discovery systems used throughout the world. VIAF was a project to look at how these variations could be related together, to create relationships between different terms that represented the same person, object, or subject. This way, a search for: 1, פו ארגד אלן 1809–1849 would locate materials under the more common heading in the United States of: Poe, Edgar Allan, 1809–1849. VIAF, for the first time, provides a way for researchers to visualize the relationships between these national authority files and create linkages between these link terms. However, given OCLC's vast amount of authority and bibliographic data, the cooperative was able to expand the project beyond authority data and begin exploring secondary relationships to a person, place, or subject—examining relationships like coauthors, related works, and publishers. Like Google's knowledge graph, VIAF utilizes data from a wide range of sources to build new knowledge through the relationships between data.

On its own, this kind of work would be exciting. But it's the open nature of linked data and the focus on machine-actionable content that has implications for the future. While Google doesn't share the underlying data that it uses to build its knowledge graphs, OCLC does. Looking at the example of Edgar Allan Poe, VIAF produces a permanent URL for the information. When requested through a browser, the system generates an HTML representation of the graph for human consumption. But if the request is made by a machine, OCLC makes the VIAF data available in various data serializations. Here's a snippet of the data when the request is for XML data (see figure 7.2).


```
viaf.org/viaf/60351476/viaf.xml
▼<ns1:mainHeadings>
  ▼<ns1:data>
     <ns1:text>Poe, Edgar Allan, 1809-1849.</ns1:text>
   ▶<ns1:sources>...</ns1:sources>
   </ns1:data>
  ▼<ns1:data>
     <ns1:text>Poe, Edgar Allan</ns1:text>
   ▼<ns1:sources>
       <ns1:s>VLACC</ns1:s>
       <ns1:sid>VLACC|000001956</ns1:sid>
       <ns1:s>DBC</ns1:s>
       <ns1:sid>DBC|87097968829984</ns1:sid>
       <ns1:s>NII</ns1:s>
       <ns1:sid>NII|DA0013993X</ns1:sid>
       <ns1:s>NSK</ns1:s>
       <ns1:sid>NSK|000039385</ns1:sid>
     </ns1:sources>
   </ns1:data>
  ▼<ns1:data>
     <ns1:text>Edgar Allan Poe</ns1:text>
   ▼<ns1:sources>
       <ns1:s>WKP</ns1:s>
       <ns1:sid>WKP|Q16867</ns1:sid>
     </ns1:sources>
   </ns1:data>
  ▼<ns1:data>
     <ns1:text>بو، إدجار آلان، 1809-1849</ns1:text>
   ▼<ns1:sources>
       <ns1:s>ISNI</ns1:s>
       <ns1:sid>ISNI|0000000121354025</ns1:sid>
       <ns1:s>EGAXA</ns1:s>
       <ns1:sid>EGAXA|vtls001060853</ns1:sid>
     </ns1:sources>
   </ns1:data>
  ▼<ns1:data>
     <ns1:text>По, Э. А. 1809-1849 Эдгар Аллан</ns1:text>
   ▼<ns1:sources>
       <ns1:s>NLR</ns1:s>
       <ns1:sid>NLR|RU NLR AUTH 773219</ns1:sid>
     </ns1:sources>
   </ns1:data>
  ▼<ns1:data>
     <ns1:text>פו, אדגר אלן, 1809-1849</ns1:text>
   ▼<ns1:sources>
       <ns1:s>NLI</ns1:s>
```


**FIGURE 7.2**
VIAF XML Representation

VIAF produces a machine-readable object about Edgar Allan Poe, and in this object, one sees not only the links between the different forms of the names, but bibliographic information, links to other numeric identifiers in other systems, and also the secondary relationships. This is a typical example of how linked data can be developed, and the transformative power that it can provide to libraries. Utilizing this data, libraries could conceivably build systems that provide better discovery, or automated authority control, or that even provide support for greater international accessibility—but we don't do this. As interesting and exciting as the work of OCLC's VIAF is, it is also exceedingly rare in the cultural heritage community. As of this writing, a large number of organizations are experimenting with or are actively building the infrastructure necessary to promote linked data use and reuse in a production environment. This work is hard and expensive, and this is one of the reasons why linked data remains an open opportunity rather than a realized promise. Even VIAF, a project that OCLC has been building and maintaining for years, lacks some of the necessary infrastructure to be a part of the current linked-data infrastructure. As we look to the future, how digital libraries support the creation of linked data services and take advantage of them will be interesting to follow.

## Sharing Metadata

Fortunately, nearly all digital repository platforms provide some method of sharing metadata. Generally, these options are limited to harvesting protocols, enabling users to download subsets of an organization's metadata for use within other systems. While this information isn't generally available in real time, this process has fueled a large number of discovery solutions that have been developed around digital libraries. More recently, libraries have been embracing standard HTTP-based operations, and developing REST-based services that utilize JSON as the primary method of communication. Moreover, new HTTP-based protocols like ResourceSync[5] and SPARQL[6] likely represent the next generation of harvest and query operations within the digital library space. These services are unique in that they seek to leverage established HTTP patterns and norms, rather than creating library-specific communication standards, thus making content more accessible to those outside of the library domain. However, since current-generation digital repository platforms primarily support OAI harvesting as a methodology for metadata distribution, much of the remainder of this chapter will focus on the tools, methods, and protocols necessary to crosswalk harvested content to different metadata schemas; on issues related to metadata crosswalking; and on the protocols used to support metadata harvesting on current digital repository platforms.

### XSLT

When considering XML metadata crosswalking, very likely one will be working with XSLT (eXtensible Stylesheet Transformation). XSLT is a W3C technology designed to work with XSL (eXtensible Stylesheet Language), which is essentially a stylesheet language for XML. XSLT was originally designed and is used primarily for the transformation of an XML document from one document language to another. On the Web, XSLT is utilized to transform XML documents into HTML documents for public display.

XSLT itself defines a list of vocabularies that can be used to manipulate an XML document. By itself, an XSLT stylesheet is no more than an XML document. Transformation commands are constructed as tags within the document, utilizing XPath to extract and reformat individual data nodes to be processed. XSLT processing instructions are defined through a namespace. Within an XML document, the namespace is a method that is used to define a set of tags through the use of an identifying URI. XSLT defines the following namespace URI, www.w3.org/1999/XSL/Transform, to define for the XML/XSLT parser a valid set of processing instructions that can be used to perform an XSLT transformation.

XSLT offers a simple method for transforming XML documents to other formats, be they another XML document or documents of another type like HTML. XSLT offers the ability to separate the display or transformation instructions from the bibliographic content, allowing the bibliographic content to be clearer and more portable. Let's look at a very simple XML document and how this document might be transformed using XSLT.

```xml
<?xml version="1.0" encoding="utf-8" ?>
<ZooTrip>
<photo title="Standing at the Elephant's pen" filename="http://oregonstate.edu/~reeset/
presentations/xml/look_elephant.jpg">
<animals />
<people>
<name>Kenny Reese, Terry Reese</name>
</people>
</photo>
<photo title="Walking Elephant" filename="http://oregonstate.edu/~reeset/presentations/xml/
elephant_boy.jpg">
<animals>
<name>Elephant</name>
</animals>
<people>
<name>Kenny Reese, Terry Reese</name>
</people>
</photo>
<photo title="Feeding the birds" filename="http://oregonstate.edu/~reeset/presentations/xml/bird1
.jpg">
<animals>
<name>Lorikeets</name>
</animals>
<people>
<name>Kenny Reese, Terry Reese</name>
</people>
</photo>
<photo title="Driving in the Savannah" filename="http://oregonstate.edu/~reeset/presentations/xml/
truck.jpg">
<animals />
<people>
<name>Kenny Reese, Terry Reese</name>
</people>
</photo>
</ZooTrip>
```

The above XML document is a simple marked-up document detailing a trip to the zoo. In the document, each object is grouped using a "photo" tag, which is enhanced with attributes providing information about the title and file name of the photo. Beneath the "photo" tag are children elements that provide some additional information about the content of the photo, specifically the animals and people in the pictures. Using this document, several XSLT transformations can be applied to generate different displays for this document. For example, if one wanted to generate an HTML document sorted by title from this XML source, one would need to utilize an XSLT document like the following:

```
<?xml version="1.0" encoding="UTF-8" ?>
<xsl:stylesheet version="1.0" xmlns:xsl="http://www.w3.org/1999/XSL/Transform">
<xsl:template match="/">
<html>
<head>
<title>Kenny's trip to the Zoo</title>
</head>
<body>
<table>
<xsl:for-each select="ZooTrip/photo">
<xsl:sort select="@title" />
<tr>
<td>
<table>
<tr>
<td valign="top">
<xsl:call-template name="print_image">
<xsl:with-param name="filename" select="@filename" />
</xsl:call-template>
<br />
<xsl:call-template name="print_title">
<xsl:with-param name="title" select="@title" />
</xsl:call-template>
<xsl:call-template name="print_animals">
<xsl:with-param name="name" select="animals/name" />
</xsl:call-template>
<xsl:call-template name="print_people">
<xsl:with-param name="name" select="people/name" />
</xsl:call-template>
</td>
</tr>
</table>
</td>
</tr>
</xsl:for-each>
</table>
</body>
</html>
</xsl:template>
<xsl:template name="print_image">
<xsl:param name="filename" />
<img>
<xsl:attribute name="src">
<xsl:value-of select="$filename" />
</xsl:attribute>
<xsl:attribute name="style">zoom:15%</xsl:attribute>
</img>
</xsl:template>
<xsl:template name="print_title">
<xsl:param name="title" />
<b>Title:</b>
<xsl:value-of select="$title" />
<br />
</xsl:template>
```

```
<xsl:template name="print_animals">
<xsl:param name="name" />
<b>Animals:</b>
<xsl:value-of select="$name" />
<br />
</xsl:template>
<xsl:template name="print_people">
<xsl:param name="name" />
<b>People:</b>
<xsl:value-of select="$name" />
<br />
</xsl:template>
</xsl:stylesheet>
```

In this XSLT sample document, we see the use of a number of common XSLT processing elements. First, there is the use of the xsl:template element. This creates a capsulized set of processing instructions that are reused whenever a specific set of criteria is met. In this case, the template is run when the root node is encountered. Looking at the document, one can get a better idea how this is utilized, looking at the print_title, print_animal, and print_people templates. Sorting is accomplished by utilizing the xsl:sort command and identifying the sort element. In this case, the sort element was the title attribute. Applying this XSLT to the source XML document produces the following HTML output (see figure 7.3).

The display in figure 7.3 could be changed quickly by making minor modifications to the XSLT document. For example, if one wanted to re-sort by a different element, one would simply need to modify the xsl:sort tag or add a conditional to print only the items that had elephants. And while this is only a simple XSLT example, it demonstrates the primary purpose for which it was developed—to transform XML structures into new and useful documents.

So how does this relate to digital repositories and their metadata? Since most digital repositories utilize XML-based data structures, XSLT can be used as a method for moving data into and out of different metadata schemas or to create new displays. The earlier examples presented a very simplistic view of XSLT—but how could this be used to translate metadata from one format to another? The answer is that the translation gets more complicated.

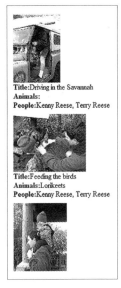

**FIGURE 7.3**

XSLT/XML Transform Output

```
<?xml version="1.0" encoding="UTF-8"?>
<xsl:stylesheet version="1.0" xmlns:dc="http://purl.org/dc/elements/1.1/" xmlns="http://www.loc.
gov/MARC21/slim" xmlns:xsl="http://www.w3.org/1999/XSL/Transform" exclude-result-prefixes="dc">
<xsl:output method="xml" indent="yes"/>
<xsl:template match="/">
<record xmlns:xsi="http://www.w3.org/2001/XMLSchema-instance" xsi:schemaLocation="http://www.loc.
gov/MARC21/slim http://www.loc.gov/standards/marcxml/schema/MARC21slim.xsd" >
<xsl:element name="leader">
<xsl:variable name="type" select="dc:type"/>
<xsl:variable name="leader06">
```

(Cont.)

```
<xsl:choose>
<xsl:when test="$type='collection'">p</xsl:when>
<xsl:when test="$type='dataset'">m</xsl:when>
<xsl:when test="$type='event'">r</xsl:when>
<xsl:when test="$type='image'">k</xsl:when>
<xsl:when test="$type='interactive resource'">m</xsl:when>
<xsl:when test="$type='service'">m</xsl:when>
<xsl:when test="$type='software'">m</xsl:when>
<xsl:when test="$type='sound'">i</xsl:when>
<xsl:when test="$type='text'">a</xsl:when>
<xsl:otherwise>a</xsl:otherwise>
</xsl:choose>
</xsl:variable>
<xsl:variable name="leader07">
<xsl:choose>
<xsl:when test="$type='collection'">c</xsl:when>
<xsl:otherwise>m</xsl:otherwise>
</xsl:choose>
</xsl:variable>
<xsl:value-of select="concat(' ',$leader06,$leader07,' 3u ')"/>
</xsl:element>
<xsl:for-each select="//dc:title[1]">
<datafield tag="245" ind1="0" ind2="0">
<subfield code="a">
<xsl:value-of select="."/>
</subfield>
</datafield>
</xsl:for-each>
<xsl:for-each select="//dc:title[position()>1]">
<datafield tag="246" ind1="3" ind2="3">
<subfield code="a">
<xsl:value-of select="."/>
</subfield>
</datafield>
</xsl:for-each>
```

The above XSLT snippet comes from a larger XSLT document capable of transforming Dublin Core metadata to MARC21XML. Looking at this snippet, a number of things become apparent. First, the XSLT document itself is a valid XML document, with a number of namespaces defined at the top of the file. A valid XSLT file must define all namespaces that will be utilized during the process—and as such, we see namespaces defined for xsl, dc (Dublin Core), and MARC21XML, which is defined as the primary namespace. Within the file, conditional operations like xsl:for-each and xsl:if are used to evaluate the current document being transformed.

The XSLT specification has evolved significantly over the past decade. While the specification still lacks many of the elements needed to be a formal programming language, it has been expanded to include a wide array of data-processing, sorting, grouping, and matching functionality. In fact, it is the richness of the feature set that remains the primary difference between the various XSLT versions. As of this writing, XSLT currently has three versions of the specification. Version 1.0 represents the most basic incarnation of the stylesheet language, and is the version supported by all modern web browsers. And while version 1.0 has not been formally deprecated, popular XSLT processors like Saxon no longer directly support this specification, but will continue to process version 1.0 documents via the 2.0 specification (which is backwards-compatible). Within the library community, most XSLT transformation documents are still written using the version 1.0 specification.

So, if the difference between XSLT versions is mainly the feature set, what does that entail? Essentially, it comes down to higher-level processing instructions. In XSLT version 1.0, data functions were primarily limited to simple math, string, and date functions. XSLT selection and grouping elements were limited to "if . . . then" statements, select statements, "for . . . next," and choose statements. The 1.0 specifications lack of grouping or matching functions would force stylesheet designers to create custom templates that replicated these operations, or encouraging XSLT stylesheet designers to rely on built-in extensions found in specific XSLT engines, which limited the portability of the solution. XSLT 2.0 filled in many of these gaps, providing true matching and grouping language elements, as well as better regular expression support. And XSLT 3.0 moves the stylesheet language closer to a true programming language, introducing error trapping and the ability to utilize functions as parameters in other functions, and introducing elements of compile-time processing into the language.

In the digital library space, XSLT wears many hats. By and large, most metadata transformation occurs through the use of XSLT processing, given the relatively easy language elements and availability of the processing engines. But XSLT is also used within some systems in place of HTML or other language elements to generate public-facing pages. Probably the best example of this use is found in the DSpace community. DSpace provides a number of different user interface technologies. There is a legacy JSP (JavaServer Pages) interface that is a mixture of pure Java and HTML. Prior to DSpace 2.0, the JSP user interface was the most common. Today, DSpace's XMLUI provides an XSLT-driven interface engine. Using this model, user interface elements are created using XSLT to manipulate the raw XML produced by the application. The shift to an XSLT model was important for libraries because it broadened the number of individuals who could work with the digital library interface, shifting the work from an organization's Java developers to more staff who are experienced in more traditional web development.

## XQuery

Within the library community, exposure to technologies other than XSLT for processing XML data is unlikely. XSLT simply meets the needs of most organizations. While XSLT has some significant disadvantages when working with large XML datasets, the majority of operations that libraries perform on XML content rarely push against these limits. However, outside the library community, the use of XSLT is often paired with another technology—XQuery.

While XSLT was designed as a stylesheet language for XML (much like CSS was designed for HTML), XQuery was created as a full-featured programming language and was designed for the search, retrieval, and manipulation of large sets of XML data. Functionally, XSLT and XQuery have a number of overlapping features. And this isn't by accident. While the XSLT and XQuery specifications are developed by different groups, they are developed cooperatively and share oversight of many technologies like XPath. This means that most operations that can be accomplished using one processing technology can likely be accomplished using the other.

Given that XQuery and XSLT have many overlapping features, one might assume that these technologies share a similar design, but in this, one would be mistaken. XQuery is an expression-based language, and shares many of the same design concepts with SQL. Its purpose is to provide a query-based language that can process large XML datasets and databases, overcoming one of the major weakness of the XSLT specification.

Within the context of digital libraries, however, XQuery has found only limited use. In surveying the most popular library metadata formats, none currently provide XQuery-based processing documents. All transformations are currently provided as an XSLT document using version 1.0 or 2.0 of the specification. In fact, as of this writing, probably the most high-profile use of XQuery within the digital library community was the use of XQuery to demonstrate the conversion of legacy MARC data to BIBFRAME 1.0, developed by the Library of Congress.[7] However, the XQuery approach was abandoned in favor of XSLT when the Library of Congress released the 2.0 version of the BIBFRAME specification.

## Metadata Crosswalking

So what is metadata crosswalking? The crosswalking of metadata is a process in which an XML document is transformed from one schema to another. The crosswalking process utilizes XSLT or XQuery documents to facilitate the movement of metadata between multiple formats. This process requires a number of decisions to be taken for how metadata elements from one schema relate to another. Metadata crosswalks are developed by examining the similarities and differences between differing schemas. Are there one-to-one relationships, that is, do elements share the same meanings, or will the data need to be interpreted? Will the conversions be lossless (unlikely) and if not, what level of data loss will be acceptable? These decisions are actually some of the most important in the crosswalking process, since they will ultimately affect the quality of the final product.

So why build metadata crosswalks? If the crosswalking of metadata will result in the loss of metadata granularity, why not just create all metadata in the desired format to begin with? Well, metadata crosswalking is done for a variety of reasons, though few are as important as remote data interoperability. Information systems today require the ability to ingest various types of metadata from remote sources. Since most organizations create metadata and metadata profiles to best serve themselves and their users, it is unlikely that data, even in a shared metadata format, will be usable without the need for some transformation or data reconciliation. When working with digital library data, it is important to remember that in most cases, an organization's decisions related to format, standards, and best practices will be unapologetically local, so captured remote metadata must be crosswalked into a format that the local system can understand. Today, metadata crosswalking remains the primary mechanism that is used to allow different systems to interoperate with each other. The crosswalking process removes data transfer barriers, allowing heterogeneous systems to successfully share data. Within the library community, this is manifested in federated search systems, which ingest metadata in various formats and provide a standardized search syntax between resources.

In addition to system interoperability, metadata crosswalking can be used to move data from an obsolete metadata schema. This type of data crosswalking has been done for decades when dealing with binary formats. Organizations routinely need to migrate image or document data from obsolete file formats. Like binary formats, metadata formats are gradually changed or replaced, and so they become obsolete with the passage of time. As formats are phased out, crosswalks can be created to provide an upgrade path for obsolete metadata schemas.

## Crosswalking Challenges

Unfortunately, crosswalking metadata is hard work. In many ways, moving bibliographic data between various metadata schemas is like trying to fit a square peg into a round hole. In the end, a crosswalk is simply a process of trying to round the square peg, so that it makes for an easier fit. Fortunately, crosswalking challenges can generally be broken down into four categories:

1. metadata consistency
2. schema granularity
3. the "spare parts"
4. dealing with localisms

## Metadata Consistency

When crosswalking metadata, consistency is the Holy Grail. The crosswalking process must assume that metadata in one format has been consistently applied if rules are to be developed for how that information should be represented in other metadata formats. Given the algorithmic nature of the crosswalking process and of digital interoperability efforts in general, data consistency remains the key to these efforts.[8] Without data consistency, crosswalking processes would need to be overly complex to deal with various data and would very likely require human interaction during or after the process. Ideally, interoperability efforts should be fully automatic, requiring few exceptions for variations in the data. However, when dealing with interoperability, the issue of data consistency is often a large hidden cost.

Within organizations, metadata practices will change over time. Shifting data models and formats have exacerbated this problem, as institutions reevaluate data scope or migrate to new digital library systems. These types of changes, while possibly advantageous within a local system, represent barriers preventing an organization from participating in larger interoperability efforts.

## Schema Granularity

Very rarely does crosswalking occur between two metadata schemas that share the same level of granularity. In part, this is due to the nature of descriptive formats—they tend to be created to meet a specific need and capture specific types of descriptive information. As a result, the crosswalking of metadata becomes a process of (1) deciphering how metadata elements are related, and (2) determining whether the crosswalk will result in a loss of data granularity. In the best-case scenario, metadata crosswalkers are looking for metadata elements that have one-to-one matches; that is, a title in one schema that matches directly with the title element in another schema so long as the granularity within the title elements is equal. In this case, metadata can be directly mapped from one element to another. This would be a lossless crosswalk—something really only achieved when moving data between MARC21XML and MARC. More likely, metadata crosswalkers will need to deal with one-to-many and many-to-many matches. This is where one metadata element in one schema matches the definition of multiple metadata elements in a different schema; for example, moving data between Dublin Core and MARC21. As noted in past chapters, Dublin Core is a relatively low granular format utilizing only fifteen core metadata elements. When crosswalking between Dublin Core and MARC, we see a number of instances where a single Dublin Core field maps to multiple MARC fields (see figure 7.4).

If we take a closer look at the Dublin Core creator field, we see very clearly how granularity can affect metadata crosswalking. The Dublin Core creator element, by definition, stores information relating to the publishers of a work. This means that any individuals or organizations responsible for the creation of the document should be tagged as a creator within the Dublin Core schema. Within MARC21, entities are tagged according to the type of entity (personal, corporate, etc.) and their relation to the work, that is, as the main entry or contributor to a work. As such, the Dublin Core creator element could theoretically map into one of seven different metadata elements within MARC21. What's more, since Dublin Core doesn't capture the

| DUBLIN CORE | MARC21 |
|---|---|
| *Creator* | 100, 110, 111, 700, 710, 711, 720 |

**FIGURE 7.4**

Dublin Core => MARC21 Author Crosswalk

entity's type or relevance to the work, any mapping into MARC21 would be prone to tagging errors or be overly generalized. Would a crosswalk of this nature be useful? It would depend on the application. Within a federated search tool, where metadata needs to be interpreted broadly, this mapping would likely be good enough. Within a more formalized metadata management system that utilizes the tagged granularity to index data, this mapping would be of minimal use.

## Dealing with "Spare Parts"

Because metadata crosswalking is rarely a lossless process, decisions often have to be made regarding what information is "lost" during the crosswalking process. Moreover, data loss isn't limited strictly to the loss of descriptive metadata, since it can include the loss of contextual metadata as well. Going back to our example in figure 7.4, the metadata being crosswalked from MARC21 to Dublin Core could be transferred in a lossless manner, since all data could be placed into the creator element. However, while bibliographic data would not be lost, the contextual metadata relating to the entity type of the creator (whether it's a personal or corporate author), as well as information relating to the entity tagged as the main entry, could be lost. So in this case, the data loss would be primarily contextual.

One of the primary tasks associated with creating a metadata crosswalk is how one deals with the "spare parts"; that is, the unmappable data that cannot be carried through the crosswalk. For example, EAD and FGDC are two examples of very hierarchical metadata schemas that contain bibliographic data and administrative data at both a collection and item level. This type of hierarchical structure is very difficult to crosswalk between metadata schemas, and in most cases, it will generally just be dropped. In these cases, metadata experts need to decide what information must be preserved, and then try to work within the confines of the crosswalking parameters.

## Dealing with Localisms

Lastly, metadata crosswalking must constantly be conscious of what I like to call "localisms"—data added to the metadata to enable data to sort or display in a specific way within a local system. Within digital repository software, many of these localisms will exist. At the Ohio State University Libraries (OSUL), a number of these localisms can be found within the library's digital collections system. When OSUL first started adding content to its digital repository, a great deal of care was put into defining how the metadata should be displayed to the user. In order to normalize the metadata displayed to the user, local, complex metadata elements were created to store and display measurement data. These data elements fell outside of the norms of the digital repository software being used at the time, but they represented the libraries' best solution for dealing with a complex issue, given the wide range of measurements that could be made on objects. Within the local content system, these localisms provide users with a normalized experience. However, harvesting this metadata for indexing outside of the local system can prove to be a challenge, since much of the context and granularity is lost through the process.

## OAI-PMH

Once an item has made it into a digital repository, how is it to be shared? Contributors likely want their work to reach the broadest audience, while digital repository administrators want to expose data in a way that will maximize its exposure at a relatively low cost. Can the repository be crawled by search engines, and can the metadata be accessed by remote systems? Within our shared information climate, digital repository software must be able to provide a straightforward method for sharing metadata about the items that it houses.

Fortunately, such a method exists in all major digital repository services. OAI-PMH (Open Archives Imitative Protocol for Metadata Harvesting) is a simple HTTP-based protocol that can be used to make a digital repository's metadata available for harvest. The protocol works over a normal HTTP Get request—allowing metadata to be harvested by the construction of a simple URL. For example, the following URL, http://kb.osu.edu/oai/request?verb=ListRecords&set=hdl_1811_29375&metadataPrefix=oai_dc, will harvest all metadata items from OSUL's 2006–07 Mershon Center Research Projects (Use of Force and Diplomacy) collection in the libraries' institutional repository. The protocol utilizes a limited set of verbs, limiting its functionality primarily to metadata harvesting and the querying of information about a specific collection or collections on the server. To simplify the OAI-PMH harvesting process, the protocol requires the support of Unqualified Dublin Core. This is what is known as the compatibility schema, so no matter what OAI-PMH repository one harvests from, one can be guaranteed that the metadata will be available in Dublin Core. However, this doesn't prevent an OAI-PMH repository from supporting other metadata formats. In fact, quite the contrary. OAI-PMH implementers are encouraged to support multiple metadata formats, so that the repositories' metadata can be provided in various levels of granularity. In the OSUL institutional repository, for example, two metadata formats are supported for harvest: Unqualified Dublin Core and RDF.

The OAI-PMH protocol recognizes five actions, or requests, that can be made to an OAI-PMH server. Attached to these actions is a limited set of arguments that can be set to limit the range of data to be harvested by date or set, as well as request the harvested metadata in a specific schema. Harvesting limits are set primarily by identifying a range of dates using the "from" and "until" OAI-PMH arguments. Within the OAI-PMH server, date ranges limit the OAI-PMH response to items whose metadata time stamp has been modified within the specified date range. The "from" and "until" argument can be used as pairs or separately to selectively harvest metadata from an OAI-PMH repository. Additional arguments that can be found in an OAI-PMH request are set, resumptionToken, and metadataPrefix. The set argument is used to selectively harvest metadata from defined sets, or collections, of items on the OAI-PMH server. The metadataPrefix, on the other hand, specifies the OAI-PMH response metadata schema. Finally, OAI-PMH allows for the use of a resumptionToken as a method to control data flow. Many OAI-PMH servers will return a maximum number of records per request. If more metadata records exist within a given OAI-PMH request, the server will provide a resumptionToken that can be used to retrieve additional requested items.

## OAI-PMH Verbs[9]

### GetRecord

This verb is used to retrieve an individual metadata record from a repository. The GetRecord verb requires the use of the identifier and the metadataPrefix arguments. To request the record id: oai:kb.osu.edu:1811/29431 from the Ohio State University Libraries' 2006–07 Mershon Center Research Projects (Use of Force and Diplomacy) collection in Unqualified Dublin Core, one would submit the following request: http://kb.osu.edu/oai/request?verb=GetRecord&identifier=oai:kb.osu.edu:1811/29431&metadataPrefix=oai_dc. This request would return the following response:

```
<?xml version="1.0" encoding="UTF-8" ?>
<OAI-PMH xmlns="http://www.openarchives.org/OAI/2.0/" xmlns:xsi="http://www.w3.org/2001/XMLSchema-
instance" xsi:schemaLocation="http://www.openarchives.org/OAI/2.0/ http://www.openarchives.org/
OAI/2.0/OAI-PMH.xsd">
<responseDate>2017-07-30T12:51:51Z</responseDate>
<request identifier="oai:kb.osu.edu:1811/29431" metadataPrefix="oai_dc" verb="GetRecord">http://
kb.osu.edu/oai/request</request>
<GetRecord>
<record>
<header>
<identifier>oai:kb.osu.edu:1811/29431</identifier>
<datestamp>2011-02-22T23:26:57Z</datestamp>
<setSpec>hdl_1811_29374</setSpec>
<setSpec>hdl_1811_29375</setSpec>
<setSpec>hdl_1811_29373</setSpec>
</header>
<metadata>
<oai_dc:dc xmlns:oai_dc="http://www.openarchives.org/OAI/2.0/oai_dc/" xmlns:dc="http://purl.org/dc/
elements/1.1/" xmlns:xsi="http://www.w3.org/2001/XMLSchema-instance" xsi:schemaLocation="http://
www.openarchives.org/OAI/2.0/oai_dc/ http://www.openarchives.org/OAI/2.0/oai_dc.xsd">
<dc:title>For Peace and Money: International Finance and the Triple Entente</dc:title>
<dc:creator>Siegel, Jennifer</dc:creator>
<dc:subject>Russian foreign debt</dc:subject>
<dc:subject>World War I</dc:subject>
<dc:description>
In For Peace and Money: International Finance and the Making and Unmaking of the
Entente Cordiale, Jennifer Siegel examines French and British bank loans to Russia
in the late imperial period, up to the Genoa Conference of 1922. The study will
```

(Cont.)

```
help explain the ways non-governmental players were able to influence policy both
domestically and across national borders in the run-up to World War I.
</dc:description>
<dc:description>Project summary</dc:description>
<dc:description>Research project funded in academic years 2004-05, 2005-06, and 2006-07.</
dc:description>
<dc:description>The University Archives has determined that this item is of continuing value to
OSU's history.</dc:description>
<dc:description>Mershon Center for International Security Studies</dc:description>
<dc:date>2007-11-05T20:32:56Z</dc:date>
<dc:date>2007-11-05T20:32:56Z</dc:date>
<dc:date>2005</dc:date>
<dc:type>Other</dc:type>
<dc:format>87068 bytes</dc:format>
<dc:format>application/pdf</dc:format>
<dc:identifier>http://hdl.handle.net/1811/29431</dc:identifier>
<dc:language>en_US</dc:language>
</oai_dc:dc>
</metadata>
</record>
</GetRecord>
</OAI-PMH>
```

### Identify

This verb is utilized to retrieve information about the repository. Sending an identify request to an OAI-PMH server will return information relating to the repository's name, the repository administrator's e-mail address, the base URL of the repository, the version of OAI-PMH supported, the time stamp of the first record placed into the repository, how it handles deleted records, and the harvesting granularity supported by the server. In regard to the harvesting granularity, this doesn't refer to the metadata schemas supported by the OAI-PMH server, but rather to the granularity relating to an item's time stamp within the repository. Granularity for harvesting can be set to any valid ISO8601 combination. Most commonly, digital repositories use a day as the level of harvesting granularity, meaning that requests would come in YYYY-MM-DD format, but could be extended to allow the specification of hours, minutes, seconds, and so on. An example of an Identify request on the Ohio State University Libraries' institutional repository server would look like: http://kb.osu.edu/oai/request?verb=Identify, and it would return the following request:

```
<?xml version="1.0" encoding="UTF-8" ?>
<OAI-PMH xmlns="http://www.openarchives.org/OAI/2.0/" xmlns:xsi="http://www.w3.org/2001/XMLSche-
ma-instance" xsi:schemaLocation="http://www.openarchives.org/OAI/2.0/ http://www.openarchives.
org/OAI/2.0/OAI-PMH.xsd">
<responseDate>2017-07-30T12:57:00Z</responseDate>
<request verb="Identify">http://kb.osu.edu/oai/request</request>
<Identify>
<repositoryName>The Knowledge Bank at OSU</repositoryName>
```

```
<baseURL>http://kb.osu.edu/oai/request</baseURL>
<protocolVersion>2.0</protocolVersion>
<adminEmail>libkbhelp@lists.osu.edu</adminEmail>
<earliestDatestamp>2001-01-01T00:00:00Z</earliestDatestamp>
<deletedRecord>persistent</deletedRecord>
<granularity>YYYY-MM-DDThh:mm:ssZ</granularity>
<compression>gzip</compression>
<compression>deflate</compression>
<description>
<toolkit xsi:schemaLocation="http://oai.dlib.vt.edu/OAI/metadata/toolkit http://oai.dlib.vt.edu/
OAI/metadata/toolkit.xsd" xmlns="http://oai.dlib.vt.edu/OAI/metadata/toolkit">
<title>OCLC's OAICat Repository Framework</title>
<author>
<name>Jeffrey A. Young</name>
<email>jyoung@oclc.org</email>
<institution>OCLC</institution>
</author>
<version>1.5.48</version>
<toolkitIcon>http://alcme.oclc.org/oaicat/oaicat_icon.gif</toolkitIcon>
<URL>http://www.oclc.org/research/software/oai/cat.shtm</URL>
</toolkit>
</description>
</Identify>
</OAI-PMH>
```

### ListMetadataFormats

This verb is used to retrieve the supported metadata schemas from an OAI-PMH server. This gives OAI-PMH harvesters the ability to see if an OAI-PMH server supports a more granular metadata schema than the required Unqualified Dublin Core. An example of a ListMetadataFormats request on the Ohio State University Libraries' institutional repository OAI-PMH server would look like: http://kb.osu.edu/oai/request?verb=ListMetadataFormats, and it would return the following request:

```
<?xml version="1.0" encoding="UTF-8" ?>
<OAI-PMH xmlns="http://www.openarchives.org/OAI/2.0/" xmlns:xsi="http://www.w3.org/2001/XMLSchema-
instance" xsi:schemaLocation="http://www.openarchives.org/OAI/2.0/ http://www.openarchives.org/
OAI/2.0/OAI-PMH.xsd">
<responseDate>2017-07-30T13:04:24Z</responseDate>
<request verb="ListMetadataFormats">http://kb.osu.edu/oai/request</request>
<ListMetadataFormats>
<metadataFormat>
<metadataPrefix>oai_dc</metadataPrefix>
<schema>http://www.openarchives.org/OAI/2.0/oai_dc.xsd</schema>
<metadataNamespace>http://www.openarchives.org/OAI/2.0/oai_dc/</metadataNamespace>
</metadataFormat>
<metadataFormat>
<metadataPrefix>rdf</metadataPrefix>
<schema>http://www.openarchives.org/OAI/2.0/rdf.xsd</schema>
<metadataNamespace>http://www.openarchives.org/OAI/2.0/rdf/</metadataNamespace>
</metadataFormat>
</ListMetadataFormats>
</OAI-PMH>
```

Note in the request that multiple metadata formats are supported on this server. In this case, the server supports the standard oai_dc metadataPrefix (Unqualified Dublin Core) as well as the rdf metadataPrefix—or in this case, a serialization of metadata wrapped in the Resource Description Framework.

### ListIdentifiers

This verb is used to return the identifiers of a set of items within an OAI-PMH repository. A request using this verb can be paired with arguments setting a date range (from and until), a metadataPrefix, a limit by set, or the use of a resumptionToken for long requests. ListIdentifier requests return no other metadata about the items in a repository but the identifier, which can later be used by the GetRecord verb to retrieve a specific item's full metadata record. An example of a ListIdentifiers request on the Ohio State University Libraries' institutional repository OAI-PMH server would look like: http://kb.osu.edu/oai/request?verb=ListIdentifiers&set=hdl_1811_29375&metadataPrefix=oai_dc, and it would return the following response:

```xml
<?xml version="1.0" encoding="UTF-8" ?>
<OAI-PMH xmlns="http://www.openarchives.org/OAI/2.0/" xmlns:xsi="http://www.w3.org/2001/XMLSchema
-instance" xsi:schemaLocation="http://www.openarchives.org/OAI/2.0/ http://www.openarchives.org/
OAI/2.0/OAI-PMH.xsd">
<responseDate>2017-07-30T13:06:02Z</responseDate>
<request metadataPrefix="oai_dc" verb="ListIdentifiers" set="hdl_1811_29375">http://kb.osu.edu/oai/
request</request>
<ListIdentifiers>
<header>
<identifier>oai:kb.osu.edu:1811/29388</identifier>
<datestamp>2011-02-22T23:26:57Z</datestamp>
<setSpec>hdl_1811_29375</setSpec>
<setSpec>hdl_1811_29376</setSpec>
<setSpec>hdl_1811_46875</setSpec>
</header>
<header>
<identifier>oai:kb.osu.edu:1811/29431</identifier>
<datestamp>2011-02-22T23:26:57Z</datestamp>
<setSpec>hdl_1811_29374</setSpec>
<setSpec>hdl_1811_29375</setSpec>
<setSpec>hdl_1811_29373</setSpec>
</header>
<header>
<identifier>oai:kb.osu.edu:1811/29432</identifier>
<datestamp>2011-02-22T23:26:57Z</datestamp>
<setSpec>hdl_1811_29373</setSpec>
<setSpec>hdl_1811_29375</setSpec>
<setSpec>hdl_1811_29376</setSpec>
</header>
<header>
<identifier>oai:kb.osu.edu:1811/29433</identifier>
<datestamp>2011-02-22T23:26:57Z</datestamp>
<setSpec>hdl_1811_29374</setSpec>
<setSpec>hdl_1811_29375</setSpec>
</header>
```

```
<header>
<identifier>oai:kb.osu.edu:1811/29435</identifier>
<datestamp>2011-02-22T23:26:57Z</datestamp>
<setSpec>hdl_1811_29374</setSpec>
<setSpec>hdl_1811_29375</setSpec>
<setSpec>hdl_1811_29376</setSpec>
<setSpec>hdl_1811_46875</setSpec>
</header>
<header>
<identifier>oai:kb.osu.edu:1811/29436</identifier>
<datestamp>2011-02-22T23:26:57Z</datestamp>
<setSpec>hdl_1811_29374</setSpec>
<setSpec>hdl_1811_29375</setSpec>
<setSpec>hdl_1811_29376</setSpec>
</header>
<header>
<identifier>oai:kb.osu.edu:1811/29438</identifier>
<datestamp>2011-02-22T23:26:57Z</datestamp>
<setSpec>hdl_1811_29375</setSpec>
<setSpec>hdl_1811_29376</setSpec>
<setSpec>hdl_1811_46875</setSpec>
</header>
<header>
<identifier>oai:kb.osu.edu:1811/29439</identifier>
<datestamp>2011-02-22T23:26:57Z</datestamp>
<setSpec>hdl_1811_29375</setSpec>
<setSpec>hdl_1811_29376</setSpec>
<setSpec>hdl_1811_46875</setSpec>
</header>
</ListIdentifiers>
</OAI-PMH>
```

### ListRecords

This verb is used to harvest a list of full metadata records from an OAI-PMH server. This verb can be paired with arguments limiting the records to be harvested by date (until and from) or by set, as well as arguments setting the metadata preference (metadataPrefix) or a resumptionToken when harvesting large datasets. In general, the ListRecords request looks identical to the ListIdentifiers request, save for the different variable usage and the fact that the response request looks similar to the GetRecord response format. An example of such a request for records in the Braceros collection in the Ohio State University Libraries' institutional repository OAI-PMH server would look like: http://kb.osu.edu/oai/request?verb=ListRecords&metadataPrefix=oai_dc&set=hdl_1811_29375, and it would return the following (truncated) response:

```
<?xml version="1.0" encoding="UTF-8" ?>
<OAI-PMH xmlns="http://www.openarchives.org/OAI/2.0/" xmlns:xsi="http://www.w3.org/2001/XMLSchema-
instance" xsi:schemaLocation="http://www.openarchives.org/OAI/2.0/ http://www.openarchives.org/
OAI/2.0/OAI-PMH.xsd">
<responseDate>2017-07-30T13:07:42Z</responseDate>
<request metadataPrefix="oai_dc" verb="ListRecords" set="hdl_1811_29375">http://kb.osu.edu/oai/
request</request>
<ListRecords>
<record>
<header>
<identifier>oai:kb.osu.edu:1811/29388</identifier>
<datestamp>2011-02-22T23:26:57Z</datestamp>
<setSpec>hdl_1811_29375</setSpec>
<setSpec>hdl_1811_29376</setSpec>
<setSpec>hdl_1811_46875</setSpec>
</header>
<metadata>
<oai_dc:dc xmlns:oai_dc="http://www.openarchives.org/OAI/2.0/oai_dc/" xmlns:dc="http://purl.org/dc/
elements/1.1/" xmlns:xsi="http://www.w3.org/2001/XMLSchema-instance" xsi:schemaLocation="http://
www.openarchives.org/OAI/2.0/oai_dc/ http://www.openarchives.org/OAI/2.0/oai_dc.xsd">
<dc:title>Rentier States and International Terrorism in Ecological Focus</dc:title>
<dc:creator>Crenshaw, Edward</dc:creator>
<dc:creator>Jenkins, J. Craig</dc:creator>
<dc:subject>international security</dc:subject>
<dc:subject>sociology</dc:subject>
<dc:subject>terrorism</dc:subject>
<dc:subject>political violence</dc:subject>
<dc:subject>use of force</dc:subject>
<dc:description>
Preliminary evidence shows that rentier states are prone to producing
international terrorism. Using OPEC nations as a rough proxy for rentier
states, one can compare the number of terrorist casualties caused by
perpetrators from OPEC and non-OPEC nations.
</dc:description>
<dc:description>Research project funded in academic years 2006-07, 2007-08 and 2008-09</dc:description>
<dc:description>The University Archives has determined that this item is of continuing value to
OSU's history.</dc:description>
<dc:publisher>Mershon Center for International Security Studies</dc:publisher>
<dc:contributor>Becker, Cathy</dc:contributor>
<dc:date>2007-10-29T18:56:44Z</dc:date>
<dc:date>2007-10-29T18:56:44Z</dc:date>
<dc:date>2007</dc:date>
<dc:type>Other</dc:type>
<dc:format>97524 bytes</dc:format>
<dc:format>application/pdf</dc:format>
<dc:identifier>Mershon Center Annual Report 2006-07, p.17</dc:identifier>
<dc:identifier>http://hdl.handle.net/1811/29388</dc:identifier>
<dc:language>en_US</dc:language>
</oai_dc:dc>
</metadata>
</record>
<record>
<header>
<identifier>oai:kb.osu.edu:1811/29431</identifier>
<datestamp>2011-02-22T23:26:57Z</datestamp>
<setSpec>hdl_1811_29374</setSpec>
<setSpec>hdl_1811_29375</setSpec>
<setSpec>hdl_1811_29373</setSpec>
</header>
<metadata>
<oai_dc:dc xmlns:oai_dc="http://www.openarchives.org/OAI/2.0/oai_dc/" xmlns:dc="http://purl.org/dc/
elements/1.1/" xmlns:xsi="http://www.w3.org/2001/XMLSchema-instance" xsi:schemaLocation="http://
www.openarchives.org/OAI/2.0/oai_dc/ http://www.openarchives.org/OAI/2.0/oai_dc.xsd">
```

```
<dc:title>For Peace and Money: International Finance and the Triple Entente</dc:title>
<dc:creator>Siegel, Jennifer</dc:creator>
<dc:subject>Russian foreign debt</dc:subject>
<dc:subject>World War I</dc:subject>
<dc:description>
In For Peace and Money: International Finance and the Making and Unmaking of the
Entente Cordiale, Jennifer Siegel examines French and British bank loans to Russia
in the late imperial period, up to the Genoa Conference of 1922. The study will
help explain the ways non-governmental players were able to influence policy both
domestically and across national borders in the run-up to World War I.
</dc:description>
<dc:description>Project summary</dc:description>
<dc:description>Research project funded in academic years 2004-05, 2005-06, and 2006-07.</dc:description>
<dc:description>The University Archives has determined that this item is of continuing value to
OSU's history.</dc:description>
<dc:description>Mershon Center for International Security Studies</dc:description>
<dc:date>2007-11-05T20:32:56Z</dc:date>
<dc:date>2007-11-05T20:32:56Z</dc:date>
<dc:date>2005</dc:date>
<dc:type>Other</dc:type>
<dc:format>87068 bytes</dc:format>
<dc:format>application/pdf</dc:format>
<dc:identifier>http://hdl.handle.net/1811/29431</dc:identifier>
<dc:language>en_US</dc:language>
</oai_dc:dc>
</metadata>
</record>
</ListRecords>
</OAI-PMH>
```

### ListSets

This verb is used to identify the current list of collections, or sets, registered on an OAI-PMH server. Only the resumption-Token argument can be paired with this verb—and only when a resumptionToken is necessary to complete a ListSets request. An example of a ListSets request would look like the following: http://kb.osu.edu/oai/request?verb=ListSets, and it would return the following truncated response:

```
<?xml version="1.0" encoding="UTF-8" ?>
<OAI-PMH xmlns="http://www.openarchives.org/OAI/2.0/" xmlns:xsi="http://www.w3.org/2001/XMLSchema-
instance" xsi:schemaLocation="http://www.openarchives.org/OAI/2.0/ http://www.openarchives.org/
OAI/2.0/OAI-PMH.xsd">
<responseDate>2017-07-30T13:09:22Z</responseDate>
<request verb="ListSets">http://kb.osu.edu/oai/request</request>
<ListSets>
<set>
<setSpec>hdl_1811_77998</setSpec>
<setName>10th&#x20;Fall&#x20;Undergraduate&#x20;Research&#x20;Student&#x20;Poster&#x20;Forum
&#x20;(2016)</setName>
</set>
```

(Cont.)

```
<set>
<setSpec>hdl_1811_54723</setSpec>
<setName>13th&#x20;Denman&#x20;Undergraduate&#x20;Research&#x20;Forum&#x20;(2008)</setName>
</set>
<set>
<setSpec>hdl_1811_54722</setSpec>
<setName>14th&#x20;Denman&#x20;Undergraduate&#x20;Research&#x20;Forum&#x20;(2009)</setName>
</set>
<set>
<setSpec>hdl_1811_24843</setSpec>
<setName>1563&#x20;Edition&#x20;Selected&#x20;Stories&#x20;(John&#x20;Foxe&#39;s&#x20;Actes&#x20;
and&#x20;Monuments)</setName>
</set>
<set>
<setSpec>hdl_1811_24844</setSpec>
<setName>1563&#x20;Edition&#x20;Selected&#x20;Woodcuts&#x20;(John&#x20;Foxe&#39;s&#x20;Actes&#x20;
and&#x20;Monuments)</setName>
</set>
<set>
<setSpec>hdl_1811_24845</setSpec>
<setName>1570&#x20;Edition&#x20;Selected&#x20;Stories&#x20;(John&#x20;Foxe&#39;s&#x20;Actes&#x20;
and&#x20;Monuments)</setName>
</set>
</ListSets>
</OAI-PMH>
```

### OAI-PMH Application

With only five verbs and a limited set of arguments, OAI-PMH presents a low-barrier method for digital repositories to make their metadata harvestable to the world. And while many people, including the authors, feel that digital repositories should make their metadata harvestable to the outside world, the obvious question for digital repository implementers is, what's in it for me? Obviously, metadata harvesting requires the allocation of resources to the harvesting process, since the harvesting of large repositories could mean the transfer of hundreds of megabytes of data. The Oregon State University institutional repository, for example, requires the transfer of about fifty megabytes of data if one was to harvest all of the available metadata. This type of data transfer could very easily start to consume significant resources if harvesting was done regularly, by multiple institutions. So while harvestable metadata may make one a good neighbor within the current information ecosystem, it does come at a real cost. So what benefits can an organization glean from supporting an OAI-PMH server?

# Facilitating Third-Party Indexing

There was a time when supporting protocols like OAI-PMH would result in a higher likelihood of a digital repository being indexed by the major commercial search providers. And this still may have some truth, since OAI-PMH provides a structural entry point into a repository, and a documented method to traverse all available content. But if this occurs, it's more due to the ability of an indexer's crawler to traverse the OAI-PMH structure, rather than to any built-in support for the format. Today, most OAI-PMH harvesting is used by aggregators within the library or cultural heritage domains to build large indexes of aggregated content, with the two largest being the Digital Public Library of America (DPLA) and OCLC.

The DPLA utilizes OAI-PMH as the primary communication standard between content providers and the aggregation of discovery and index metadata related to an item. Given that OAI-PMH provides incremental harvesting based on time and the number of records, it provides the minimal functionality for the DPLA to keep metadata related to a specific collection current. OCLC, on the other hand, utilizes OAI-PMH as a method for automatically generating MARC data for items in a digital collection. Using this server, OCLC can enable users to map metadata elements harvested through the OAI-PMH interface to their MARC record equivalents. The process is messy and often produces very minimal records, but the process does enable organizations to quickly create metadata records for inclusion into OCLC's WorldCat database, which then is made available through search engines and a wide range of OCLC discovery products.

For search services outside of the library domain, indexing has moved away from OAI-PMH to other technologies like site maps or embedded linked data using formats like Schema.org. Site maps are essentially special text files that provide minimal metadata about an item and a durable URL that can be crawled and indexed. This simplifies the indexing process for search providers, particularly when working with resources that generate a lot of dynamic content or are primarily database-driven. Today, most modern digital library software supports this level of functionality.

The use of microformats, like Schema.org, enables organizations to embed linked data at the meta tag level. This information is only read by the indexer and is used to enrich their knowledge graphs within their systems, and promote relationships between content. While the use of these formats doesn't necessarily lead to better indexing, the use does enable greater findability, since the embedded microdata enables providers to better classify content and build relationships to items that might not have otherwise been obvious. For example, tagging an item about fishing on the Ohio River with a geographical tag would enable the search provider to know that this image may be relevant to a user in Ohio, regardless of whether that information shows up anywhere within the visible metadata. This kind of linking is often done outside of the library community, particularly in the business community, to easily surface and categorize information related to locations, websites, hours of operation, and types of services provided.

# Metadata Repurposing

Digital repositories supporting OAI-PMH also offer an organization a number of opportunities to repurpose metadata between various systems. Within the library community, many organizations still create MARC records for items housed within their digital repository for indexing with the organization's ILS (integrated library system). This often means that organizations are creating multiple copies of a metadata record—an original record created in MARC and a record created within the digital repository. However, by utilizing their OAI-PMH server, organizations can reduce the need for duplicate metadata creation by simply deriving all metadata surrogates from the metadata stored within the digital repository.

## *The Oregon State University Electronic Theses Process*

Like many organizations, the Oregon State University Libraries (ORST) requires graduate students to submit their thesis into the libraries' institutional repository (IR). The IR is where the primary metadata record for an individual thesis is created; however, a MARC metadata record still must be created for indexing into OCLC's WorldCat database and the local ILS. Previously, library technical services staff would simply re-create the MARC records by hand utilizing the metadata from the IR as a template. And while this process took only a handful of minutes to complete, when multiplied over the course of 50–100 documents, it was found that a significant number of resources were being used to re-create these metadata records.

In order to streamline the process of generating MARC metadata, a process was developed that allowed technical services staff to utilize the OAI-PMH server to output an item's metadata and automatically generate the necessary MARC records. Moreover, given the ability to harvest sets of records in one-month increments, the harvesting process would only need to be done at the end of each month, or twelve times a year.

To develop the process, ORST developed a custom XSLT crosswalk that is specific to the electronic theses collection[10] and MarcEdit's[11] built-in OAI-PMH harvester. Utilizing MarcEdit, library staff simply initialize the built-in OAI-PMH harvester and provide the necessary harvesting information.

Using the MarcEdit OAI-PMH harvester, technical services staff are able to set the harvesting range and the desired character set of the MARC records. In figure 7.5, one can see that MarcEdit's OAI-PMH harvester enables the user to harvest from multiple known metadata types, as well as convert XML data encoded in the UTF-8 character set into the more traditional MARC-8 character set. With the options set, staff simply run the harvester, which returns a file of generated MARC records.

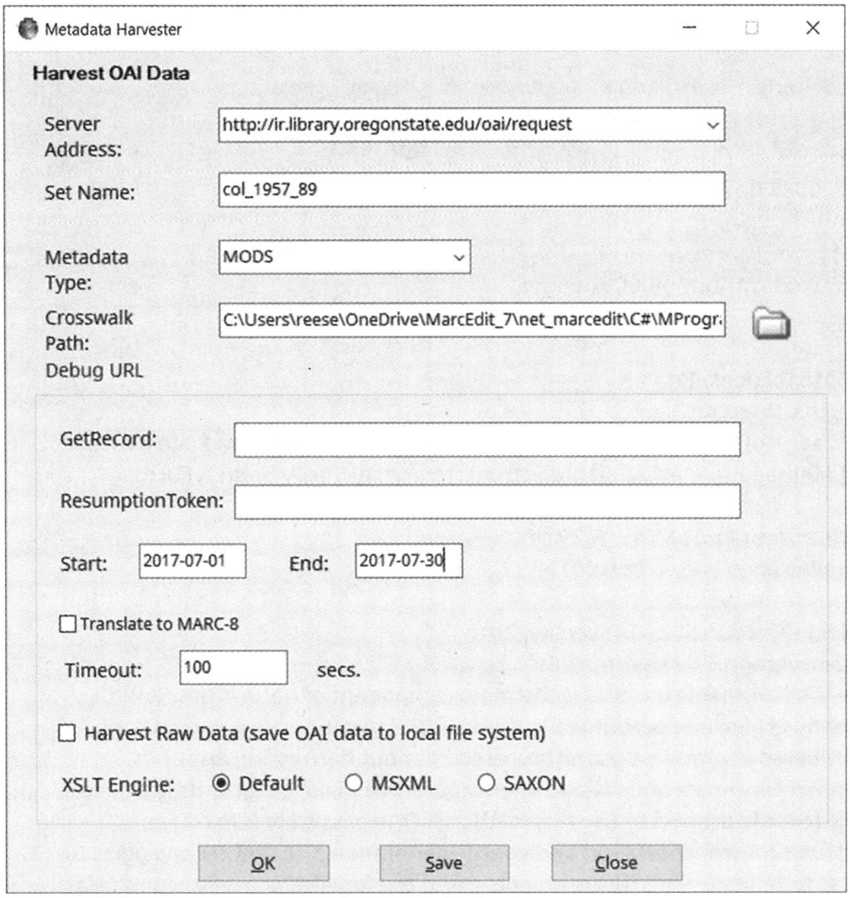

**FIGURE 7.5**

MarcEdit OAI-PMH Harvester

Once generated, files are loaded into a MarcEditor, as seen in figure 7.6. Files harvested from the IR present a number of challenges. The problems primarily fell into two categories: (1) a system process will modify an item's metadata time stamp, incorrectly marking it for harvest, and (2) both controlled and uncontrolled subject terms are stored in the same MODS element, requiring additional processing to produce a good record. Once within the MarcEditor, staff have the ability to edit records individually or globally using one of a number of built-in tools. At ORST, the process of editing the generated metadata has varied from utilizing external scripts to clean up the generated metadata content, to utilizing MarcEdit's built-in macro language to edit content strictly within the application.

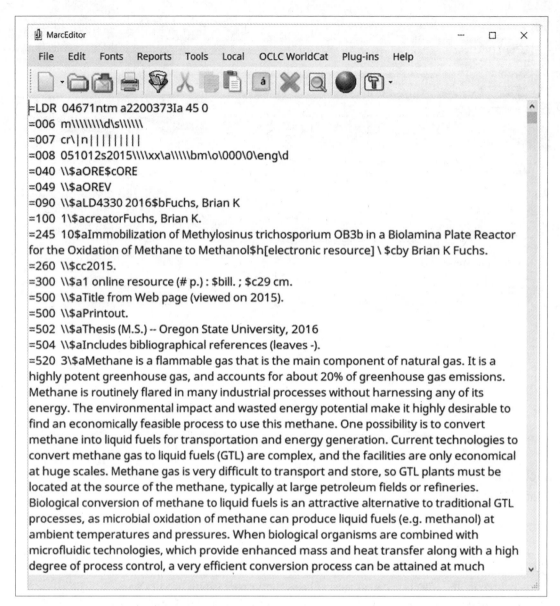

**FIGURE 7.6**

Generated Records in MarcEdit's MarcEditor

### The Ohio State University Libraries: Automatic Data Transfer of Digital Content between the Internet Archive and the HathiTrust

However, OAI-PMH isn't the only way in which data can be repurposed for use in other systems. So long as a system has a documented method for extracting data, a process can be developed around it. This has been the case with the Ohio State University Libraries' partnership with both the Internet Archive and the HathiTrust.

Like all libraries in the Big Ten, OSUL participated in the Google Book Project, providing approximately one million titles for digitization, with the digitized content being made available through the HathiTrust. When selecting materials to be digitized, the libraries used a wide range of criteria to ensure that the materials selected were of significant value, and unique to the HathiTrust. Additionally, participants had to evaluate the condition and form of the content to be digitized, since Google's process was optimized to handle only the most common material forms in fair to good condition. This meant that at the conclusion of the project, most libraries had thousands of items that were identified as good candidates for digitization, but had been disqualified due to the condition or form of the items. OSUL was no different; the libraries had identified a wide range of materials to contribute to the HathiTrust, but they would need a different workflow to digitize and upload the content.

To move the project forward, the libraries partnered with the Internet Archive. Materials were digitized with scanners, and software was purchased from the Internet Archive which would streamline depositing the materials in the Internet Archive's management system. This would allow the libraries to use the Internet Archive's OpenLibrary platform in order to provide wide access to the content. Moreover, once the content had been ingested into the Internet Archive, materials could be identified and provided to the HathiTrust through a partnership agreement between the Internet Archive and the HathiTrust. To make the transfer, OSUL would just need to generate a specially formatted XML file which included the metadata for the digitized item in MARCXML, and a specially coded set of fields that provided the necessary identifier information for the digitized materials at the Internet Archive.

In early testing, the libraries utilized staff to hand code these transfer files. MARC data would be converted to MARCXML using a range of tools, and then a staff member would code the information related directly to the Internet Archive files that were slated for data transfer. The problem was that this process didn't scale up. The libraries had identified hundreds of thousands of potential items to digitize and transfer in this manner, meaning that an automated process needed to be developed.

To facilitate the process, a plug-in was created in MarcEdit to leverage the Internet Archive search API. The Internet Archive provides an API that returns information about items in an XML format. Using this information, the libraries could create a process that would query the Internet Archive, retrieve the list of digitized materials over a specified period of time, extract the specific item data, and then automatically generate the transfer file. (See figure 7.7.)

Using the plug-in, the process for deposit shifted from a manual process that could handle a few dozen records a month to an automated process that was limited only by the organization's capacity to digitize content. And because the process was developed utilizing shared API and communication standards for both the Internet Archive and the HathiTrust, the plug-in was purposefully developed so that its use and output wouldn't be tied just to OSUL's local workflow, but would be made generic, so that it could

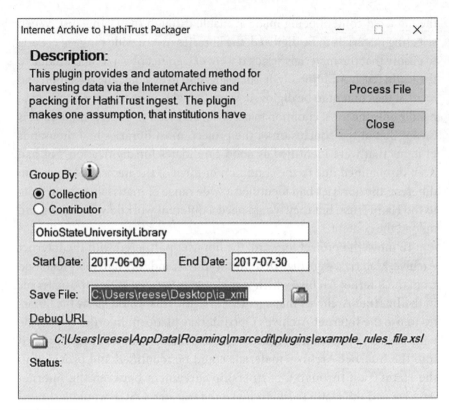

**FIGURE 7.7**

The Ohio State University Internet Archive to HathiTrust
Data Transfer Plug-in

be used by any HathiTrust partner that was using the Internet Archive for
digitization.

## Summary

Digital repositories offer the library community an opportunity to interact
with a growing number of information providers within today's information
ecosystem. This offers the library community an opportunity to build upon
its shared legacy of data-sharing and serve as an example for other members
of the information community. This means providing the technical support
needed to enable metadata harvesting, as well as giving up control over how
that metadata is used once it has been harvested. Of course, other organizations benefit from this data-sharing as well, since more of their repositories'
content will be made available to a global audience through multiple access
points. The library community and digital repository implementers should
be moving in a direction that will enable users to access content within their
chosen workflow. Finding ways to free one's metadata from the confines
of its digital repository or content management system offers a first step
towards this goal.

# Notes

1. This quote is often attributed to Steward Brand, who was recorded making this statement during a hackers conference in 1984: https://en.wikipedia.org/wiki/Information_wants_to_be_free.

2. Wikipedia, "MARC Standards," https://en.wikipedia.org/wiki/MARC_standards.

3. Europeana, www.europeana.eu/portal/en.

4. DPLA Apps, https://dp.la/apps.

5. Open Archives Initiative, "ResourceSync Framework Specification," www.open archives.org/rs/toc.

6. W3.org, "SPARQL 1.1 Query Language," www.w3.org/TR/sparql11-query/.

7. Library of Congress, "MARC2Bibframe," https://github.com/lcnetdev/marc2bib frame.

8. Tony Gill and Paul Miller, "Re-Inventing the Wheel? Standards, Interoperability and Digital Cultural Content," *D-LIB Magazine* 1, no. 1, www.dlib.org/dlib/january02/gill/01gill.html.

9. Open Archives Initiative, www.openarchives.org/OAI/openarchivesprotocol .html.

10. Terry Reese, "Oregon State University Electronic Theses Dspace (OAI-PMH) to MARC21XML Crosswalk", Oregon State University. http://hdl.handle .net/1957/6300.

11. Terry Reese, "MarcEdit," Terry Reese, http://marcedit.reeset.net.

# Access Management

**8**

Managing collections has always required managing access to them. Libraries navigate copyright and fair use issues every day when handling interlibrary loan and electronic-reserves requests. However, libraries' experience with access management is overwhelmingly from the perspective of the information consumer rather than the information publisher and distributor. Digital repositories require libraries to take on both of these roles: that of the entity which secures rights for publication, and the entity which enforces access rights for materials.

Unless your repository exclusively contains open-access resources, repository administration requires time and resources dedicated to access management. Articles and documents may need to be embargoed in order to satisfy publishers' or patent needs. Photos may need to be restricted because they contain personal or proprietary data. Access may need to be changed because signed releases have expired. Individuals and groups contributing content to the system may need to limit access to specific individuals and communities. For most repositories, access management requires balancing the rights of authors with the mission of the library.

## IN THIS CHAPTER

✓ Copyright

✓ Access Control Mechanisms

✓ Implementing Access Control

## Copyright

Unless a repository is used only for internal purposes, access management involves a copyright dimension. Copyright is a set of legislative rights that allows content creators and those they authorize to control the dissemination of their work. Copyright applies differently in different countries, particularly in regard to the types of works that can receive copyright. For example, within the United States, no materials created by local, state, or federal governments can be copyrighted, while in the United Kingdom, all government works are copyrighted as the property of the Crown. Likewise, the duration of copyrights and the applications of fair use differ, though nations have traditionally respected copyright law across borders.

Copyright is ultimately a matter of defining and managing acceptable risk—eliminating risk is not possible. No copyright law is clear enough to not be open for interpretation. Staff and content providers might not be aware of an outside party's legitimate interest in a resource. People make mistakes. Even if your repository contains only items that are within the public domain, it is still possible to encounter copyright issues, as the photographer Carol Highsmith learned in 2016 when Getty Images sent her a letter accusing her of copyright infringement and demanding payment for a photo she took and donated to the public domain.

It is important to be aware that people do not necessarily own the rights to things they create—and they may be unaware of this when they contribute materials to a repository. Especially in academic settings, authors often transfer reproduction rights to publishers, but they may not ever have had rights to the work if it was done for hire, contains proprietary information, or other circumstances apply. Fortunately, many publishers explicitly allow works to be added to institutional repositories or posted on personal web pages. However, libraries can still unknowingly infringe upon the copyright holder's reproduction and archival rights, and they need to respond quickly when this occurs.

When setting up a repository, it is also important to consider how coauthored materials will be handled. Ideally, the primary content creator submits materials. Coauthored materials require all authors to authorize the archiving and redistribution of a work. How does the organization secure these rights or ensure that the content submitter has secured redistribution rights for the repository? An organizational policy on copyright and the submission of works into the repository must define what documentation is necessary when content submitters place questionable materials into the digital repository. An organizational copyright policy helps to protect the institution in cases where proper rights were not secured, but the item was still submitted to a repository. It gives the organization a process they can follow and simplifies the submission process. What's more, organizational policy can lay out how proper documentation will be retained and stored in the case of future disputes.

As a repository evolves and becomes more widely used within an organization, questions regarding the inclusion of materials not specific to an organization or content creator are sure to come up. Can a website or a group of web documents be archived for long-term access in the digital repository? Can digitized slide collections be made available through the digital repository? The archiving and redistribution of materials for which the organization has no direct ownership or rights present a prickly problem for repository administrators, particularly if this content is not vetted.

Organizations need a clear understanding of how materials enter the digital repository, and the problems that may arise throughout the submittal process. Having a policy in place empowers repository administrators to make informed decisions regarding the types of items that can and cannot be submitted to the repository, while giving content providers a clearly documented path for submitting content. A policy helps to resolve disputes and protect both the content submitter and the digital repository from potential legal challenges over the redistribution of an item.

This book dedicates considerable discussion to planning and implementing a digital repository platform. Likewise, organizations must create an equally careful plan for addressing copyright issues with regard to the digital repository platform. As a content provider, digital repository administrators need to be concerned with issues relating to how materials are assigned copyright, as well as the access-management requirements required by specific licenses. Repository planners will also need to create a plan to deal with the inevitable problems relating to the access of individual materials. Your library can reduce its legal exposure by setting guidelines for the types of licensed content allowed in the digital repository and by creating a policy for reviewing submitted work.

Risk can be minimized if your library observes due diligence with copyright and access control issues and responds quickly to complaints. If your repository contains resources that are subject to different rights and permissions, errors will be less likely and will be easier to identify and resolve if the ingest process requires proper documentation such as releases and permission forms which are linked to individual resources.

One of the most difficult aspects of hosting a digital repository is managing the license restrictions. Today, a number of license families exist that grant or restrict a broad range of rights regarding the reproduction and use of a work. As a content provider, it is the responsibility of the digital repository to provide access mechanisms that faithfully protect a document according to the license terms supplied by the document's author. A model that allows users to set their own distribution terms will potentially prove to be untenable, since access to documents could become uneven and difficult to manage.

Organizations hosting a digital repository need to take the proactive step of defining the license terms under which authors may distribute their works within the digital repository. This means defining the types of materials the repository is willing to accept to meet its overall goals and mission. Defining these terms gives the digital repository administrator the ability to administer documents more easily, since access-management restrictions become narrowly defined by the acceptable distribution terms. The challenge for the institution comes in selecting a set of licenses that allows authors the freedom to share or restrict their work, while still meeting the goals and mission of the repository.

Fortunately, digital repository developers can use standard licenses. Standard rights statements make it easier for users to understand what they can and cannot do with a resource, and these licenses can be processed by harvesters, search engines, and computer programs.

The purpose of the repository determines which standard licenses might be most appropriate. For example, the Creative Commons license family provides a set of license options that grant the redistribution of a work or publication, but allow the author to specify terms regarding the redistribution and use of a work. Creative Commons licenses are appropriate for documents, images, and certain other resources where the author of the resource is the copyright holder and the terms of use are both simple and unchanging. The Creative Commons license family provides licensing on four separate dimensions to form six different license types, with their terms detailed at https://creativecommons.org/licenses/, plus a public domain license. These dimensions are:

**Attribution (BY):** Others who use the work in the manner requested by the author, but not in a way that suggests endorsement. Permission is required to use the work without assigning credit or implying endorsement.

**ShareAlike (SA):** Others may copy, distribute, display, perform, and modify the work, so long as all modified work is distributed on the same terms. Permission is required to distribute the work under other terms.

**NonCommercial (NC):** Others may copy, distribute, display, perform and modify the work unless NoDerivatives is also chosen for any noncommercial purpose. Permission is required for commercial use.

**NoDerivatives (ND):** Others may copy, distribute, display, and perform only original copies of the work. Permission is required to modify the work.

**Public Domain:** This allows all users to distribute, share, and modify an existing work without restrictions. The Creative Commons license is ideal for digital repositories because it makes the assumption that a work can be reproduced and shared. Since one of the primary purposes of a digital repository is to allow for the distribution of digital materials, requiring authors to acquire a Creative Commons license for inclusion within a digital repository allows the organization to solve a number of distribution-related challenges. Moreover, the Creative Commons organization itself provides a wizard at http://creativecommons.org/license/ to help authors select the specific type of Creative Commons license that best reflects how they want their materials used. For example, to make the most restrictive license that prohibits creation of derivative works, restricts all commercial use, and requires attribution as requested by the creator, the symbol and textual representation would be:

ⓒ ⓘ ⓢ ⊜ BY-NC-ND

Creative Commons licenses are an excellent choice for many repositories because:

- Creative Commons licenses are well-known and widely used outside of the library community for dealing with electronic documents.

- A number of tools embed the Creative Commons license directly into resources. For example, Microsoft and the Creative Commons organization worked together to create a plug-in specific to Microsoft Office that allows a user to automatically sign created documents with a particular Creative Commons license variant. Likewise, Open Office, and open-source productivity software, also provide a mechanism for automatically applying the Creative Commons license to created documents.

It is important to be aware that all Creative Commons licenses assume that the creator owns the copyright. It's also important to be aware that these licenses are useful only in situations where standardized messages that don't require access controls meet repository and author needs. As such, the licenses are not appropriate for a wide variety of materials, including those that:

- Have been submitted for publication and need embargoes enforced

- Contain sensitive information that must be limited to particular user communities

- Consist primarily of data. The impact of Creative Commons licenses can be unpredictable upon researchers who depend on data from many sources. When data providers dictate what research can be done, by whom, for what purposes, and how they can be combined, the effect can be to impede research.

- Are subject to terms that expire, such as releases that only allow dissemination during particular periods of time

For situations when Creative Commons licenses are not appropriate, a variety of other standard rights statements are available—including statements developed expressly for specific types of resources. For example, http://rightsstatements.org provides twelve different rights statements that are specifically designed to communicate the copyright status of cultural objects. These rights statements fall into three broad categories: those that are subject to copyright; those that are not subject to copyright; and those for which copyright is not clear. The Open Data Commons Public Domain

Dedication and License at https://opendatacommons.org/licenses/pddl/ was designed specifically for data. An organization can also create its own licenses. However, adopting widely used licenses simplifies interoperability and future migrations.

Access control and copyright controls differ significantly among repository platforms, which in turn affects what types of materials and services a repository can support. For this reason, it is important to detail the collections, users, and needed access control when selecting a repository platform as outlined in chapter 2.

## Access Control Mechanisms

Even if the purpose of your repository is to make items freely available, you'll probably need to implement access control. Graduate students may need embargo support so that their theses, dissertations, or supporting data comply with publication, research, or employment obligations. Researchers must often suppress or control all or portions of their work for reasons relating to privacy, security, or intellectual property. In a corporate setting, some materials may be unsuitable for general access. There are many scenarios in which access to submitted content may be delayed, temporarily available, or indefinitely limited to a specific user group.

Getting your repository running requires you to implement access control that meets your repository's needs. To accomplish this, you need to determine:

- Which authentication mechanisms your institution supports—including those that are not currently in use
- Which authentication mechanisms can potentially be used with the repository
- Who you need to talk to in order to implement mechanisms that will work for your repository

When implementing access control, it's important to distinguish between authentication and authorization. Authentication is the process of verifying someone's identity. For example, when you log into your computer or e-mail with a user name and password, you prove you are the owner of that user name. Authorization is the process of determining what someone may access. For example, once you log into your computer, you may only be able to see and modify certain directories and files on network drives, depending on which ones you are authorized to work with.

Repository administrators often are charged with implementing specific access-control mechanisms that provide authentication and authorization functions based on their organization's infrastructure—that is, they often have little choice over which mechanisms they can use. Libraries often serve many groups that cannot be authenticated using the library's authentication system. For example, academic libraries often serve affiliated faculty, community users, and other groups that are not in their organizational directories, so alternative mechanisms must be implemented to provide access to these users. Historically, this has been a difficult process.

Repository users usually need to access multiple services managed by the library and parent institution. You can improve security and convenience by leveraging an authentication system they already use at your institution rather than setting up and managing a new system that requires users to manage another set of credentials. Coordinating a repository's authentication with other systems can be handled in a variety of ways, depending on the specific repository platform and the authentication systems available. Today, many organizations turn to federated authentication, which allows multiple authentication systems to be used.

Access control is a complex and jargon-laden topic. This chapter discusses terms and concepts you're likely to encounter. A wide range of authentication methods exists, ranging from authentication tied directly to the repository platform, to IP authentication, to directory and SSO (single sign-on), to social media log-ins. Given the varied authentication methods utilized over a networked environment, a standard access-control mechanism such as Shibboleth, OpenID, Central Authentication Services (CAS), Lightweight Directory Access Protocol (LDAP), Athens, or a vended solution that manages multiple methods can make the authentication process simple or even transparent to the user.

As you consider authentication mechanisms for your repository, keep the following considerations in mind for each mechanism:

- What advantages does it offer?
- What disadvantages does it present?
- What systems are involved for the purposes of providing data and authentication services, and who maintains them?
- What policy and technical prerequisites must be satisfied to implement the system?
- Who needs to be involved in its implementation?
- How difficult is it to set up and how long will that take?
- How difficult is it to maintain?
- What users is it unable to provide access for, and what alternatives will be available?
- What additional data or functionality does it require to function? For example, if patrons authenticate via SSO, what data will you need to augment repository accounts with, and how will you include this information?

## Lightweight Directory Access Protocol (LDAP)

LDAP is an application protocol for querying specialized directory services such as Active Directory (AD). Although LDAP itself is only a protocol, the term "LDAP" is often used to refer to directory services that can be queried with LDAP. Directory services are used to manage a wide array of objects, but for repository purposes, they can be thought of as specialized databases that are used for authentication and storing information about users and groups.

LDAP can be relatively convenient and secure because it can maintain credentials centrally outside of the repository. LDAP is commonly used for authentication—particularly for e-mail services and address books, and it is particularly useful as an authentication mechanism because it often reveals information about the user or the structure of the organization, thus allowing the assignment of role- or group-based permissions. Having said this, LDAP authentication often faces the following challenges:

- LDAP requires users to log in for each service separately, so they may be prompted for the same credentials multiple times for each additional service they access.
- Repository software often cannot leverage user attributes or organizational units in LDAP records for access control.
- If the library does not control the LDAP server:

  Organizational units or attributes are defined differently than needed by the library

  Getting all necessary users included can become a political as well as a technical complication

  The LDAP server may contain individuals who should not have permissions, and these cannot be distinguished from those who should

- If the repository is hosted, campus or organizational regulations may prohibit outside connections to the LDAP server.

### Single Sign-On (SSO)

Many institutions support single sign-on (SSO) authentication—so named because the user only needs to log in once to access multiple systems. SSO is like "cloud computing" in that the term has no specific technical meaning. Rather, SSO refers to a property of how authentication systems can be used. A few of the most common SSO implementations are discussed in this section, but dozens are available as of this writing and can be found listed at https://en.wikipedia.org/wiki/List_of_single_sign-on_implementations.

For example, a Shibboleth SSO might query Microsoft Active Directory services using the LDAP protocol to allow users to authenticate once in order to access multiple systems without being prompted for new credentials. Theoretically, SSO can be used to authenticate virtually anything, and Shibboleth can consult multiple authentication systems. In this example, SSO can only authenticate users in Active Directory. This means you still have to figure out how to authenticate users who are not in Active Directory, but those who are in Active Directory will only have to log in once rather than retype their credentials each time they access a new service, as they would had the repository queried Active Directory using LDAP to authenticate users.

If your organization offers SSO that is supported by your repository, SSO offers a better user experience and better security than the alternatives, so it is normally the preferred access mechanism.

SSO provides the following benefits:

- Users can log in with credentials they use for other services, and once they've logged into an SSO service, they won't be asked to log in again when they access another SSO service.

- Users can access multiple systems (including LDAP), allowing more flexibility in the authentication process.

- Sensitive information such as user passwords is not stored in the repository system and is therefore not a security burden for the repository itself.

### Central Authentication Service (CAS)

CAS is an open source protocol for SSO authentication that validates users against a database such as LDAP. CAS centralizes authentication and is appropriate if you want to ask all users to log into a single service. CAS is easier to implement than Shibboleth, though it has less functionality because it cannot express user attributes as richly, nor does it have federated capabilities. However, it is a good option when available if it meets the needs at hand.

### Security Assertion Markup Language (SAML)

SAML is similar to CAS in that it is also an open source protocol developed for SSO that can authenticate using a number of forms of authentication, including LDAP. The important difference between SAML and CAS is that SAML has federated authentication and better authorization capabilities. SAML is most commonly used with Shibboleth. If you are using SAML only for authentication, it may be easier to implement CAS if you have a choice in the matter.

### Shibboleth

Shibboleth is similar to CAS in that both are open source technologies that can be used to implement SSO. However, it is different from CAS in multiple respects:

- Shibboleth is a service that relies on the SAML protocol while CAS is a protocol.

- Shibboleth is designed for sharing authentication data between organizations in a distributed environment, so it federates authentication and distributes the management of user information across organizations over the SAML protocol to exchange authentication and authorization data.

- Shibboleth is generally more difficult to configure than CAS.

### OpenID

OpenID is different from SAML or CAS in that there's no trust relationship with the provider—you accept whatever it tells you and associate with a placeholder identifier in the repository. Like Shibboleth, OpenID is a federated identification management protocol. However, it differs from Shibboleth in several key respects. First, OpenID has been designed under the premise that user-identification management can function essentially like a URI. Within the OpenID model, a user signs in using a unique URI, which is resolved by a service run either by the user or by the authenticating organization. Like Shibboleth, the protocol defines how user information is securely transmitted between resources, as well as what attributes are needed to authenticate users between targets. What makes OpenID different from many other authentication services is the notion of a secure URI that acts as a user's user name and password. Within the OpenID model, the URI provides the authentication mechanism for the protocol, meaning that how one proves ownership of the URI directly relates to how authentication is verified within the system.

### OAuth and Social Media Authentication

OAuth allows third parties such as social media services to authenticate to another system. Unlike OpenID, which has a primary purpose of authentication in a web environment, the primary purpose of OAuth is to allow users to permit API authorization for application. As such, the two are complementary.

An example of a repository application of OAuth would be that a user would authenticate using a social media account and then be asked for permission to share her e-mail address with the repository software. Upon the user granting that permission, the e-mail address would be matched to an account.

OAuth and social media authentication offer the following advantages:

- Many users won't be asked for credentials after logging in because simply being logged in to their favorite services grants them access.

- If your organization won't allow vendors outside your firewall to connect to your LDAP or other authentication system, OAuth offers another way to allow users to associate an organizational network address with a password they remember.

- These mechanisms can often be used instead of local authentication for users who cannot be authenticated with SSO or the preferred mechanism, and so they are potentially an attractive option even for organizational users.

However, OAuth also possesses disadvantages as well:

- A separate mechanism must be used to manage accounts because only authentication is provided. Functionality authorizing who can access what, when, and how must be developed separately.

- Users may not have accounts on any of the OAuth or social media services your repository supports. If they do have accounts, they may be unwilling to link them.

- Allowing even a user name or e-mail from an unapproved third-party service may violate organizational policy.

## Athens

Athens is fundamentally different from Shibboleth and OpenID in that it is proprietary as well as both a communications protocol and authentication scheme. Whereas Shibboleth is a distributed authentication service, Athens is a centralized authentication service. Within the Athens framework, there is a single authentication origin that authorizes all incoming requests from a target resource that provides centralized user administration. In addition, it's important to note that unlike Shibboleth and OpenID, which are both open source projects that can be used with diverse systems, Athens is a commercial authentication method that can only be utilized by products that support it.

## Active Directory

Active Directory is a commercial product developed by the Microsoft Corporation that is widely used to provide authentication and authorization services in Windows environments, but it also supports directory, domain, rights management, certificate, and federated services. Active Directory can provide SSO services, and it can also work in concert with a variety of proprietary and open source technologies to provide directory services.

## Internal Authentication

Most systems support local users who are authenticated by a password. However, this mechanism is undesirable except when the system is intended for a small number of regular users because of the administrative overhead it entails for repository managers and users who have to keep track of yet another account. In addition to administrative concerns, best security practice is to avoid storing any information about staff and users that isn't absolutely essential.

Even if your organization supports SSO or another convenient form of authentication, you may need to create internal accounts that are associated with user names from those other systems. For example, if the group attributes in your organization's Shibboleth or LDAP services don't correspond with your access control needs, the group attributes need to be defined in the local system and associated with local user names, which in turn are authenticated by Shibboleth, LDAP, or some other service.

## IP-Based Authentication

Many systems support IP authentication, and even those that don't can often be made to do so via web server configuration. IP authentication is easy to implement, but it presents the following challenges:

- IP addresses are associated with computers rather than individuals.
- IP numbers for computers are subject to change.
- IP authentication fails when users or staff connect from an unexpected address. This can be mitigated with a proxy server, but then everyone who logs into the proxy server has the same address.
- On a related note, firewalls and Network Address Translation (NAT) require assigning the same permissions to all people from a particular IP address whether or not they should all have the same permissions.
- IP authentication is a rough tool that is normally used to control access to entire areas of a system rather than provide more fine-grained permissions.

## Vended Authentication

A variety of vended authentication options are available that support individual or multiple methods outlined above, as well as others. Commercial services can allow libraries to support multiple authentication methods with much lower overhead and expertise. Some libraries may be able to authenticate repository use by leveraging products they've already purchased for other purposes such as proxying. Make sure your organization's policies and security practices allow connections with local and vended services and exposure to user data before assuming that this is a viable option.

# Implementing Access Control

The process of setting up access control varies greatly with the repository and its needs, where and how it's hosted, what mechanisms your organization supports and how they're set up, your relationship with those responsible for working on the repository, and the organizational goal. As such, the process of implementing access control normally involves the following basic steps:

- Ensuring communication between those charged with technical implementation and those providing authentication for the organization.

- Setting up the accounts and and groups that are needed to achieve the necessary functionality. For example, even if your organization supports SSO, a mechanism for associating those accounts with appropriate privileges and groups needs to be set up in the repository, which may require semiautomated or even manual work.

- Configuring and testing authentication in the repository. Testing requires verifying that:

  All users are in expected groups

  If multiple authentication mechanisms are necessary, the process for logging in is clear

  Everyone can sign in

  SSO and external authentication systems link with repository accounts properly

  Permissions function properly at individual and group levels

  All aspects of the account life cycle can be performed. Accounts can be created, maintained, disabled, archived, or deleted as required by library and institutional requirements as users come and go.

Unless your repository provides the exact same access to everyone who can authenticate with an external system, you will need some mechanism to add user data to the system. Some users such as staff and community users may need to be added manually, but others may require data loads. In the case that data loads are necessary, you need:

- A unique identifier that serves as a match point with the authentication system. Under most circumstances, this is straightforward because you can use a network name, but be aware that these can change (e.g., when they change their real name).

- A mechanism to extract data from the source system
- To transform the data into a format the repository can understand
- A mechanism to load the data into the repository

Setting up authentication is usually fairly simple in terms of the number of steps involved and the technical complexity of implementing those steps. However, access control is also very detail-oriented, so tiny details often have a huge impact on how well authentication and authorization work—and if they work at all.

# Thinking about Discovery

**The ability to create,** store, and curate digital content means very little if robust access and discoverability aren't a key part of the system. In this respect, digital preservation and library systems are very different from their analog cousins. For example, consider a book on a shelf. If one takes the book and reshelves it into a different location in the library, access is definitely affected. But unlike digital content, access isn't completely removed. Users could still find the book, or the library may stumble across the material during an annual shelf reading. The point is, the physical content is still accessible to the user. Digital content is very different in this respect. Because the digital object has no physical placeholder, items that are not indexed simply don't exist. The same is true for items that cannot be found. While serendipitous discovery does happen in the digital space, it cannot happen when materials are invisible to the user. Content must be discoverable if it is to be accessible to users. But unlike the past, concerns related to discovery are no longer limited to one's local system or environment. Current research shows that most users discover digital content not through the systems in which they are housed, but from outside tools like search engines.[1,2] At the Ohio State University Libraries, this is reflected in how users access content in the libraries' institutional repository. Access logs demonstrate that search engines, particularly Google, direct most users to content on the system. This means that one needs to think about discovery very differently, or at least view discovery beyond the horizons of one's own local organizational web presence.

In earlier chapters, this book has discussed the necessity of having a cohesive collection development policy in place in order to ensure a logical development of collections within the digital repository. This ensures that the digital repository doesn't become a virtual attic full of cobwebs and stale materials—but is constantly being refreshed and weeded as the collection continues to grow.

In the same manner, responsible digital repository administrators need to consider what level of discovery their digital repository will support. In chapter 6, a great deal of attention was given to the development of services around a digital repository and the benefits associated with allowing the harvesting of one's repository's metadata. The sharing of metadata goes a long way towards promoting the open-access culture that the library community continues to cultivate—but it doesn't relate directly to discovery. In many cases, individuals will harvest and reindex metadata to create new research tools or services, offering yes, a separate set of access points, but providing the content within a different contextual framework. Ultimately, allowing the sharing and harvesting of metadata requires organizations to give up some level of control over the metadata and content as individuals mix and mash their services with other materials.

Discovery is a different animal altogether. While metadata harvesting does promote the discovery of materials within different contexts and services, it's not explicitly used, nor should it be solely relied upon, for outside discovery. Successful digital repositories offer a multiplicity of discovery avenues—allowing users the ability to choose the searching methodology. Digital repository administrators need to consider what additional searching protocols they are willing to support to provide the necessary access points for both users and what we today refer to as "federated searching." In some cases, support for library protocols like SRU/W or OpenURL may be provided by the digital repository software platform—but if not, what and how is support added? Likewise, does the organization wish to support emerging search protocols from outside the library community like OpenSearch, or create locally developed RESTful API, or leverage new open standards like SPARQL? Ultimately, the question that repository owners need to consider is how any of these services will benefit users and aid in the long-term findability of the organization's content. Likewise, how does a digital repository administrator decide what legacy protocols to continue to support, and when should these legacy protocols be deemed obsolete? Repository administrators have a wide range of potential protocols and search standards that could be supported by their repository software— meaning that an evaluation of how the repository will be searched should be conducted to meet this need. This chapter, however, will highlight many of the protocols that are most often supported within the library community, and it will describe the current crop of federated search software packages.

## Unpacking Discovery?

Before we jump too far ahead in this chapter, we need to deal with the sticky issue of discovery. Within the current literature, the terms "federated search," "metasearching," "integrated searching," "cross-database searching," "parallel searching," "discovery systems," and likely many other terms are all utilized to represent the same set of concepts. For the purposes of this book, the terms "discovery," "metasearch," and "federated search" will be used interchangeably to represent the same set of technologies and concepts. So, what is a discovery system? Well, it depends on the type of system being evaluated. Discovery systems tend to fall into one of three categories of systems: federated systems, hybrid systems, and managed systems.

Federated search systems provide a normalized method for searching multiple databases through a single query. It's important to note that conceptually, federated search systems have been available for a very long time. Since the late 1990s, a number of federated search systems have been used within the library community[3] and outside the library community.[4] Federated search tools like OCLC's SiteSearch and search engine metasearch tools like Metacrawler are good examples of these early federated search tools. These tools served as a searching portal, allowing users to query a large number of resources through a single interface.

In figure 9.1, we see a diagram of a traditional federated search system. These systems utilize a single query form that sits on top of the actual federated search engine. This engine handles the actual communication with the various databases to be queried. Moreover, this engine will traditionally handle tasks related to normalizing the resulting information from the various databases. This would include handling tasks like sorting, merging, and deduping the results from various databases. Today, this diagram has changed slightly. With the advent of OAI (Open Archive Initiative) and other metadata-harvesting protocols, many federated search systems have become hybrid search systems—harvesting, normalizing, and locally indexing metadata for some systems—while maintaining the broadcasting search components for resources that cannot be harvested.

Hybrid federated search systems, as diagrammed in figure 9.2, utilize a local data store to improve indexing and response time. These systems use a just-in-case philosophy and harvest, index, and normalize metadata from a set of diverse databases prior to the user's query, in much the same way that a web search engine crawls and indexes the Web. Today, many libraries use the hybrid search method when creating "bento"-style discovery systems. These tools mix locally indexed content with content retrieved via APIs to generate a contextual-based discovery experience. This approach is somewhat unique to the library community, in that it seeks to replicate the different silos of library content, recognizing that library content is very difficult to surface without some context placed around the results. This approach attempts to provide that context by shifting the results paradigm from a long list of results to content buckets that are separated by the type of material being queried.

Managed systems work by indexing all content into a central index, as diagrammed in figure 9.3. Unlike federated or hybrid systems, managed systems harvest and index all content locally,

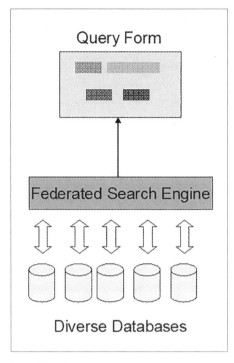

**FIGURE 9.1**

Federated Search Diagram

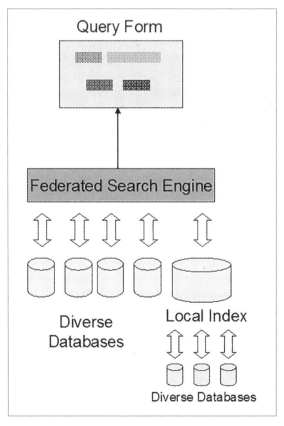

**FIGURE 9.2**

Hybrid Federated Search Diagram

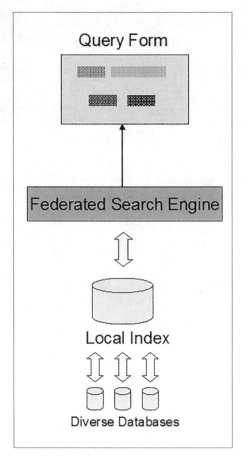

**FIGURE 9.3**
Managed Search Diagram

allowing the service to create specialized indexing, facets, and ancillary services around the content being mined. Outside the library community, search engines are excellent examples of a managed search. Search engines utilize crawlers to capture and index websites. One of the direct benefits of this approach is that managed systems provide total control over issues like relevancy, indexing, and query languages. At the same time, the primary disadvantage is that unless the content is indexed, it cannot be found. Within the library community, this is very much how third-party comprehensive discovery tools work. Tools like ProQuest's Summon or EBSCOhosts's EDS index large sets of library content. These tools provide a high level of relevance and speed to the user, but the search is limited to the content that has been indexed.

## Federated Search and Digital Libraries

How federated search fits into the larger picture of digital libraries may not be readily apparent at first glance. For most organizations, how a federated search product will interact with their digital repository infrastructure is likely the farthest thing from their minds—but by neglecting this consideration, they put their digital collections at a distinct disadvantage and ultimately shortchange their users' overall experience. Federated search tools are often thought of only in relation to electronic serial content. Organizations purchase access to thousands of journals online, and federated search tools have been springing up since 2000 that promise to provide a single search interface for all of these resources. However, as a digital repository program develops, collections and projects will often become siloed. The development of these information silos is often unintended, and often occurs because of funding sources or software platform choices. For example, an organization may use DSpace for their electronic theses collection, use Sufia to house their archival image collection, and use ArchivesSpace to house their EAD content. Separated by software platform, each of these projects represents three separate interfaces that a user would need to query in order to locate content from these digital projects. These separate interfaces marginalize these collections by placing them outside of the organization's mainstream query interface. What's more, this would represent three new query interfaces existing on top of a library's traditional search tools like the integrated library system and electronic journal pages. In all, a user may have to search 8 to 10 different locations just to cast a net that is broad enough to query most of the important organizational resources for a topic.

While federated search tools certainly have the ability to provide a more unified search interface for vended serial content, they are probably best suited for the unification of discovery for locally developed digital collections. This is due in large part to the fact that an organization has the ability to control how outside resources interact with its local tools. This can give institutions the ability to create or support standard web services' APIs to enable better integration with their federated search software. Likewise, local digital projects are more likely to accommodate local data harvesting, enabling tools to harvest collections into a single repository for faster searching.

Digital repository programs can also take advantage of a federated search program to expand their acquisition and collection development resources. Many digital repository developers will often make the mistake of considering only their organization's digital content and projects as "collectable" digital resources. However, a good federated search program allows an organization to fully utilize digital collections from not just its own digital resources but digital resources from other organizations, removing the barriers of organizational ownership and distance for its patrons. This allows users at one organization to query resources from not only their institution, but from selected digital collections held by other institutions. In this way, an organization could potentially leverage the Library of Congress's American Memory Project and OAIster alongside local and vended content. Finally, federated search tools offer an organization the ability to provide value-added services for its users. Federated search tools can allow organizations to capture search history and document click-counts in order to augment their ranking algorithms and provide context to search results.

## Why Think about Discovery

Given the improvements made by search engines like Google and Bing, one is left to wonder if organizations still need to provide their own discovery systems. Within the library community, discovery tools have traditionally been used to link vended content with other resources—which to some degree is starting to happen at the search engine level through Google Scholar and other aggregated research-focused portals. Given the development of these portals, should local discovery even be a consideration for digital library administrators? The answer would be a resounding yes. While traditional search engines continue to do a better job of indexing and surfacing academic content, the reality is that large swaths of digital content remain outside of their view. Whether this information is vended content purchased by the library or is in locally managed digital collections, organizations must make an active effort to ensure that content is discoverable by these tools—and even then, there is no guarantee that one's materials will show up when queried. Certainly, organizations should be actively working to ensure that their content is accessible and indexable within the traditional search engine infrastructure—but these systems utilized closed relevancy algorithms that make it difficult to know how one's content will be searched. The best way to ensure that local content remains findable is to create a local discovery system that works hand in hand with the traditional search engine systems. By producing content that will work in both, organizations can improve their chances of being indexed and optimize their content for ease of discovery.

## Current Research

While the concept of federated searching and discovery systems is not new, active participation by libraries in the creation of new ways of displaying and conceptualizing the user's experience with a discovery system is a relatively recent phenomenon . . . and we'd argue a welcome one. Prior to the entry of library-vended discovery systems, cultural heritage institutions led the way in developing new ways of visualizing the search and retrieval of heterogeneous content. But around 2006, this changed; content providers like EBSCOhost and ProQuest developed large managed discovery tools that worked directly with academic content providers to enable libraries to do full-text searching of nearly all of their vended content. These tools represented a leap forward, and essentially stopped much of the homegrown development and research that had been occurring around discovery system development.

Interestingly, this started to change around 2010 when North Carolina State University introduced users to its bento search experience. Leveraging both vended and local data stores, NC State challenged the current paradigm by providing results in contextual buckets rather than in a long list . . . and the approach worked. Since that point, cultural heritage institutions have reentered the fray, doing new and exciting research around results management, linked data usage, language agents, and much more.

### Recommender/collaborative filtering

Current federated search services query preselected or user-selected groups of information. This assumes that the user community making use of a particular tool consists of expert users or others who are familiar with the resources being queried. One of the strengths of federated search is the ability to serendipitously discover information within larger datasets—something that the current crop of federated search tools does poorly. Within the federated search community, there is a current drive to understand how the collaborative filtering of results and databases can lead to a better understanding of how target databases can be transparently selected or recommended to the user based on query terms.

### Deduplication of results

Most of the current generation of federated search tools currently provide some form of deduplication of items from a given results set. However, how each tool provides this deduplication service varies in both technique and effectiveness. Given the varied nature of data recovery from target databases, deduplication techniques based solely on titles, dates, or authors are prone to be spotty at best. Federated search developers continue to research better and more normalized methods for providing better deduplication of resources and ways of displaying duplicate results.

### Knowledge-base management

Before vendors' federated search systems became mainstream, a number of larger academic institutions like the University of California system created and managed their own federated search tools. However, many of these tools have since been abandoned due to the fact that the creation and long-term management of the knowledge base is expensive and time-consuming, given that available content and providers are always rapidly changing. Vendor-based solutions provided a method to outsource much of the technical knowledge-base management to a third party. Even with this outsourcing, knowledge base management still consumes a great deal of time for organizations—making this an area that federated search vendors are constantly looking to improve. Within the open source community, this issue is also getting attention, as researchers looking to develop community-oriented federated search tools are examining methods to create shared knowledge-base systems[5] in order to reduce management tasks for all users.

### Automatic data classification

As hybrid discovery systems become more widely utilized, a growing need for the automated classification of resources will continue to develop. Given the varied nature of access points, vocabulary, and classification, research relating to the normalization and automatic classification of items based on concepts is a growing field of research for federated search developers. What's more, large aggregators like VIAF provide a tremendous opportunity to mine local data and enrich that content through the building of linked data relationships. Tools like VIAF could possibly enable discovery system developers to create new methods for building facets and classifying content, while at the same time developing infrastructure to enable local systems to close the data loop and provide reciprocal relationship information as open data.

### Ranking systems

All discovery systems provide some methodology for doing some relevance ranking of items within a result set. However, often this ranking is user-initiated, and done after the items have been queried. Given the inherent speed limitations built into a broadcast search system, federated systems traditionally print results as they are returned from target databases, meaning that unlike traditional search engines which provide the most relevant items at the beginning of a results set, federated search systems require some user interaction to replicate that result. What's more, given the varied nature of the data returned by target resources, ranking items within a larger result set can be a challenge in and of itself, and this continues to be fertile ground for further research and discovery.

### Development of language agents

Cultural heritage organizations' primary research and user communities are more diverse and international than ever before. This diversity has significant benefits, since new users are approaching the evaluation of primary digital content from a wider cultural lens. At the same time, it has exposed some significant challenges, particularly in the United States, where materials and metadata are overwhelmingly available only in English. This lack of language diversity has a major impact on the findability of content for users, creating significant barriers to access for many within the international community.

To address these challenges, research into the development of language agents seeks to build a bridge between users and systems, and to overcome traditional language barriers. This work is possible due to the continued improvement of the real-time translation services that are being used to power personal digital assistants. Both Google and Microsoft are investing significant resources in the development of artificial intelligence services to power their personal digital assistants. Researchers interested in language development have benefited from this work, since both Google and Microsoft provide open web services to interact with these systems. This has enabled researchers to delve into the creation of intelligent agents that could be used to improve the library discovery experience by removing language as a barrier to discovery. The work is still in its initial stages, but this seems like fertile ground for continued development.

## Searching Protocols

As the library community has become more dependent on new and emerging technologies to deliver and maintain services, so too have libraries found themselves becoming more dependent on specific technical metadata standards and protocols. Chapters 5 and 6 discussed the library community's current reliance on XML and XML-based metadata schemas within current-generation digital repositories for bibliographic description. These chapters discussed the various ways that XML-centric metadata systems are changing the way that systems and individuals can interact with their descriptive data, and the chapters discuss the major technologies currently being utilized in conjunction with these XML-centric descriptive systems. Likewise, the library community has come to rely on a specific set of communication protocols to allow the remote searching of local systems.

Since the late 1990s, the library community has seen an explosion in the number of communication protocols being utilized for library services. Protocols like LDAP for authentication, OAI for data harvesting, and OpenURL and DOI for linking are playing a key role in how the library of the twenty-first century interacts with its users. And what's more, for the first time, the library community isn't just looking within its own community, but is looking outside of that community for communication and data transfer protocols that are easy to implement and can provide a robust level of search and integration. Digital repository administrators need to carefully consider both what communication protocols they wish to support, and at what level they want to support real-time federated searches of their content. Given the array of protocols available, this analysis will focus on the three search protocols that enjoy the widest support within the library community and beyond: Z39.50, SRU/W, and OpenSearch. While other protocols exist, these three protocols are nearly universally supported by federated search systems and provide a great deal of flexibility in terms of query support and metadata formats.

## Z39.50

Z39.50 is the grandfather of federated searching within the library community. The protocol traces its roots back to the early 1970s as a way for large bibliographic databases like the Library of Congress and OCLC to share bibliographic data between systems. In 1979, a National Information Standards Organization committee was formed to investigate the development of a standard data protocol that could facilitate bibliographic data-sharing. These efforts culminated in the development of Z39.50–1988, or Z39.50 Version 1. As documented later by Clifford Lynch,[6] Version 1 was basically a theoretical concept draft that was virtually unimplementable. In retrospect Lynch, one of the original members of the Z39.50 committee, would call the first Z39.50 draft an utter fiasco that should never have been approved by the committee.[7] Following the approval of Version 1, the Library of Congress was appointed as the maintenance agency for the protocol.

The protocol was subsequently revised again in 1992 (Z39.50–1992), expanding the protocol's capabilities and borrowing heavily from work that was internationally published as ISO 10162/10163. However, like the previous version of the protocol, Z39.50 was still tied to the OSI framework. The OSI (Open Systems Interconnection) model is a seven-layered conceptual

| Application |
|:---:|
| Presentation |
| Session |
| Transport |
| Network |
| Data Link |
| Physical |

**FIGURE 9.4**

OSI Model

model that describes how information moves from the application level in an environment, through the network level, and to the application level of a target (see figure 9.4).

For practical purposes, the Z39.50–1992 draft was practically unimplementable due to the draft's continued reliance on the OSI framework—particularly a desire to make use of the presentation layer within the OSI model. This coupling hamstrung developers, and continued to be a barrier for implementation. Recounting his work with the Z39.50 community, Clifford Lynch notes:

> By 1992, it was already clear to most implementers that OSI had failed, but this was not yet a politically acceptable statement within international standards bodies or certain US government and library circles. There was at least one OSI-based implementation of Z39.50–1992, which was developed but never exercised because there was nobody to talk to—and no way of talking to anyone. To move Z39.50 from theory to practice it was necessary to move it into the TCP/IP based environment of the Internet, despite the political controversy that this would entail.[8]

Given OSI's failure to gain traction, CNI initiated the development of Z39.50 over a TCP/IP connection, leading to the subsequent revision (Version 3) in 1995. Z39.50–1995 (Version 3) expanded the available attribute set for searching, and also provided guidelines for implementing Z39.50 over a TCP/IP connection.[9] These changes allowed Z39.50 to be utilized for the first time in widespread deployment by software and content developers alike within the library community. Z39.50–1995 was quickly adopted by the major library ILS vendors and became the standard by which records could be shared and contributed to remote library systems. Content providers would later provide support for Z39.50 as a means for building citation applications and facilitating basic levels of remote searching in the content repositories. Citation software like EndNote would later be developed as a robust citation management application utilizing Z39.50 to query and retrieve metadata about specific titles within a database.

So, what is Z39.50? Z39.50 is a stateful connection between a client (or origin) and a server (target). Z39.50 supports two levels of search—what are known as a SCAN and a SEARCH. SCAN requests retrieve result sets containing minimal metadata—basically an item's title. These requests provide a quick mechanism for retrieving a results list within a selected target. Once an item has been selected, a request for the full item's metadata can be made on the server. The second type of request is SEARCH. A SEARCH differs from a SCAN request in regard to the data being made available within the results set. Unlike a SCAN request, which returns a list of item titles, a SEARCH request returns the entire metadata record for each item within the results set.

Given the nearly universal support for the Z39.50 protocol within the library community, one would think that the protocol has been a stunning success—but this is not necessarily the case. While Z39.50 is widely supported within the library community, the protocol itself has failed to realize its full potential. Even in the absence of viable alternatives, Z39.50 has remained more of a fringe protocol, supported primarily in response to the perceived need within the library community for its support, rather than the actual utilization of the protocol. In part, this is due to the complexity of the protocol itself. In the not too distant past, adding Z39.50 support required the development of a Z39.50 server, including components for encoding and decoding/encoding ASN.1/BER messages between the host and target. Given the obscure nature of the protocol (i.e., it is used primarily by the library community), this process was often a major barrier to implementation, since only a handful of individuals outside of the vendor community knew how to create the necessary components to utilize the protocol. What's more, the protocol itself is expensive in terms of the system resources that need to be deployed. And with that said, Z39.50 has enjoyed a reawakening of sorts—though this time, outside of the library community. Within the GIS (geographic information systems) community, the Z39.50 protocol is being used to build shared information networks like the Federal Geographic Data Committee (www.fgdc.gov) and to create small organizational networks through GIS software solutions that use Z39.50 as the networking protocol.[10]

While issues relating to the relatively expensive nature of the Z39.50 protocol have not been significantly overcome, adding support for the protocol has no longer become the primary barrier to implementation. This is thanks largely to the open-source library community and the development of a number of toolkits designed specifically for the integration of Z39.50. Much of the credit for the simplification of the Z39.50 protocol goes to the ZOOM[11] (Z39.50 Object-Oriented Model) initiative. Started in 2001, the ZOOM initiative defined a set of object-oriented APIs that has been adapted and ported to a wide variety of development languages. Toolkits such as YAZ[12] (Yet Another Z39.50 component) have provided the open source community with professional tools for creating or interacting with a Z39.50 server. Code examples utilizing these components can be found in numerous languages like PHP,[13] Ruby,[14] PERL,[15] C#,[16] and so on. Digital repository administrators looking to implement Z39.50 support in their repositories now have a simple set of toolkits that can be plugged into their repository software, allowing quick Z39.50 integration. Of course, nowadays one must evaluate if Z39.50 support is still valuable to one's user community, since more Internet-friendly protocols have begun to emerge and find a footing within the library community.

## SRU/SRW

While Z39.50 has been and continues to be an important protocol within the library and digital library communities, the protocol's reliance on ASN.1/BER encoding makes it incompatible with the various XML-based systems that are being developed today. And while many tools continue to support and rely primarily on Z39.50, the execution and processing of the protocol is disruptive, since these resources cannot be fully integrated into an XML-based system. Moreover, while Z39.50 does include authentication control mechanisms, they pale in comparison to the authentication methodology currently being developed and deployed within today's current-generation web services. In response, the Z39.50 International Maintenance Agency began the development of ZING, the next generation of Z39.50. ZING was to be an XML-based, object-oriented form of Z39.50 that could be utilized within today's web services infrastructure. Originally developed as a web services protocol, ZING was eventually expanded and renamed as SRU/SRW.

SRU (Search/Retrieval URL) and SRW (Search/Retrieval Web Service) represent the next generation in Z39.50 development. It's important to note that SRU/W was not developed with the intent to supersede the Z39.50 protocol, but to provide a protocol that would give users and developers easier access to bibliographic data. SRU/W continues to share a number of concepts with Z39.50, most notably the EXPLAIN, SEARCH, and SCAN services—as well as retaining data in results sets.

### EXPLAIN

The SRU/W EXPLAIN protocol provides developers with an avenue for querying a server for the types of metadata schemas and query methods currently supported by the server. Moreover, this option provides users with administrative information about the server—providing contact information and information relating to the current configuration of the SRU/W instance. While this command set can be utilized by developers attempting to design a service around an SRU/W server, its greatest use is as an automatic discovery method for machine-to-machine processing. Since SRU/W utilizes a form of response structure, automated processes, much like the web crawlers used by search engines, can be used to automatically capture and utilize an SRU/W server's configuration information for current and future queries.

### SCAN

The SCAN command is a holdover from Z39.50, providing access to a quick hits list. SCAN searches return a minimal amount of metadata (primarily title and creator), as well as information regarding the number of items in the SCAN list. Within Z39.50, the SCAN command provided a lightweight mechanism for querying a Z39.50 server for fast results, forgoing the more time- and research-intensive process of retrieving actual datasets. However, within the SRU/W context, the SCAN command's value is lessened due to the inexpensive nature of the request, coupled with the absence of a significant performance penalty for retrieving an item's full metadata.

### SEARCH

Like the SCAN command, the SRU/W SEARCH command is very analogous to the SEARCH command within Z39.50. Like Z39.50, the SRU/W SEARCH command returns a record set that contains access to the item's full bibliographic metadata. Unlike Z39.50, SRU/W allows for a finer granularity of control over how metadata is returned to the user in regard to the record set's size and number of records. What's more, SRU/W is a stateless protocol by virtue of its reliance on the HTTP communication protocol, meaning that record sets are created dynamically on each SRU/W request.

However, unlike Z39.50, SRU/W is a fully XML-based protocol that returns XML-encoded data. What's more, queries within SRU/W are made as string queries using textual tags to represent indexes as defined by a supported context set. A context set works essentially like a namespace within an XML document—it defines the list of indexes available for search. Currently, SRU/W recognizes a number of common context sets, including CQL (Common Query Language), DC (Dublin Core), and bath (Z39.50 Bath Profile), but SRU/W is not restricted to the use of just these common sets of context sets.[17] SRU/W allows the server to define the context sets that are currently being supported.

The greatest difference between Z39.50 and SRU/W is the method of communication. Unlike Z39.50, SRU/W primarily communicates between the client and server over an HTTP connection. SRW provides a more robust version of the protocol by encoding responses between the client and server using SOAP messages, while SRU simplifies the communication process by utilizing simple URLs (HTTP GET requests) to issue queries and retrieve results in XML. For example, a developer wanting to utilize an SRU/W server would make an initial request to the server asking for an explanation of the services supported. Using SRU, this request can be made using a simple URL. Utilizing the Library of Congress's catalog, we can send the following EXPLAIN request: http://lx2.10c.gov:210/LCDB?operation=explain&version=1.1, to the server to discover the supported services: http://lx2.10c.gov:210/LCDB. (See figure 9.5.)

From the response, we can discern a number of things about the Library of Congress's SRU/W service. First, the server supports a number of different context sets. Within the IndexInfo tag, we find the following:

```
<set identifier="info:srw/cql-context-set/1/cql-v1.1" name="cql"/>
<set identifier="info:srw/cql-context-set/1/dc-v1.1" name="dc"/>
<set identifier="http://zing.z3950.org/cql/bath/2.0" name="bath"/>
<set identifier="http://zing.z3950.org/cql/local/1.1" name="local"/>
```

These tags define the context sets that will be utilized for query. Further examining the EXPLAIN request, we can see how these context sets are defined. Within the EXPLAIN response, we can see that a "subject" index has been defined.

```
▼<zs:explainResponse xmlns:zs="http://www.loc.gov/zing/srw/">
   <zs:version>1.1</zs:version>
 ▼<zs:record>
     <zs:recordSchema>http://explain.z3950.org/dtd/2.0/</zs:recordSchema>
     <zs:recordPacking>xml</zs:recordPacking>
   ▼<zs:recordData>
      ▼<explain xmlns="http://explain.z3950.org/dtd/2.0/">
        ▼<serverInfo>
            <host>mprxyvlp01.loc.gov</host>
            <port>210</port>
         </serverInfo>
        ▼<databaseInfo>
            <title>LCDB -- Library of Congress Online Catalog</title>
          ▼<description lang="en" primary="true">
             SRU/Z39.50 Gateway to LCDB Z39.50 server. Records in UTF-8 encoding.
           </description>
         </databaseInfo>
        ▼<indexInfo>
            <set identifier="info:srw/cql-context-set/1/cql-v1.1" name="cql"/>
            <set identifier="info:srw/cql-context-set/1/dc-v1.1" name="dc"/>
            <set identifier="http://zing.z3950.org/cql/bath/2.0" name="bath"/>
            <set identifier="http://zing.z3950.org/cql/local/1.1" name="local"/>
          ▼<index id="1016">
              <title>Keyword Anywhere</title>
            ▼<map>
               <name set="cql">anywhere</name>
             </map>
           </index>
          ▼<index id="4">
              <title>Title</title>
            ▼<map>
               <name set="dc">title</name>
             </map>
           </index>
          ▼<index id="1003">
              <title>Creator</title>
            ▼<map>
               <name set="dc">creator</name>
             </map>
            ▼<map>
               <name set="dc">author</name>
             </map>
           </index>
          ▼<index id="21">
              <title>Subject</title>
```

**FIGURE 9.5**

SRU EXPLAIN Response

```
<index id="21">
<title>Subject</title>
<map>
<name set="dc">subject</name>
</map>
</index>
```

These indexes define the supported query types or indexes supported on the SRU server. Looking at the EXPLAIN result, we can see that a number of different query types are supported by the server. For example, a subject query of "Columbus Ohio" could use any of the following searches:

```
▼<zs:searchRetrieveResponse xmlns:zs="http://www.loc.gov/zing/srw/">
   <zs:version>1.1</zs:version>
   <zs:numberOfRecords>447</zs:numberOfRecords>
 ▼<zs:records>
   ▼<zs:record>
      <zs:recordSchema>marcxml</zs:recordSchema>
      <zs:recordPacking>xml</zs:recordPacking>
    ▼<zs:recordData>
     ▼<record xmlns="http://www.loc.gov/MARC21/slim">
        <leader>03609nkd a22004935a 4500</leader>
        <controlfield tag="001">19440000</controlfield>
        <controlfield tag="005">20170112101255.0</controlfield>
        <controlfield tag="007">kh |||</controlfield>
        <controlfield tag="008">960502s1958 xxunnn | | kneng</controlfield>
       ▼<datafield tag="035" ind1=" " ind2=" ">
          <subfield code="a">(DLC)lmc1996001341/PP</subfield>
        </datafield>
       ▼<datafield tag="906" ind1=" " ind2=" ">
          <subfield code="a">0</subfield>
          <subfield code="b">cbc</subfield>
          <subfield code="c">orignew</subfield>
          <subfield code="d">u</subfield>
          <subfield code="e">ncip</subfield>
          <subfield code="f">20</subfield>
          <subfield code="g">y-printpho</subfield>
        </datafield>
       ▼<datafield tag="010" ind1=" " ind2=" ">
          <subfield code="a">2016714571</subfield>
        </datafield>
       ▼<datafield tag="040" ind1=" " ind2=" ">
          <subfield code="a">DLC</subfield>
          <subfield code="c">DLC</subfield>
          <subfield code="e">gihc</subfield>
        </datafield>
       ▼<datafield tag="050" ind1="0" ind2="0">
          <subfield code="a">LOOK - Job 58-8100</subfield>
        </datafield>
       ▼<datafield tag="245" ind1="0" ind2="0">
          <subfield code="a">All America cities</subfield>
          <subfield code="h">[graphic].</subfield>
        </datafield>
       ▼<datafield tag="260" ind1=" " ind2=" ">
          <subfield code="c">1958 Nov. 12 (date added to Look's library)</subfield>
        </datafield>
```

**FIGURE 9.6**

SRU Subject Query

1. Dublin Core Query: http://lx2.10c.gov:210/LCDB?ope
   ration=searchRetrieve&version=1.1&query=dc.subject
   =%22columbus%200hio%22&recordSchema=marcxml&
   startRecord=1&maximumRecords=5

2. Bath Query: http://lx2.10c.gov:210/LCDB?operation=
   searchRetrieve&version=1.1&query=bath.subject=%22
   columbus%200hio%22&recordSchema=marcxml&startR
   ecord=1&maximumRecords=5

In both cases, the subject request would return the record shown in figure 9.6. One might also notice that the record in figure 9.6 is in MARCXML. This is defined through the use of the recordSchema argument in the query URL. Like the context sets, the supported record schemas are also defined in the EXPLAIN request. In the case of the Library of Congress's SRU server, the following recordSchemas are supported: marcxml, dc, and mods.

```
<schemaInfo>
<schema identifier="info:srw/schema/1/marcxml-v1.1" sort="false"
name="marcxml">
<title>MARCXML</title>
</schema>
<schema identifier="info:srw/schema/1/dc-v1.1" sort="false" name="dc">
<title>Dublin Core</title>
</schema>
<schema identifier="info:srw/schema/1/mods-v3.5" sort="false"
name="mods">
<title>MODS v3.5</title>
</schema>
</schemaInfo>
```

Given all the benefits associated with SRU/W, it has been puzzling why so few applications, tool sets, or organizations currently support the protocol. By contrast, after nearly fifteen years, the Z39.50 protocol, despite its cryptic communications format and spotty character-encoding support, still remains the predominant method for searching and retrieving bibliographic data in the library environment. This isn't to say that a handful of large SRU/W implementations doesn't exist. The Library of Congress provides a robust SRU/W API for its library catalog, as do projects like the European Digital Library (www.theeuropeanlibrary.org). Additionally, vendors like Ex Libris encourage users to utilize their built-in SRU service over the traditional Z39.50 connection (though both exist). However, after being available and in production for nearly fifteen years, the tools or software to support the SRU/W standard remain few and far between. What's more, given the inconsistent implementation of SRU services and the trend among digital library developers to create more RESTful-based services, it appears that the desire to provide long-term support and maintenance for existing tools capable of working with the SRU/W standard is very much on the wane.

### OpenSearch

OpenSearch is an intriguing protocol when one considers how quickly it has been adopted by developers outside the library community. OpenSearch was developed in early 2004 by Amazon.com to allow resources to be integrated into its A9 search engine. However, the simplicity of the protocol's search and response syntax has led to a very quick adoption within the corporate community. So ubiquitous has OpenSearch become that all major web browsers use it to configure new search endpoints in the browser.

As a protocol, OpenSearch functions very much like SRU/W in that it works over an HTTP GET connection utilizing a very simple URL query structure. What makes OpenSearch different is the response format. OpenSearch utilizes RSS (Really Simple Syndication) and the Atom Syndication format as the response format. By utilizing these two formats, OpenSearch has been able to successfully leverage tools that have traditionally been used for blogging to quickly develop tools and services that can serve and consume an OpenSearch query and response. Like SRU, OpenSearch utilizes an easy-to-understand query syntax that can be expressed through a URL.

Probably OpenSearch's greatest strength is the ease with which the protocol can be implemented. Utilizing a minimalist approach, OpenSearch uses a minimal number of arguments for query. Couple this with the known RSS/Atom response format, and most systems can be retrofitted to support OpenSearch queries and responses in the course of a couple of hours. For example, at Ohio State University, the local digital collections system has been created using the Samvera technology stack. The URL to create a query into the digital collections system is fairly straightforward:

- baseURL: https://library.osu.edu/dc/catalog
- encoding: utf8=%E2%9C%93
- Query string: q=test
- Reurn format: format=json

Using this structure, any request made to the digital collections system will return back JSON results. Since JSON is a format that is easily parseable by most web-based programming languages, implementing an OpenSearch data feed is relatively easy. What's more, by providing an OpenSearch feed and creating the necessary autodiscovery link, for example (see figure 9.7),

```
<!DOCTYPE HTML PUBLIC "-//W3C//DTD HTML 4.01//EN" "http://www.w3.org/TR/html4/strict.dtd">
 <html xmlns="http://www.w3.org/1999/xhtml" xml:lang="en" lang="en" dir="ltr">
   <head profile="http://a9.com/-/spec/opensearch/1.1/">
     <link rel="search"
           type="application/opensearchdescription+xml"
           href="http://linktoyourcontentsearch.xml"
           title="Your content search" />
   </head>
   <body>
    <!--- ... --->
   </body>
 </html>
```

**FIGURE 9.7**

OpenSearch Autodiscovery Link Syntax

a user's web browser would be able to automatically recognize the search profile and make it accessible directly within the application.

Implementing the OpenSearch protocol proved to be simpler than initially expected in part due to the protocol's minimalist specifications (www.opensearch.org/Specifications/OpenSearch/1.1) and the wide variety of example code that is currently available and shows OpenSearch's integration within other applications. In all, the process took about ten minutes to produce the following plug-in:

```php
<?php
/**
* Version 1.0
*—initial version
*—supports OpenSearch 1.0, http://opensearch.a9.com
*
* @Based on the WordPress opensearch plugin
* @http://williamsburger.com/wb/archives/opensearch-v-1-0
*/
function extract_description($s, $max) {
$words = explode(" ", htmlspecialchars($s));
if (count($words)>$max) {
return implode(' ',array_slice($words, 0, $max-1)) . "[ . . . ]";
} else {
return $s;
}
}
//Constants
define("CONST_TITLE," "title");
define("CONST_DESCRIPT," "descri");
define("CONST_SUBJECT," "subjec");
define("CONST_CREATOR," "creato");
if (isset($_GET["searchTerms"])) { $searchTerms = $_GET["searchTerms"]; } else { $searchTerms = ""; }
if (isset($_GET["startIndex"])) { $startIndex = $_GET["startIndex"]; } else { $startIndex = 1; }
if (isset($_GET["startPage"])) { $startPage = $_GET["startPage"]; } else { $startPage = 1; }
if (isset($_GET["count"])) { $count = $_GET["count"]; } else { $count = 10; }
$records = array();
if (!empty($searchTerms)) {
$total = 0;
$contents = file_get_contents("https://library.osu.edu/dc/catalog?utf8=%E2%9C%93&per_page=$count&
q=$searchTerms&format=json");
$contents = utf8_encode($contents);
$contents = json_decode($contents, true);
if (count($contents) > 0) {
$totalResults = $contents["total"];
$records = $contents["docs"];
}
}
?>
<?php header( "Content-type: text/xml;\n\n " , true ); ?>
<?php echo '<?xml version="1.0" encoding="utf-8" ?' . '>'; ?>
<rss version="2.0"
xmlns:content="http://purl.org/rss/1.0/modules/content/"
xmlns:wfw="http://wellformedweb.org/CommentAPI/"
xmlns:dc="http://purl.org/dc/elements/1.1/"
xmlns:openSearch="http://a9.com/-/spec/opensearchrss/1.1/"
>
<channel>
<title>Test Title</title>
<link>http://reeset.net/anonymous/osu_dc.php</link>
<description>Test Description</description>
<pubDate><?php echo date( 'D, d M Y H:i:s +0000'); ?></pubDate>
<generator>OSU PHP Sample Generator</generator>
<language>English</language>
<openSearch:totalResults><?=$totalResults?></openSearch:totalResults>
<openSearch:startIndex><?=$startIndex?></openSearch:startIndex>
<openSearch:itemsPerPage><?=$count?></openSearch:itemsPerPage>
<?php if ( $records ) {
$items_count = 1; ?>
<?php foreach ( $records as $record ) {?>
<item>
<title><?=$record["title"][0]?></title>
```

```
<link>https://library.osu.edu/dc/concern/generic_works/<?=$record["id"]?></link>
<dc:creator><?=$record["creator"][0]?></dc:creator>
<? $word_count = explode(" ", $record["description"][0]); ?>
<?php if ($word_count > 50) {?>
<description><![CDATA[<?=extract_description($record["description"][0], 50)?>]]></description>
<?php if ($word_count > 255) {?>
<content:encoded><![CDATA[<?=extract_description($record["description"][0],255)?>]]></
content:encoded>
<?} else { ?>
<content:encoded><![CDATA[<?=extract_description($record["description"][0])?>]]></content:encoded>
<? } ?>
<? } else { echo "<description></description>"; } ?>
</item>
<?php $items_count++; ?>
<?php } ?>
<?php } ?>
</channel>
</rss>
```

This plug-in implements basic OpenSearch functionality, which now allows the collection to be natively searched from within a web browser using the autodiscovery syntax within an HTML page. For example:

```
<html>
<head>
<link rel="search" type="application/opensearchdescription +xml"
href="http://example.com/open-search.xml"
title="Search Example.com via OpenSearch" />
```

Since its development in 2006, OpenSearch has found significant traction both within the web community and the library community. Large library resources like the Library of Congress's Linked Data Service (http://id.loc .gov) and OCLC's VIAF (www.viaf.org) have used OpenSearch to provide a nonlibrary-specific programming interface. Given its wide acceptance, digital repository administrators would be well-served to see how this protocol can be utilized to expose their own collections to wider audiences. What will be more interesting is how the library community responds over the long term to the use and support of protocols like OpenSearch. While SRU/W offers a greater level of granularity in terms of search, protocols like OpenSearch offer the library community a way to interact with developers outside the library community on their terms, allowing individuals and organizations a much straighter path for resource integration.

## Linking Protocols

Linking protocols specify a standard method for generating URIs for materials outside of one's repository. When we consider current-generation digital repository platforms, nearly all provide some method for generating a permanent URI for an item. For many platforms, this involves utilizing

PURLs (Persistent URLs) or the Handle System. In theory, these persistent URIs provide a permanent access point for a resource. However, what happens when a link should be generated from a digital repository to an item outside of the resource? For example, a preprint of an article has been placed into a repository, but a link to the published article is desired—how would this type of linking take place? In general, two primary linking methods are emerging. The first method, OpenURL, uses a protocol that queries an outside service to determine if an organization has access to a specific resource from any of its vended content. The second method, DOI (Digital Object Identifiers), represents a type of fingerprint for digital documents. This is a widely utilized identifier in the publisher community that can be used to link directly to a resource. The use of either of these linking solutions requires interaction with an outside server or service—and digital repository administrators would be well served to evaluate both protocols if linking to external items is required.

### OpenURL

The original version of OpenURL (now called version 0.1) developed out of a research project at Ghent University in Belgium in early 2000. The concept was the product of a research project by Herbert Van de Sompel and Patrick Hochstenbach that looked at ways to solve linking issues when dealing with digital articles.[18] As more and more academic research moved into the online area, libraries and other information organizations were having increasing difficulty locating journals and articles within the various aggregated journal packages. Van de Sompel and Hochstenbach's research focused on exploring a linking system that could facilitate the discovery of access points for a digital item by evaluating all of an organization's digital subscriptions or open access resources. The process would generate a linking URI, allowing a user access to the resource if the organization had any valid access to that resource.[19] In late 2001, Van de Sompel and Hochstenbach sold this concept to Ex Libris, which developed the first OpenURL resolver, SFX. Given the simple nature of the OpenURL protocol, the specification enjoyed a quick adoption rate, quickly becoming the de facto format supported by data vendors and leading a number of library vendors to produce OpenURL products.

The OpenURL protocol itself works as a resolution system. A request is sent from a user to an organization's OpenURL resolver, which stores information relating that organization's digital assets holdings. The request is processed by the OpenURL resolver, generating a link to the resource if it exists.

Figure 9.8 illustrates very simply how an OpenURL request is handled by a generic OpenURL resolver. The resolver engine utilizes a holdings database to evaluate the incoming request. If the resource appears within the holdings database, a link can be generated to the item—if not, then a link is not generated and in most OpenURL systems, a set of alternative access methods is provided to the requester.

The OpenURL protocol itself is very much like Open-Search in that it is executed over an HTTP GET connection. Requests are made using a specially crafted URL that includes citation-level bibliographic data which will be used by the resolver to identify the resource. For example, the following URL represents a simple OpenURL request to Oregon State University's OpenURL server for an article entitled "Information Professionals Stay Free in the MarcEdit Metadata Suite":

> http://osulibrary.oregonstate.edu/digitalcollections/
> openurl/open.php?url_ver=Z39.88–2004&amp;ctx_tim
> =2006–12–31T15%3A36%3A37–0800&amp;ctx_ver
> =Z39.88–2004&amp;ctx_enc=info%3Aofi%2Fenc%
> 3AUTF-8&amp;ctx_id=&amp;rft.isbn=&amp;rft.atitle=
> INFORMATION+PROFESSIONALS+Stay+FREE+in+
> the+MARC+EDIT+METADATA+SUITE.&amp;rft.title=
> Computers+in+Libraries&amp;rft.spage=24&amp;rft
> .date=20040900&amp;rft.issn=1041–7915&amp;rft.issue
> =8&amp;rft.volume=24&amp;rft.aulast=Reese&amp;rft
> _val_fmt=info%3Aofi%2Ffmt%3Axml%3Axsd%3Ajournal

Currently, OpenURL exists in two flavors, the original OpenURL 0.1 specification and the more recent OpenURL Framework for Context-Sensitive Services (OpenURL 1.0), which was adopted as a NISO/ANSI standard (Z39.88–2004) in April 2005[20] and revised in 2010. OpenURL 1.0 expands the OpenURL protocol beyond that of simple item linking, allowing the context of an item to be described, as well as providing an XML specification for the protocol. This has made possible the exploration of new ways to use OpenURL to promote resource discovery, including auto resource discovery[21] and integration with microformats through example micro formats like COinS (Context Objects in Spans)[22] and unAPI.[23] What's more, OpenURL is a very complementary standard, in that it integrates well with other linking technologies. For example, handle id's, PURLs, OAI identifiers, DOIs, and so on can all be used in concert with the OpenURL protocol.

Fortunately for digital repository administrators looking to use OpenURL as a linking system, OpenURL resolvers have become fairly ubiquitous, and likely will be available at one's organization. Administrators then will simply need to be responsible for ensuring that their software can generate the relevant OpenURL requests to the resolution server.

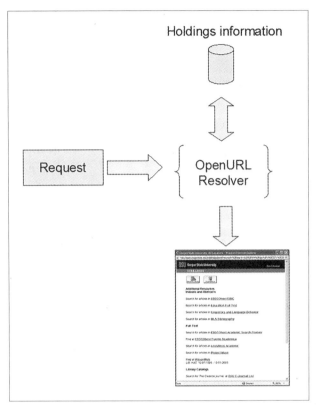

**FIGURE 9.8**

OpenURL Resolution Diagram

## DOI (Digital Object Identifiers)

Digital Object Identifiers (DOIs) are a special implementation of the Handle System. The Handle System provides a digital object architecture for managing items within a networked environment.[24] It provides a unique digital identifier that, once registered, is permanent for a particular item. In many ways, these identifiers are very much like an ISBN or a government document classification number in that a DOI is a string of characters making up a unique identifier for a resource.

10.0001/9876541

Like a government document number (SuDoc), a DOI is made up of two components—a prefix and a suffix.[25] In the above example, the prefix would be the information before the slash: 10.0001. The prefix itself is made up of two parts. The first part of the prefix is the first two digits, "10." This first part of the prefix identifies the identifier as a DOI. The second part of the prefix, "0001," is an assigned organization code. The organizational code is assigned by a DOI registration agency to an organization. This value is unique to an organization—and all documents published by an individual organization will utilize the same prefix. The suffix of the DOI, "9876541," is a user-defined character string that uniquely identifies the resource. This string can contain any alphanumeric string so long as the data is unique to the organization. This could range from an ISBN to a local control number.

DOIs are different than other control numbers such as ISBNs in that they are:

- associated with metadata that can be changed
- designed to be created and maintained independently in a distributed environment
- resolvable—they can connect people directly to resources
- can be assigned to any digital object rather than specific types such as books, journals, and articles

For more information regarding the DOI numbering scheme, developers or potential DOI implementers should consult the DOI Handbook (www.doi.org/hb.html).

So how do DOIs and OpenURL fit together? Does one supersede the other? Actually, no, the two are complementary technologies. At this point, current-generation browsers cannot natively resolve a DOI. Rather, DOIs must be sent to a DOI resolver, like http://doi.org, where the identifier can be resolved directly to an article. However, direct resolution to an article again raises the issue related to organizational holdings and access to the item. Fortunately, DOIs can be used in conjunction with OpenURL. OpenURLs can wrap a DOI and utilize a service resolution service to resolve a DOI to an OpenURL for processing against the OpenURL resolver's holdings database. Currently, a number of such resolution services exist—the most widely used likely being CrossRef (www.crossref.org). CrossRef is a DOI linking service that is free for library and nonprofit organizations, and provides a web services-based interface that can be integrated into the OpenURL process.

Figure 9.9 updates the resolution diagram from figure 9.7 by adding a resolution service like CrossRef to the infrastructure. In this diagram, the OpenURL resolver acts as the DOI resolution agent, transparently communicating with a DOI registry to resolve the submitted DOI to data that can be used within an OpenURL service. This data allows the OpenURL resolver to then query the resolver's holdings database to locate an accessible copy of the item or push data to an OpenURL-aware service like an interlibrary loan service.

### Search Engine Support

While search engines continue to improve their ability to index dynamic and database-driven content, digital library systems interested in ensuring that content can be indexed by the current search engine systems must actively ensure that their systems are generating site maps. Initially started by Google, site maps[26] are currently the best method for ensuring that search engine crawlers can locate and index content within a digital content system. Site maps are simple XML files that provide linking information to the documents within a collection. These maps are utilized by the search engine to "program" how a search engine's web spiders crawl and index a site. This gives search engine crawlers the ability to index resources with dynamic URLS—items that are generally outside of a web spider's field of vision.

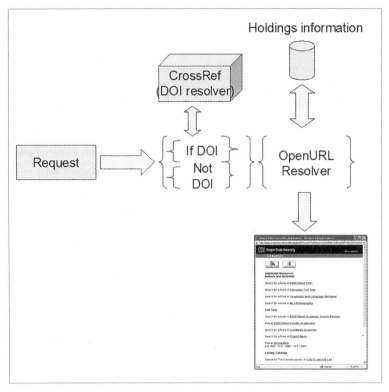

**FIGURE 9.9**

Modified OpenURL Diagram with DOI Resolution

In addition to site maps and metadata harvesting, commercial search engines are providing access to OpenURL linking and resolving of resources. Originally found in Google Scholar, these services allow organizations to embed OpenURL links in electronic resources held by the organization. These links could link to electronic articles, print books, or items within a digital repository. Unfortunately, unlike the site map concept, each commercial search engine supports this service in a different way, requiring organizations' OpenURL and electronic holdings information to be stored in differing formats.

## Evaluating User Needs

Given the wide variety of protocols and metadata formats, how does one decide which ones to support? Since no current digital repository package supports every potential protocol or access point, any evaluation of digital repository packages should include a discussion of which protocols and metadata need to be supported to meet the needs of one's organization and user community. But how to evaluate need? Ultimately, the evaluation process needs to involve members from throughout the organization to ensure that the widest range of necessary services is offered to both encourage organizational development and meet long-term user needs.

## Developmental Needs

Within an organization, a digital repository will likely be only one type of digital resource supported by that organization. This means that the organization will need to consider how the digital repository fits into the larger information infrastructure of the organization and what protocols will need to be supported to allow for the development of services around the collection. Will the digital repository need to interact with a federated search tool? Should the tool be harvestable by commercial search engines? Will the metadata need to be repurposed outside of the digital repository system? These are just a few of the questions that digital repository administrators need to consider when selecting a digital repository package for their organization. The digital repository administrator should work closely with the individual responsible for planning out the corporate information infrastructure—as well as developers within the organization—to discover and plan for the necessary modes of access to support continued development.

Ideally, this evaluation is an ongoing process, since protocols and standards will change over the lifetime of the digital repository. A good digital repository administrator will need to keep the lines of communication open between him/herself and the organization's development community to ensure that the repository platform continues to grow with the needs of the organization. Very likely, this might necessitate the local customization of a digital repository platform through code customization or the purchase of subsequent software, but evaluation of the repository software is a task that must remain ongoing.

## User Needs

Unlike past generations, today's user presents a welcome problem for organizations. Many users today are very familiar with the concept of mashups; that is, utilizing code API from various services to create their own custom services. These services may be very personal, serving a very specific need or a more general one that is open to a wider audience. But unlike years past, users have become more active in looking for ways to search, store, and link to data within library collections. A digital repository will not be immune to this user tendency and will need to consider what level of user interaction the organization is willing to support. Should the repository support RSS or the Atom publishing protocol? Should the repository be searchable in commercial search engines or linkable from outside resources like blogs? Users' needs will vary widely between organizations—and it's up to the digital repository administrator to discern what tools and protocols users find necessary. For example, many users will require the presence of some type of citation service. Since different organizations will utilize different types of citation services like EndNote or RefWorks, how a digital repository provides citation support will vary given the needs of its user community.

Discerning those needs may not be a simple process, however. Functions like citation services, OpenURL linking, and cross-database linking are very general user services that are likely to be supported by most digital repositories—but issues like a user API or support for syndication protocols are more individual to an institution. Digital repository administrators will likely need to look to public services librarians and organizational usability studies to get a better idea of what is necessary to support their users' research and development needs.

## Summary

The widespread implementation of discovery systems is changing the way that the library community views digital services. In past years, web services were viewed as anything available over the Web. Web journals, databases, and so on provided a way to expand access to users in ways that had not been previously available. Discovery systems offer this capacity, and in addition, organizations now have the ability to build services that can query multiple resources, saving the user the frustration of trying to locate a single item within an ocean of digital assets. Even with their warts and shortcomings, current-generation discovery systems offer users a set of tools that can be used to query all (or most) of an organization's resources.

## Notes

1. Kenning Arlitsch and Patrick S. O'Brien, "Invisible Institutional Repositories: Addressing the Low Indexing Ratios of IRs in Google Scholar," *Library Hi Tech* 30, no. 1 (2012): 60–81.

2. Kenning Arlitsch and Patrick S. O'Brien, *Improving the Visibility and Use of Digital Repositories through SEO* (Chicago: American Library Association, 2013).

3. Early examples of federated search tools would include resources like Federated Searcher, a Java-based application used for federated searching of theses (1998); Stanford University's START project (1997); Virgina Tech's Federated Search (1998); and OCLC's SiteSearch.

4. The FGDC (Federal Geospatial Data Committee) initiated a Z39.50-based search portal for geospatial data in 1996.

5. Terry Reese, "Building a Shared, Metadata-Driven Knowledge Base System," *Ariadne* 47 (2006), www.ariadne.ac.uk/issue47/reese/.

6. Clifford A. Lynch and Cecilia M. Preston, "Internet Access to Information Resources," in *Annual Review of Information Science and Technology (ARIST)*, vol. 25 (New York: Elsevier, 1990), 263–312.

7. Clifford A. Lynch, "The Z39.50 Information Retrieval Standard," *D-Lib Magazine*, April 1997, www.dlib.org/dlib/apri197/041ynch.html.

8. Ibid.

9. Ibid.

10. ESRI, "Metadata and GIS: An ESRI White Paper," October 2002, www.esri.com/library/whitepapers/pdfs/metadata-and-gis.pdf.

11. ZOOM Initiative, http://zoom.z3950.org/.

12. IndexData, www.indexdata.dk/yaz/.

13. http://us2.php.net/manual/en/ref.yaz.php.

14. http://ruby-zoom.rubyforge.org.

15. http://search.cpan.org/~mirk/Net-Z3950-ZOOM/.

16. http://sourceforge.net/projects/zoomdotnet/.

17. Library of Congress, "Context Sets," www.loc.gov/standards/sru/cql/index.html.

18. H. Van de Sompel and O. Beit-Arie, "Open Linking in the Scholarly Information Environment Using the OpenURL Framework," *D-Lib Magazine* 7, no. 3 (2001), www.dlib.org/dlib/march01/vandesompel/03vandesompel.html.

19. O. Beit-Arie et al., "Linking to the Appropriate Copy," *D-Lib Magazine* 7, no. 9 (2001), www.dlib.org/dlib/september01/caplan/09caplan.html.

20. National Information Standards Organization, "Z39.88–2004: The OpenURL Framework for Context-Sensitive Services," www.niso.org/standards/standard_detail.cfm?std_id=783.

21. D. Chudnov, R. Cameron, J. Frumkin, R. Singer, and R. Yee, "Opening Up OpenURLs with Autodiscovery," *Ariadne* 43, www.ariadne.ac.uk/issue43/chudnov/.

22. E. Hellman, "OpenURL COinS: A Convention to Embed Bibliographic Metadata in HTML," http://ocoins.info/.

23. D. Chudnov et al., "Introducing unAPI," *Ariadne* 48, www.ariadne.ac.uk/issue48/chudnov-et-al/.

24. The Handle System, www.handle.net/.

25. DOI Handbook, www.doi.org/hb.html.

26. Google, "Google Site Maps," www.google.com/webmasters/sitemaps/.

# Planning
# for the Future

**Cheap technology and network** computing have fundamentally altered the way that information is created, distributed, organized, and used. For libraries, the most important of these effects has been the rapid decentralization of information and its storage in volatile formats. Since the function of libraries has traditionally been to preserve information resources and provide centralized access, technological developments have changed the primary function of the library from preserving physical information that it owns to providing access to electronic information that is often maintained by others.

The digital repository will play a very interesting role in the future. Although locally maintained by individual libraries, the repository's true value lies in the role it plays as part of a network consisting of high-value resources. Consequently, even when libraries create substantial digital collections that they own and maintain, the library of the next generation will still need to achieve a high level of interoperability with digital repositories maintained by others, as well as other information sources. Nonetheless, as time passes, digital repositories will play a progressively greater role in local library services.

## Providing Information That People Need

Now that most information is created and used exclusively in an electronic format, libraries must confront the challenges that digital repositories present if they are to maintain a prominent role in preserving and organizing information. Because most libraries have access to information that is unique to their organization or area, they also need to be familiar with methods that will allow them to share that information with others. In the process of learning to share information with other institutions, libraries will also become proficient with the methods necessary to integrate information from many remote sources. As the geographic range and number of people who access libraries remotely increases, the use of aggregated databases, electronic books, digital repositories, and websites will continue to grow. To serve these users, libraries must develop tools so that users can search all these resources without having to know which one contains the information they need.

This is not to say that libraries will only provide access to digital information. For a variety of reasons, paper and other physical formats will continue to play an important role for the foreseeable future, even if the use of these materials is waning. Too much information that will never be digitized has accumulated over the years. Even if copyright were not an issue, there will never be enough money and labor to do the work of digitizing print resources because of the sheer amount of physical processing required in relation to the demand for some of these resources—especially with low-use special collections. In some cases, paper is simply the most practical and efficient format to serve certain information needs. It is easier to quickly browse and read paper, and sometimes it is impractical to have an electronic device that requires special care and a continuous power supply. For these reasons, many libraries will continue to maintain and develop their paper collections despite the wealth of information available online and the online access to excellent subscription databases.

Nonetheless, it is clear that people will expect and need mostly electronic information in the future. It is simply too convenient to use—especially in an environment characterized by the wide geographic dispersal of information resources. Users' need to access a wide variety of electronic resources makes the creation of digital repositories inevitable. Libraries must embrace this new role or they will soon find themselves limited to maintaining paper collections that receive progressively less use over time. In fact, even completely physical collections need electronic collections of metadata to preserve the context and meaning of the collection. People expect to discover information through electronic searches because of how easy and expedient this method is. Information that is not at least indexed electronically will increasingly become disused and inaccessible. Despite the fact that many large libraries will never have their entire collections in their online catalog because the cost of converting the remainder of the cards would be prohibitive, few people use card catalogs anymore, even when these are the only access mechanism to significant parts of the collection. Even many librarians who are aware of this problem still use the online catalog exclusively.

## Libraries' New Roles

Given the extensive transformation of the information landscape in recent decades, the core services that libraries provide must be reexamined. A growing trend over the past few decades has been to contract external entities to provide library services. In the past, library personnel chose which materials to acquire. They ordered, cataloged, and processed resources. When patrons needed help, librarians provided assistance.

Today, it is common for libraries to use vendor-provided approval plans to select books and other materials in all formats for their collections. Many libraries include vendor catalogs in their searchable collections and purchase or rent items that patrons request. Most cataloging is performed by downloading records from OCLC, loading sets of vendor-provided records, or activating collections of records in shared systems. As collection budgets have failed to keep pace with inflation, libraries have increased their reliance on group purchases of electronic packages and interlibrary loan for electronic and physical materials alike. It is expected that other libraries will maintain many resources that users need. In other words, many tasks that used to be regarded as core functions have been outsourced.

In recent years, this trend has accelerated, and libraries have started relying on outside parties to maintain the collection and provide reference as well as access services. Electronic collections are rarely managed directly by libraries. Rather, access to them is licensed through vendors, and in many cases, the library is not even responsible for providing proxy access or authentication. Vendors are becoming increasingly responsible for determining what belongs in a collection and for ensuring that the resources are adequately protected. If current trends continue, and libraries provide access to increasingly larger collections provided by a shrinking number of vendors, eventually a point will be reached where one could argue that the library is merely acting as a purchasing agent and that the vendor is performing the acquisition, preservation, and access functions that have been traditionally associated with libraries.

Progressively fewer services require a librarian's mediation. Desktop access circumvents the reference interview and assistance finding items—a patron might well have his or her reference question answered by someone thousands of miles away rather than by the local librarian. If librarians interact with patrons remotely and rely exclusively on digital information to answer questions, there is no reason why libraries cannot follow the example of many businesses and contract 24/7 phone and chat-style reference from centers around the world that have been optimized to service a global market spanning many time zones. Systems are being maintained outside the library as well as services. When campus or municipal IT departments do not absorb the responsibility for system administration, libraries frequently opt to purchase hosted solutions. Libraries join progressively larger consortia, and in recent years, the number of shared catalogs has rapidly expanded. Libraries rarely maintain their own systems directly, and a growing number of services are hosted by an outside provider.

In short, almost all aspects of library work—selection, acquisitions, cataloging, interlibrary loan, reference, preservation, and systems—are increasingly being provided outside the library. As libraries' dependence on licensed content increases and libraries purchase fewer resources in any format that they care for directly, it is clear that the library's role in archiving and preserving information is gradually diminishing—or that the individuals who actually perform these functions work for these "outsourced" entities, requiring us to change our view of what a library is. It is not clear what the future holds, but it is evident that the stereotypes of librarians shelving books or gently warning patrons to work more quietly will soon have little basis in fact. Libraries already look very different than they did just a few decades ago, and more dramatic changes loom on the horizon.

Although many library administrators and staff have become very concerned by the transfer of responsibilities traditionally performed by the library to outside organizations and to the users themselves, these trends should be welcomed. Rather than representing a "dumbing down" of services and a reduction in quality, these trends represent a chance for libraries to provide a higher level and quality of service than was possible before. As an analogy, let's consider the travel industry. Before people could use the Internet to plan trips and make reservations, the only way consumers could purchase an airline ticket was through a travel agency or directly from the airline. Tickets could be obtained by mail or in person, but losing them often resulted in significant headaches and charges to replace them. On the day of travel, the customer had to stand in a long line because the gate agent had to enter information from the ticket into the system to issue a boarding pass.

Now, customers can compare fares on airlines quickly and receive automated alerts when routes they are interested in can be bought at desirable prices. The customer enters all of the relevant information into the system, chooses seats, obtains boarding passes, and can check in using a mobile phone which can also be used as a boarding pass. The new system is faster, easier, and more flexible for the customer despite the fact that he or she does most of the work, and moreover, the airline can provide its service at significantly lower cost.

Likewise, online library services have improved to the point that users can now find many things they would have needed help accessing only a few years ago. When librarians are freed from more basic tasks, they can serve more effectively as information advocates for users without the conflicts of interest that travel agents faced.

## Learning from the Past

Like the people who used to process paper tickets for airlines, librarians must adapt their skills to match user needs and new realities. Most people now type their own documents, dial phone numbers, and press the buttons when they enter an elevator despite the fact that decades ago secretaries typed documents, operators dialed phone calls, and elevator operators selected floors for people. Improved technologies and trends towards self-service have led to the automation of many tasks and have made it easy for people to serve themselves. As a result, people can easily use their mobile phones to perform tasks and obtain services that once were provided by career professionals.

Libraries serve as cultural institutions as well as information resources, so it's essential to retain knowledge that has emerged over time. However, it is also necessary to embrace the future and recognize the difference between maintaining a connection with the past and clinging to practices that have lost their relevance. Every service that is now considered a part of "traditional" library service was at one time new and innovative, and it is important to realize that new traditions will continue to emerge. The long-term outlook for libraries that anticipate and respond to user needs is much better than it is for those that try to define user needs in terms of what services they provide now.

History teaches many lessons. For libraries, one of the most important of these lessons is that change is inevitable, so the repository of today must be designed with this in mind. Digital resources have existed for only a few decades, and not enough time has passed for libraries to know what formats, methods, and systems are best suited to archiving and serving these digital materials. No system lasts forever, and it would be a mistake to presume that the best tools for running a digital repository have even been developed yet. Every generation believes it has attained the pinnacle of scientific knowledge and technological achievement. Great advances have occurred throughout the ages, and there is every reason to expect that future generations will continue to improve current methods, tools, and knowledge.

The Great Library of Alexandria contained hundreds of thousands of items over two thousand years ago, but classification systems that members of the public can use to find related books together have only been in general use for a little over a century. Consistent authority files have only been in widespread use for a few decades—until network computing made producing collective authority files convenient, each library maintained its own separate authority files. As a result, headings varied from one environment to another. As much as librarians and users take electronic resources for granted, online catalogs have been in widespread use for only a few decades.

Digital repositories are still in their infancy and demand considerable staff and technical resources, considering the number of resources they contain and how often they are used. Although many if not most libraries have some sort of digital repository, these resources are usually seen as auxiliary rather than as essential to library services. Some repositories look very polished on the surface, but contain very few resources. Those that contain many items frequently have collection development policies that add materials because they are free rather than because they are particularly useful. Even though libraries have built repositories for decades, we are still at a stage where repositories are often treated as concept demonstration projects rather than as true components of the library collection. However, there have been successes, and libraries are pursuing more ambitious projects that address larger-scale and more sophisticated information needs.

Although digital repositories still play a relatively minor role in the information landscape, a growing number of significant electronic collections are becoming available. The Library of Congress's American Memory Project is a well-funded endeavor to make unique and rare materials that document the American experience available online. Other institutions also make extensive collections of unique materials available online. Clearly, digital repositories are becoming more of a core service.

Successful repository projects normally have well-defined scopes. The Library of Congress's American Memory Project does not simply gather any information relating to American history. Rather, it focuses on primary documents that are of particular historical or cultural significance. Successful university repositories typically make a special collection available online, or focus on very specific locally produced resources, such as theses and dissertations. Other digital archives focus on preserving access to specific titles or resources.

It is easy to imagine that libraries will collect all resources that their patrons use digitally, just as they traditionally have with physical formats. However, there are a number of reasons why the emergence of repositories that serve relatively specialized needs may be part of a growing and permanent trend. Identifying content that the library can reasonably expect to store and have the right to distribute is very difficult. Copyright regulations put severe limitations on the types of materials that libraries can store in digital repositories. Rights management issues are complex. There is a strong incentive for libraries to focus on providing access to those items that they own the rights to distribute.

Even when copyright is not an issue, a number of technical and organizational challenges place significant constraints on what kinds of resources can be archived. As chapters 2 and 3 explained, certain types of resources lend themselves poorly towards the archival procedures normally used in repositories. It is important to keep a sense of perspective. Although there has been a great deal of hand-wringing about what is lost when digital information is archived, libraries have always limited their collections to what could be stored and managed properly. Few libraries accept materials they cannot preserve and provide access to, and it is difficult to argue that those that do are providing better service. Even when information is recorded on paper, most libraries provide minimal access at best to physical information that does not conform to a very rigid structure. On the rare occasions when significant efforts are made to store paper resources that do not have the properties of books or serials (e.g., correspondence, notes, etc.) in a special collection, access is often provided via sketchy information in a specialized finding aid or a collection-level catalog record, and finding the desired item requires searching through boxes of paper materials. In short, libraries have traditionally addressed the problem of which resources they preserve by limiting their collections to items they can work with. It is perfectly reasonable to continue this same practice for digital resources.

# Adapting to Change

Libraries must evolve if they want to remain relevant for serving people's information needs. The amount of information that people want access to is increasing, but the funding and number of library staff are not. As time passes, information will increasingly be maintained and controlled by parties outside of the library. Given that libraries have traditionally served as centralized repositories of information, the trend toward users' needing decentralized electronic information has major implications for the delivery of library services.

As users require an increasing number of specialized information resources that are available only on specialized platforms, it's clear that the library's role in the information ecosystem is diminishing. Libraries even face significant competition in their core business of providing patrons with books—online services deliver electronic and physical books, videos, and audio resources quickly and cheaply to patrons.

In response, many libraries have started adopting popular services and methods that were developed by businesses. It's appropriate for libraries to incorporate certain ideas from the business world, but libraries need to maintain their own niche. Simply emulating models adopted by for-profit entities that have more efficient supply and distribution systems is not an effective long-term strategy for libraries. If the library provides a similar service to the one provided by business, but does so less effectively, the logical outcome is for libraries to fade away while users turn to other information providers to meet their needs. If libraries are to remain relevant, they need to do more than simply mimic the services provided by others.

The key to libraries' continued success is to identify which services they are uniquely positioned to provide. There has been endless discussion in the library community about features such as recommending other materials, or letting users place comments in online catalogs and repositories, recommend other resources, use social media accounts to share what they're doing, and other practices. However, it is highly unlikely that libraries will be able to perform these tasks as well as large businesses do. Making accurate recommendations requires a great deal of statistical data about individual as well as group preferences and behavior. Libraries use a large number of separate and often incompatible systems, so it would not be technically feasible for them to combine their data so that it could be used for local purposes, even if they wanted to. Moreover, libraries do not track user behavior for many reasons, including a professional commitment to protect users' privacy and freedom to explore without surveillance. And even if libraries did track user behavior, they would never achieve the scale necessary for it to be useful, since major Internet services have detailed data on what hundreds of millions of people have looked at, bought, shared, and have been sent.

Some popular features of online systems that do not rely on statistics might be difficult to implement in local systems. For example, it is unlikely that enough patrons would attach thoughtful comments in a local system to affect more than a tiny minority of resources. Online booksellers have millions of users, yet the number of comments is relatively small, and they appear mostly on popular books that sell many copies. If libraries focus on copying business practices such as these, they will find that the product they deliver will be inferior and have a higher cost. Consequently, these services seem poorly suited for repositories and may not be well suited for any but limited library applications.

As a practical matter, libraries cannot expect to rely on any method that requires sophisticated and large-scale technological integration. All examples of technologies that have proven successful for the purposes of integrating library collections are very simple. Even moderately complex technologies such as Z39.50, SRU, and OAI-PMH are rarely used despite widespread vendor support, a lack of viable alternatives, and strong advocacy on the part of the library community. Because technology skills vary so widely from one library to the next, and many library staff can't spend significant amounts of time developing technical skills and debugging software, all technological integration must use robust protocols and standards that are simple enough to be understood and implemented very quickly by people without highly specialized technical knowledge.

For libraries to thrive, they must concentrate on services that they can provide better and more efficiently than anyone else. As a practical matter, this means that services requiring specialized expertise and technical infrastructure that are not normally found in libraries are best delivered by other entities. Libraries excel at services that require large-scale cooperative efforts or the human evaluation of information resources. One inherent advantage that libraries have over any other information provider is that they have cataloged and organized materials that have been created over a period of centuries. In addition, libraries have established practices that allow them to quickly identify what materials other libraries have, as well as where a particular resource can be found. Consequently, even if a library does not have what a user needs, chances are that it can be quickly obtained through interlibrary loan.

Although digital information will continue to increase in importance, an enormous amount of valuable information from the past will be available only in physical formats such as paper, and the only way to find it will be through a library. Library catalogs have their faults, but the methods they use to organize materials have proven effective for organizing hundreds of millions of unique items. People may rave about Amazon.com, but it is far easier to find all of the books written by an author in a library catalog, particularly if he or she has a common name with multiple spelling variations. Major academic libraries frequently provide access to millions of titles directly, and they can obtain materials they don't own from libraries around the country or even the globe. Now that greater numbers of libraries participate in large consortium catalogs where their holdings can be collectively searched and group purchases of electronic resources become more common, it is clear that libraries still have much to offer.

In addition to the well-organized materials they have collected over the years and the cooperative arrangements they have made to maximize the use of these resources, libraries are well-positioned to provide certain services better than businesses do. If a user does not know what he or she needs, a reference librarian is still much more helpful than a search engine or a vendor database. A reference librarian will know which content providers are most likely to have resources that could help the user, and will not fail to recommend materials to a user because a competitor owns them or because they are not listed near the top of a keyword relevancy search. By leveraging these and other strengths, libraries will continue to provide critical information services well into the future.

## Consolidation and Specialization

Just as it has transformed other institutions and businesses, the global Internet economy is changing how libraries operate. Patrons expect libraries to deliver a greater variety of materials than ever before, and they want these faster, cheaper, and better. Libraries must pool resources and enter cooperative agreements to take advantage of economies of scale, consolidated purchasing power, and other efficiencies. Fortunately, libraries have been doing exactly this for many years. Thousands of libraries use the OCLC cooperative to share cataloging and holdings information. This makes efficient copy cataloging, large-scale authority control, and interlibrary loan possible. Large library consortia provide a shared catalog and distribution system to make it possible to share materials almost seamlessly. Consortia and cooperative organizations can also take advantage of combined purchasing power to negotiate better terms for licensed and purchased products.

The Internet has enormous value because it allows millions of computers to communicate with each other. Individually, even the most powerful computers have limited value. Collectively, they comprise an incredibly powerful resource that allows a user at an inexpensive workstation to do things that would be impossible even with a non-networked supercomputer. Digital repositories are also more valuable when they are part of a greater network. Just as a coin, stamp, card, or a book has more worth as part of a collection than by itself, documents, images, videos, and other resources are more useful as part of a greater collection. As the collection becomes richer and more extensive, the value of the component parts continues to increase. For this reason, a repository is far more valuable as part of a great network of information resources that can be searched conveniently than it is as a silo of information on the Internet.

At the same time that we build large collections to impart more value to materials, we must also ensure that the collections contain things that truly belong together. Coins and stamps are more valuable as part of a collection because the collection provides a context for these materials, while the individual items provide context for other items in the collection. Users can already search the Internet, so the collection must provide context that can't be found elsewhere to be valuable. The most important difference between a museum and a landfill is that the former selects and presents items within meaningful contexts, while the latter can include just about anything—both of them collect old stuff. The value of a repository is measured by the context it provides to the materials it contains and how it makes those materials fit in the greater information ecosystem.

Consolidating services, employing technologies to share metadata and information, and collaborating with other organizations enables libraries to take advantage of the work and resources at other institutions so that they can serve their patrons better, cheaper, and faster. By specializing in services and materials that a library is well-positioned to provide and by turning to partners and vendors for addressing other needs, libraries can maintain and even expand their niche well into the future.

A good repository does much more than store and provide access to a collection of digital materials. Rather, it represents a unique archive of useful materials that serve the library community as well as other users. Just as libraries have banded together to provide collective cataloging and even reference, the logical path for libraries is to collectively capture information so that it can be made accessible.

A number of high-profile library initiatives reflect the trends towards leveraging the collective value in diverse library collections. For example, the Digital Public Library of America (DPLA) represents an effort to provide open access to books, images, records, and audio cultural heritage materials drawn from the collections of libraries, archives, and museums into a single national digital library. The DPLA is possible because of enthusiastic support within the library community for Dublin Core, OAI-PMH, and other generic standards discussed in chapters 6 and 7 that help libraries to conveniently share unique resources.

## The Shared Environment

If libraries want their digital repositories to represent more than a fringe of special collections, a model based on the premise that libraries individually manage the resources that patrons use only puts them at the same status as other individual content providers. Users need all kinds of information, and an individual library can only own the rights to a small fraction of the resources that a community of users is likely to want. Thus, for repositories to play an important role in the future, it must be possible to discover materials in them by using patrons' preferred search mechanisms.

It is unreasonable to expect users to search thousands of repositories located around the globe or individual silos for materials of interest. Just as most users find what they want on the Web by consulting one of a small number of search engines, they will most likely want to find all library materials in a single search. Repositories that lack the capability for sharing information with systems that users want to use have the effect of hiding important resources from all users, except those who are especially persistent or lucky enough to stumble upon what they need. Web search engines play an important role in discovery, so it's important to build systems that work well with them. Good repositories must allow users to search for what they want across multiple information sources at the same time, preferably without the user having to know which information sources need to be searched.

Efforts have been made to incorporate library materials in web search engines, but it is unlikely that this approach will provide effective access to entire categories of content that are essential for many library users. Web search engines cannot provide links that provide users with immediate access to resources in subscription databases, nor can they automatically place interlibrary loan requests for materials that must be obtained from other libraries. Web search engines cannot display local holdings or availability information, nor can they perform searches when the search target is an item that has a common title (e.g., reports, bulletins, proceedings, etc.), or when all items are by a specific author.

It is clear that as time passes, other libraries and organizations will maintain a growing proportion of the resources that individual libraries have traditionally owned and maintained. Thus, the management of library collections will ultimately be based on access to rather than ownership of materials.

A well-managed repository that contains unique and useful information is a critical component of the next-generation library. Just as the Internet decentralized computing, it is also decentralizing library services. Figure 10.1 illustrates how libraries have traditionally managed and provided information to users. According to this model, the library owns all materials

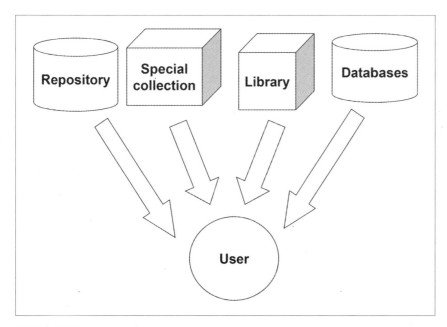

**FIGURE 10.1**
Traditional Library Service Model

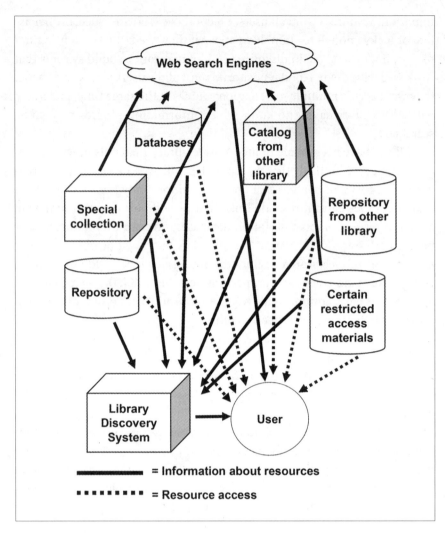

**FIGURE 10.2**

Next-Generation Library Service Model

and provides what is requested. When the user needs something, he or she searches the appropriate collection directly to find resources.

Figure 10.2 depicts how the next-generation library will serve patrons. There are two important differences between this diagram and the traditional model. The first difference is that users don't need to search individual resources, nor do they need to know which resources are being searched. Rather, they search their favorite search engines and library discovery interfaces that include information from many sources. The second difference is that in many cases, the user does not obtain the resource from the library. The library acts as an intermediary in some cases, such as interlibrary loan or proxy access to subscription materials, but its primary function is to secure access rights and integrate metadata from a variety of sources and make it searchable in a way that helps the user.

Figure 10.2 is displayed from the user's perspective and has been simplified for clarity. In this diagram, the user's home library compiles information about resources (i.e., metadata) from a number of sources. Viewed from a universal perspective, there is no "main" library except from the perspective of an individual user. Notice that this model potentially allows access to access-controlled resources that are maintained by other entities. This is possible because of distributed access-control mechanisms such as those discussed in chapter 8.

The proponents of a vision where all libraries both collect and distribute metadata must ask why all metadata is not simply included in a single repository. The answer is simple: for information to be useful, it needs context. By allowing individual libraries to choose which metadata is harvested, searched, and presented, users may browse and search different virtual collections. Just as many shoppers would be better served by a small store that specializes in a particular type of product than by a shopping mall containing dozens of stores of all sizes that sell goods expected to appeal to the vast majority of consumers, many people will need specialized information spaces that are optimized toward their needs. While it would be technically feasible for all information providers to keep all metadata in a single physical location, the organizational and technical challenges are considerable enough that the disadvantages outweigh the benefits of doing so. By sharing metadata, libraries can use the operating environments and software that best serve their specific needs in order to provide access to all materials.

In this next-generation model, the number of information providers has greatly expanded, and a service point can be provided anywhere a user has network access. This means that many users will never see the inside of a library, and librarians will not see their most loyal customers. Just as the Internet has made it possible for people to maintain close relationships with people they have never met in person, it also allows libraries to make resources scattered all over the globe seem as if they were part of a single collection, and provide highly personalized services to users who will never enter the building.

To move toward the next-generation library, where information is stored in distributed repositories around the world, library systems must invest in common protocols and standards that allow information to be discovered, transmitted, and used. Library standards and protocols such as SRU/SRW, OAI-PMH, OpenURL, and Dublin Core are mostly unknown outside the library world and are not generally supported by digital asset-management systems designed for specific use cases. However, these systems typically do support standards relevant to the communities and uses that the systems are designed to support. As the number of resources that require mediated access for rights-management reasons increases, distributed access-control mechanisms discussed in chapter 8 rather than library-managed solutions may prove necessary.

In many ways, the most important aspect of the digital repository is not that the information is being stored in electronic format. Rather, it is that otherwise insignificant repositories will be able to play a role in a large peer-to-peer network containing a rich collection that can be used to serve diverse needs. Once the technical and organizational challenges of creating digital repositories are overcome, the next critical hurdle will be to make sure that these systems can share information seamlessly with each other.

Libraries will distinguish themselves by providing federated content management. The complexity of this task is significant, but the basic tools and methods necessary to achieve it already exist, and libraries know how to use them. For example, librarians have long taken relatively sophisticated authority control mechanisms for granted. Although it is common for naive technologists to claim that authority control is not necessary when sophisticated keyword searching is available, people usually quickly discover through experience that it is indeed necessary.

To illustrate this point, Wikipedia uses a process called "disambiguation" that is not only functionally equivalent to authority control, but which also uses the same mechanisms. Among other things, disambiguation specifies rules for qualifying common terms, and expressing relationships between different entries, and it even prescribes how the headings for certain types of resources are constructed. A disambiguation page has a structure very similar to that of an authority record.

## Federated Vocabularies

Effective searching is difficult to achieve without vocabularies that allow users to specify what they need. Algorithms based on resource popularity may work well for general web searching, but when highly specialized resources are needed that do not have equally unique vocabularies, these materials become difficult, or even impossible, to find. For this reason, vocabularies that allow users to search for items within a knowledge domain are necessary for searching across multiple repositories.

The maintenance of vocabularies implies authority control. However, just as resources become more decentralized, vocabulary maintenance will also become decentralized. While it would be impractical for librarians to maintain vocabularies using committees, as is currently done with Library of Congress Subject Headings (LCSH), it would be perfectly feasible for them to identify vocabularies maintained by appropriate bodies that could be used to manage access across multiple repositories. As repositories and library services mature, it seems a natural extension for librarians to manage vocabularies belonging to different domains.

The technical infrastructure to manage vocabularies has been in place on the Internet for many years. Namespaces are based on this same concept of managing vocabularies belonging to different domains. However, namespaces present multiple challenges. For example:

- Presuming that you could work with multiple namespaces simultaneously, what would that look like in an ideal world?

- As a practical matter, how could a system that works with more than a small number of namespaces be built and maintained?

- If vocabularies are merged for the sake of simplifying both maintenance and the user experience, how is this accomplished?

- All namespaces must be maintained. Despite very strong support and assistance from the worldwide library community, LCSH has very limited ability to express concepts, and even then it can be very outdated.

- It takes domain knowledge and metadata expertise to apply metadata.

- The sheer amount of resources being created means that only a tiny percentage of them can have metadata manually assigned.

However, libraries have a vested interest in presenting information resources within the context of a larger collection. This dynamic explains why most libraries obtain the vast majority of their catalog records from OCLC WorldCat rather than by creating new ones themselves. Library staff are trained professionals, so although there are certainly discrepancies in how they describe things, the level of consistency is very high. Even when they lack domain expertise or time to assign metadata, they can use analytical tools and automation to enrich specialized materials with high-quality metadata. If there is one thing that the library community recognizes, it is the importance of consistency in organizing a collection. As has been described throughout this book, the standards that make the participation of repositories in federated collections possible also allow finding and using the materials that these collections contain. Consequently, the prospects of success are very good.

## Summary

Libraries have traditionally served as centralized repositories of information, so the rapid decentralization of information brought about by the Internet and cheap technology presents significant challenges to libraries. To maintain a prominent role in the provision of information services, libraries must develop digital repositories and other services to provide access to distributed resources so that user needs can be met.

Among other things, such a shift requires librarians to focus more on providing access to materials owned and maintained by others. It will also require librarians to identify and expand those services that libraries are uniquely positioned to deliver. By leveraging the enormous amount of experience that librarians have in evaluating, organizing, and identifying information, libraries will continue to be critical components of the infrastructure that people need to find what they want. While librarians can learn from popular features of the online services and search engines, they should not simply try to emulate successful commercial entities that have developed business models based on relative strengths and weaknesses that are different from those of libraries.

Digital repositories maintained by libraries will perform an important function in this new, decentralized environment since they will contain a wide variety of specialized and unique collections. To be useful to local users as well as to the greater library community, these repositories must support common protocols for sharing metadata so that libraries can effectively manage federated collections. To support robust federated searches, libraries will also have to identify and develop vocabularies that describe their local collections but that also translate well into generic standards such as Dublin Core. Just as libraries have shared cataloging for many years to provide better service at lower cost, they will need to share the collections stored in digital repositories on a large scale.

Physical libraries have traditionally limited their acquisitions to materials that they can effectively preserve and process. Likewise, digital repositories will need to define their collections in terms of what they have rights to provide access to and what can be preserved. As a practical matter, this implies that most successful digital repositories will serve specialized needs because the best tools and methods for acquiring, storing, and accessing digital resources depend on the type of resource.

## References

Doctorow, Cory. "Metacrap: Putting the Torch to Seven Straw-Men of the Meta-Utopia." Last updated August 26, 2001. www.well.com/~doctorow/metacrap.htm.

Networked Digital Library of Theses and Dissertations. "Networked Digital Library of Theses and Dissertations." www.ndltd.org.

# INDEX